infinite
POSSIBILITY

infinite
POSSIBILITY

CREATING CUSTOMER VALUE
ON THE DIGITAL FRONTIER

B. Joseph Pine II
Kim C. Korn

BK
Berrett–Koehler Publishers, Inc.
San Francisco
a BK Business book

Berrett-Koehler Publishers, Inc.
235 Montgomery Street, Suite 650
San Francisco, CA 94104-2916
Tel: (415) 288-0260 Fax: (415) 362-2512 www.bkconnection.com

Ordering Information
QUANTITY SALES. Special discounts are available on quantity purchases by corporations, associations, and others. For details, contact the "Special Sales Department" at the Berrett-Koehler address above.
INDIVIDUAL SALES. Berrett- Koehler publications are available through most bookstores. They can also be ordered directly from Berrett-Koehler:
Tel: (800) 929-2929; Fax: (802) 864-7626; www.bkconnection.com
ORDERS FOR COLLEGE TEXTBOOK/COURSE ADOPTION USE. Please contact Berrett-Koehler: Tel: (800) 929-2929; Fax: (802) 864-7626.
ORDERS BY U.S. TRADE BOOKSTORES AND WHOLESALERS. Please contact Ingram Publisher Services, Tel: (800) 509-4887; Fax: (800) 838-1149; E-mail: customer.service@ ingrampublisherservices.com; or visit www.ingrampublisherservices.com/Ordering for details about electronic ordering.

Berrett-Koehler and the BK logo are registered trademarks of Berrett-Koehler Publishers, Inc.

Printed in the United States of America

Berrett-Koehler books are printed on long-lasting acid-free paper. When it is available, we choose paper that has been manufactured by environmentally responsible processes. These may include using trees grown in sustainable forests, incorporating recycled paper, minimizing chlorine in bleaching, or recycling the energy produced at the paper mill.

Library of Congress Cataloging-in-Publication Data

Pine, B. Joseph.
    Infinite possibility : creating customer value on the digital frontier / B. Joseph Pine II, Kim C. Korn. – 1st ed.
      p. cm.
    Includes index.
    ISBN 978-1-60509-563-9 (hbk. : alk. paper)
  1. Technological innovations–Management.   2. Digital media–Management.   3. New products.   4. Customer relations.   I. Korn, Kim C.   II. Title.
    HD45.P536 2011
    658.5′75–dc22
                          2011009376

First Edition
16 15 14 13 12 11   10 9 8 7 6 5 4 3 2 1

BOOK PRODUCED BY: Westchester Book Group
COVER DESIGN: Mark van Bronkhorst, MvB Design
COPYEDITOR: Rick Camp
INDEXER: Robert Swanson

To Stan Davis, who inspired this book, and to my wife, Julie, who inspires me.

—*Joe Pine*

To my wife, Annie, for her good humor and tireless support, and to Joe for his trust.

—*Kim Korn*

contents

foreword

September 1, 2010. On my guestroom doorsill at the Hilton Orlando Bonnet Creek. The *USA Today* cover story: "Stadium vs. Home: Can the NFL make being there match what's on TV?" The newspaper quoted fans who said they would rather stay put—saving money, avoiding traffic, having easier and cheaper access to food and beverage, as well as enjoying a better overall football-viewing experience via their HDTVs. (One former season-ticket holder boasted of having five television screens—and presumably five different games—on simultaneously.) NFL Commissioner Roger Goodell, recognizing the rising competition between the in-person and from-home experiences, commented, "We have to bring technology to our stadiums to make that experience better."[1]

This dynamic between the real and the virtual, between atoms and bits, between other-staged and self-directed time, defines the competitive landscape that Joe Pine and Kim Korn so richly explore in the pages that follow. Today, nearly every business must join the NFL in tackling its own "digital media strategy" to contend with the disruptive forces that accompany our electronic age. Pine (my business partner of fifteen years at Strategic Horizons LLP) and Korn (whom I've come to know through his in-person participation at our firm's annual thinkAbout events) provide an invaluable service in expanding the purview for navigating the digital frontier. Many people today merely view this new dynamic in terms of the physical and the virtual. Pine and Korn go beyond these dual domains of (what they term) *Reality* and *Virtuality* to define six additional realms that together form octants in a "Multiverse" of infinite possibility that stands before us. The model they present is not easy to digest, for they split three perpendicular coordinate planes (of time, space, and matter) to create a 2×2×2 framework—enough to frighten away any casual reader. But I urge you to approach the model and their tome like Yogi Berra: When you come to a (three-pronged) fork in the road, take it! Take it: for the journey will open up myriad new ways of thinking more richly about the future of your business.

Knowing Joe Pine has long found inspiration from the work of Stan Davis, I went back and reread the foreword that Stan wrote nearly two decades ago for Joe's first book, *Mass Customization*. In it Davis shared two interrelated perspectives: first, how management often mistakenly sees the world in terms of "parts/wholes" instead of holistically pursuing new value-creating forms of business; and second, how executives usually frame most of their decisions around false dichotomies.[2] This faulty thinking continues to this day: Physical vs. Virtual, Atoms vs. Bits, Stadium vs. Home.

To date, most enterprises have treated new digital technologies as an incremental part tacked onto the existing whole. The results all too frequently intrude on the experience, rather than more subtly and holistically enriching it. A retail bank sticks plasma TVs up on the wall behind its tellers to stream video content irrelevant to the transactions being performed, rather than use digital media in an interactive way to speed up the line. A museum places freestanding kiosks at every turn, unused or abused until sitting in disrepair, instead of designing new ways of technologically introducing context or inciting action that draws patrons into its core exhibits.

Instead of making the real-world experience better, digital technology often worsens it. I'm not one to go to many NFL games, as baseball is my sports passion. After twenty-five years of being a (full) season ticket holder with the Cleveland Indians, I've recently discontinued the purchase. Why? Not because my beloved Tribe has lately fielded weaker teams (I actually like watching the young talent develop over time), but because the electronic output on the team's new $8 million scoreboard—"Whack a Mole" and "Pong" contests, movie trivia, dance competitions, as well as other non-baseball "fan-cam" features—and the blasting of unsolicited music (why is it that sports arenas with these jumbo TVs usually have such poor *sound* systems?) too greatly detracts from the actual baseball experience. If I want a video experience, I'll stay at home and watch the MLB Network; for real baseball, I plan to take in the Lorain County Ironmen of the Prospect League top college prospects playing a summer schedule using wood instead of aluminum bats and more importantly, no digital-experience intrusions.

Surely you've encountered similar digital intrusions in your life: your teenage children (or your spouse!) texting in their laps at the dinner table; colleagues taking a cellphone call that suddenly and rudely interrupts the face-to-face conversation you were having; high-def screens distracting your dining companion during a restaurant meal; pop-up ads popping up online; and the like. It's not that new digital content cannot enhance an experience—Virgin America's use of an animated cartoon in the seatback screens to share flight safety instructions is a vast improvement on the typical audio announcements (again, via poor sound systems) on most other airlines. But too often in too many places the digital element fails to satisfy the objective that Joe Pine and I put forward in *The Experience Economy* when we called for the creation of experiences (and specifically ones with themes) that "integrate space, matter, and time into a cohesive, realistic whole."[3]

Consider the themed place that does just that in the homes of the most fervent NFL fans: the "man cave." The TV broadcasts scroll scoring updates across the bottom of the screen, with many viewers taking yet further steps to keep up with the action by having multiple TVs or using picture-in-picture to follow more than one game. The room's furnishings—the deeply cushioned armchairs and recliners, the nearby refrigerator, the ubiquitous cup-holders—enhance the viewing experience. Undoubtedly, colorful team logos and other sports paraphernalia grace the room. Viewers donning customized jerseys manage fantasy football teams and have handheld devices at the ready to check their make-believe rosters at websites like myfantasyleague.com. Between Sundays, the room is used to play PlayStation or Xbox, often replicating game-play of the entire NFL season via EA Sports' *Madden NFL*. And if a real NFL game is missed, a Digital Video Recorder allows for watching real games at a different time. (Such well-equipped venues indeed beg the question: Can the NFL make being there match what's on TV?)

If such man caves demonstrate anything about the whole of life— and the lives of your customers—it's that more and more of our existence now takes place with a screen. Time with the screen began with our *eyes*: first the TV screen, then a computer screen, and now a screen held in our hands. And today, we increasingly engage these screens with our *hands*—not just holding devices containing screens, but touching the screen itself as the means of interacting with digital content. What's next? The inevitable result: more and more of our *minds* concerned with what's on the screen instead of something, anything, (everything?) off the screen. Interestingly, this impact on the eyes-hands-mind mirrors the dimensions of space-matter-time that underlie Pine and Korn's model: our eyes focus on the space of the screen, our hands manipulate the matter on the screen, and our minds focus upon the content emanating from the screen.

Am I presenting here a false on-/off-screen dichotomy? Well, yes I am, but only because purveyors of the screen have largely treated the digital world as something completely displacing life as we know it.[4] Consider for example the comments that Jeff Bezos, founder and CEO of Amazon, made in an interview with *Newsweek* in late 2009 concerning Amazon's Kindle e-reader:

> Q: Do you think that the ink-and-paper book will eventually go away?
> *Bezos:* I do . . .
> Q: Do you still read books on paper?
> *Bezos:* Not if I can help it.[5]

This perspective serves as the self-fulfilling prophecy with which Bezos evidently hopes to affix the future state of a world without physical books. His aspirations for Amazon's electronic-book container reflect the underlying dichotomy that motivates much of what is offered by Amazon and myriad other digital innovators in the marketplace.

But consider some alternative possibilities, ones that reject this either/or physical/virtual trade-off. What if Amazon, instead of offering e-books as a lower-cost alternative *versus* purchasing physical books, had bundled the physical-and-virtual together and made the purchase *of both* the lowest cost option for readership. (After all, an electronic copy of any book has an incremental cost of zero, as the digerati like to remind us.) What if they charged more to *not* send one version or the other? What if certain electronic capabilities were then offered to those who purchased an enhanced version of its Prime membership program? And what if that program actually offered membership to both electronic and physical experiences that fostered conversations between those reading the same books—instead of just providing a cheaper way to ship (more expensive) physical books? What if Amazon saw the electronic world as the primary means of encouraging more people to build physical libraries—promoting greater appreciation for knowledge—instead of just the vehicle to eliminate bound books altogether?[6]

I raise these questions as an expression of my fear concerning the world that may emerge if nontechnologists give Pine and Korn's book

but a cursory read—or worse, if they ignore it altogether and the only serious students of their tome are technologists who believe "there's nothing special about the place of humans" as "the distinction between the
roles of people and computers is starting to dissolve,"[7] who see any
Multiverse as an ideal world where "the intravidual—has multiple selves
competing for attention within his/her own mind, just as, externally,
she or he is bombarded by multiple stimuli simultaneously,"[8] and who
dedicate nearly every waking hour to producing new technologies that
do not really meet "basic human needs, because, at bottom, they are . . .
rather aimed at the loftier goal of transcending such mortal concerns
altogether."[9]

I implore readers to ask themselves a series of questions about their
businesses (and of themselves as humans working in business enterprises):
Do you seek and serve to ultimately have people (including yourself)
spend more or less time before a screen? Does your introduction (and
personal use) of the digital exist to improve real lives? Or does the non-
digital exist primarily to improve digital lives? (There is a point when
people do "crossover" this threshold; think of the person who more
highly values time in *Second Life* than in real life; more broadly, consider how many people now spend more waking hours with screens than
without them.) Time is the currency of experiences. So how is the value
of the experiences you enable as a producer (or enjoy as a consumer)
realized—by increasing or decreasing the amount of time devoted to
interacting with atoms (or bits), in real (or virtual) space?

Negotiating the future uses of time is precisely what Pine and Korn's
book is about. They are right to point out just how radically different
digital technology compares to old analog media. Therefore Think Opposite! Recognize that as the world becomes more customizable,
reconfigurable, convergent, instantaneously accessible, and univer-
sally connected, what people might value most are offerings that have
been customized specifically for them (sparing the hassle of incessantly
self-configuring), that diverge from predetermined categories of use,
that make customers at certain times and in certain places inaccessible
to particular matters. I suspect this is what lies at the center of the
Multiverse.

Finally, as more "conversations" are enabled by "social media" (surely
the term must soon fade away), recognize that talking past each other is
not the same as talking with each other. My hope is that this book will
spark many true conversations. Otherwise, as a local ad agency in

Cleveland prints on the back of its business cards: "I look forward to ignoring you on LinkedIn."[10]

JAMES H. GILMORE

Coauthor of *The Experience Economy* and *Authenticity*
Shaker Heights, Ohio
January 2011

acknowledgments

There were several seminal events in the creation of this book, the first being when I (Joe) again looked through Stan Davis' *Future Perfect* and flashed on No-Matter as an extension of Matter in the three-dimensional graph of the Universe. That immediately led to the depiction of the Multiverse just as shown in Figure 1.2, but I had no idea what any of the octants were other than Reality and Virtuality (which underwent many name changes as the work progressed).

That was over a decade ago. I continued to play around with the framework off and on, figuring out Augmented Reality and Mirrored Virtuality (thanks to David Gelernter's wonderful *Mirror Worlds*, the original name for that octant), but I still had trouble with the rest. The next key event came with the announcement of the Nintendo Wii in 2006, and then I knew that's what [No-Time – No-Space – Matter] was all about—and also that there would be true power in the framework.

The third event was when Don Tapscott's New Paradigm Learning Corporation (now Moxie Insight), after showing them the framework in its then-current state, hired me to think and write about how digital technology could be applied to experience staging. Mike Dover took on the task of shepherding me through the process, and with the able assistance of Nikki Papadopoulos, we had a great thinking session in my office to flesh out the Multiverse and find examples across all the octants. Without this session and continued time with Mike working through the ideas—resulting in "How to Think About Technology and Media in Staging Compelling Experiences," New Paradigm Learning Corporation, Big Idea Project, Information Technology and Competitive Advantage (IT&CA) Program, September 2007—this book never would have been written.

The last seminal event was showing the framework to Kim Korn, who loved it so much he took it on himself to delve into its details, understand its nuances backward and forward, and make sure it was logically consistent. I came to depend on his thinking and his analysis so much the only logical conclusion was to make him coauthor—a title he richly deserves for his work in leading the writing of Chapters 10 and 11 as well as reviewing, commenting, and making better (not to mention logically consistent) the rest of the book. Thank you, Kim. Without you, this would be a much inferior work.

We two would also like to thank those who have come before in explicating the digital frontier. Their work is acknowledged already in the text and endnotes, but we single out here the particular contributions to our thinking made by not only Stan Davis and David Gelernter but Brenda Laurel, Nicholas Negroponte, Jane McGonigal, Wade Roush, Sherry Turkle, Brian Arthur, Jaron Lanier, Tom Boellstorff, Edward Castronova, David Weineger, Henry Jenkins, Jesse Schell, and Gary Hayes, plus John Smart, Jamais Cascio, Jerry Paffendorf, and the rest of the group behind the Metaverse Roadmap, who deserve great kudos for their framework showing how the real and virtual could be fused.

During the writing of this book, I (Joe) became a Visiting Scholar with the MIT Design Lab, to which I owe a debt of gratitude to the late Bill Mitchell, Betty Lou McClanahan, and Ryan Chin. Ryan graciously introduced me around the MIT Media Lab, which led to many new discoveries and examples, particularly from meeting Turkle, Joe Paradiso, Pattie Maes, Hugh Herr, and Neil Gershenfeld. The very first presentation of the ideas was in fact to Henry Jenkins' Comparative Media Studies group at MIT, thanks to Sam Ford.

Many companies and people supported the ideas by providing us with venues for speaking and conducting workshops, every one a crucible for testing the ideas and sharpening the arguments. Of special note here are Yuri van Geest and the rest of the Mobile Mondays Amsterdam organizers; Risto Nieminen, CEO of Veikkaus, who commissioned the very first Infinite Possibility workshop; Risto Lahdesmaki, Mikko-Pekka Hanski, and board member Kaija Pöysti of Idean; Teemu Arina of Dicole; Sanna Tarssanen of the Lapland Experience Organization; Mark Hansen, Lisbeth Valther Pallesen, Conny Kalcher, and Hanne T. Odegaard of LEGO System; Ian Turner, Shannon Galphin, and Justin Carlson of Duke Corporate Education; Ian Jan-Hein Pullens and Pieter Aarts of NedSense; Al Ramadan, then of Adobe; Kris and Laila Pawlak Østergaard of DARE2; and Sonia Rhodes, Mark Tomaszewicz, and Jack Abbott of TEDx San Diego.

We also owe a debt of gratitude to all those who reviewed the manuscript and/or an earlier white paper and provided us with their thoughts and comments. We are sure we're forgetting some people here (our apologies), but thank you to Asta Wellejus, Ayesha Khanna, Bob Jacobson, Bob Rogers, Chris Parker, Dieke Schultz, Doug Sweeny, Kevin Clark, Kevin Dulle, Mark McNeilly, Mark Tomaszewicz (again), Mike Dover (again), Mike Kraft, Peter Funke, René van Dijk, Rick Schuett, Sonia Rhodes (again), and Stewart Hayes. There were also a number of people who replied on Twitter to our queries and retweeted our thoughts on the subjects in this book to their followers.

Other folks who deserve special mention: Albert Boswijk of the European Centre for the Experience Economy for his support of all things Experience Economy; Conny Dorrestijn of Shiraz Partners for so taking to the ideas that she took them to her client NedSense and incorporated them into a white paper for them; Ronald van den Hoff of C.D.E.F. Holding for helping to spread the word on the ideas in general and our search for the right cover in particular; Jorgen van der Slot of Freedom-Lab BV for creating a way of explaining them through his Penny For Your Thoughts program; Gary Adamson of Starizon for instilling in me (Joe) an understanding of true experience exploration (and in particular inspiring the notion of relating the Multiverse to the maps of explorers of old); Nadine Kano of Microsoft for her great support of researching experience and computing; Margie Adler for helping us think through the realms and for helping us write the early drafts of the first few chapters; and Nathan Rice for helping us with our own social media strategy and implementation.

We also thank Johanna Vondeling, our first editor at Berrett-Koehler, for recognizing the value in this book and bringing us into the BK author fold. Neal Maillet took over as our editor halfway through the project and provided invaluable advice, and Jeevan Sivasubramaniam provided great support throughout. We did not get to know everyone else at BK as well, but to a person each has been more than helpful, and we know they did a great job because you're reading about it right now. And we are especially grateful to Edward Wade of Westchester Book Services for his good work and great patience with us throughout the entire copyediting and visual style processes.

I (Joe) would also like to thank my father Bud Pine—an electrical engineer and programmer since the late 1950s who worked on the Arpanet, the Internet's precursor—for instilling within me a love and knowledge of computers, and acknowledge my partners at Strategic Horizons LLP: Doug Parker for keeping the business running and engagements coming

in while I write; Scott Lash, for promoting and running all of our offerings, especially thinkAbout and Experience Economy Expert Certifica-
tion; and Jim Gilmore, for his thinking and provocations. Thank you,
Jim, for providing invaluable feedback on this book, and especially for
writing the forward.

Finally, we both thank our immediate and extended families for their
encouragement and support. We would not be able to do what we do
were it not for all that Julie Pine and Ann Korn do for us.

JOE PINE
KIM KORN

Dellwood, Minnesota
Stillwater, Minnesota
March 2011

part I

PREPARATION

Introduction

INNOVATION ON THE DIGITAL FRONTIER

A number of years ago I (Joe) gave a boardroom talk in Milan, Italy, to a number of executives from different companies. One was the vice president of a global coffee manufacturer, who said something that amazed me: "There's been no innovation in the coffee industry in fifteen years." I responded: "Have you never heard of *Starbucks*?" This gentleman could only conceive of innovation in physical *goods,* not in *experiences—* a particularly ironic stance given we were in one of the foremost coffee meccas of the world, the very city that inspired Howard Schultz to create the Starbucks coffee-drinking experience.

That is what we desperately need in business today: experience innovation. Why? Because we are now in an Experience Economy, where experiences—memorable events that engage people in inherently personal ways—have become the predominant economic offering. It eclipsed the Service Economy that flowered in the latter half of the twentieth century, which in turn superseded the Industrial Economy, which itself supplanted the Agrarian Economy.[1]

Experiences are not new, just newly identified as distinct economic offerings. They have always been around—think of traveling troubadours, Greek plays, Roman sporting events, *commedia dell'arte* performances— but now encompass so much of the economy that every company faces a stark choice: innovate goods and services ever faster as their productive lives get ever shorter, or focus on offering innovation further up the "Progression of Economic Value" (Figure I.1), on experiences that engage customers, or even transformations, built atop life-changing experiences, that guide customers in achieving their aspirations.[2] These higher-order offerings create greater value for customers, generally have longer

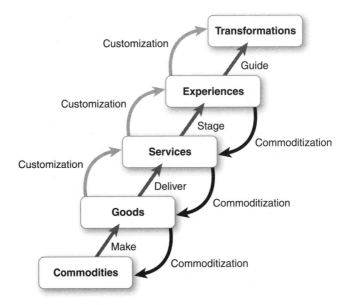

Figure I.1 The Progression of Economic Value. From B. Joseph Pine II and
James H. Gilmore, *The Experience Economy*, Updated Edition
(Boston: Harvard Business Review Press, 2011), 245.

life spans as they prove more difficult for competitors to imitate, enable
premium prices, and let companies capture more economic value.

Innovation is the great decommoditizer, for by definition if it is truly
new, it is truly differentiated, as no one else has the same capability;
competitors cannot create that same value at any price. And today, taking either innovation path to stay ahead of the commoditization steam-
roller seeking to squeeze margins and flatten profits, a company must
attune itself to the greatest source of offering innovation ever devised:
digital technology.

The Digital Frontier

As coffee manufacturers the world over missed the shift to the Experience
Economy, so too have many companies missed how digital technology
has been remaking the competitive landscape. Consider Motorola, once
the king of cellular phones. Its stay atop the pinnacle of the industry,
however, resulted from *analog* phones; once the shift to digital washed
over the industry in full force, it was Nokia that took over the crown.
Nokia innovated far better in function and styling, providing more of

what customers wanted from the new capabilities digital technology brought to mobile phones and services. Motorola fought back and produced occasional successes, such as the RAZR, but could not consistently outperform Nokia and spun off the business into Motorola Mobility as it became one of many also-rans in the industry.

But so, really, did Nokia. For what both companies missed was the intersection of digital technology and experience innovation pioneered by Apple. When Apple entered the smartphone industry and took it over—in worldwide global mindshare if not in market share—it thought long and hard about the *phone-using experience* and created a device not just highly functional but a joy to use. It thought long and hard about how the experience we have *with* our phone could be a great part of its value, and then about how the experiences we have *on* our phone, via apps, could overwhelm every other consideration. It thought long and hard about how to turn the *purchasing* of the phone (and of course all its other technological offerings) into an experience itself and innovated the one-of-a-kind Apple Stores, which today generate over half the company's revenues. It even thought long and hard about the *box-opening* and *guide-reading experiences,* for goodness sake, and innovated ones for the iPhone and its App Store, respectively, about which people wax poetic![3] Apple still primarily *sells* digital-based goods (with many services, such as the iTunes store, and a few membership-based experiences, such as One to One), but it *markets* digitally infused experiences, and thereby reaps the rewards.

Thinking long and hard about using digital technology to create unique customer value—that is the theme of this book. The digital frontier, lying at this intersection of digital technology and offering innovation, beckons companies seeking to create new customer value by mining its rich veins of possibility. For digital innovations enrich our lives by augmenting and thereby enhancing our reality; by engaging us through alternate views of reality that make us active participants in the world around us; by letting us play with time in ways not otherwise possible; by engrossing us in virtual worlds that enchant and capture our time; by allowing us to interact with those worlds through material devices and even gestures; by letting us physically realize whatever we imagine; and by enabling virtual representations that mirror our reality to enlighten us from a new vantage point. Digital innovations can even give us a greater appreciation and desire for Reality itself, whenever we take the time to unplug and just be. But by far the greatest value will come from those innovations that create *third spaces* that fuse the real and the virtual.

Why Digital Technology Changes the Game

As far back as 1984, pioneering computer scientist Alan Kay recognized the unique power of digital technology "The computer is a medium that can dynamically simulate the details of any other medium, including media that cannot exist physically. It is not a tool, although it can act like many tools. The computer is the first metamedium, and as such it has degrees of freedom for representation and expression never before encountered and as yet barely investigated."[4] Around that same time, one of those investigating the power of this new medium, Jaron Lanier, coined the term "virtual reality" as he envisioned the creation of a "virtual world with infinite abundance."[5] And less than a decade later, Brenda Laurel, in her wonderful exploration *Computers as Theatre,* told us that "computers are representation machines" and that designing the "human-computer experience" is "about creating imaginary worlds that have a special relationship to reality—worlds in which we can extend, amplify, and enrich our own capacities to think, feel, and act."[6] Now, what these visionaries foresaw two and three decades ago has become impossible for us to ignore because it underlies so very much of the value companies create today, so much of the value customers seek.

Digital technology differs from all other kinds of man-made technology due to the distinctive characteristics of the bits at its digital core. Although most readers will be familiar with these characteristics (and others that could be cited), it still is worth recognizing the following:

∞ *Bits are immaterial.* They weigh nothing, cost little or nothing to store or replicate, and do not "age" with time. They require no ongoing maintenance, are always as good as they were the first day they were produced, and do not wear out with use. For example, music recordings replicated on vinyl albums may get dirty, scratched, and wear a little each time a needle slides down the groove bouncing off the molded pattern of matter holding the analog information about the music. Even the CD, an intermediate technology somewhere between the analog vinyl record and the digital music file on a computer or iPod, is subject to damage, misplacement, and general deterioration over time. But much to the chagrin of the music industry, music in a lossless digital format can be replicated without limit and stored indefinitely while every copy remains as good as the original recording.

∞ *Bits are easily integrated, again at little or no cost.* Any digital device can talk to any other digital device—at the speed of light—in a wave of ongoing digital convergence. Your PC or Web-enabled mobile phone can now be used to control your home's lighting, pools, heating, air conditioning, and DVR (digital video recorder) from wherever you are in the world. And if you want to go out to eat while on the road, there's an app for that, as your iPhone can take your verbal request to locate a restaurant, give you the latest reviews, show it on a map, email the result, and get you a reservation. Apps even allow you to ask open-ended questions about what is available to do in your area today, tonight, or this weekend. Such capabilities come about from the mashup of a wide variety of once distinctly separate analog technologies, including telephone directories, road maps, newspaper and magazine reviews, and so forth, to provide a seamless, simpler, and more complete experience.

∞ *Bits are cheap when it comes to imagining, experimentation, and prototyping.* With purely digital offerings you can play around with them to your heart's content and market's readiness without every incurring the cost of physical production. Even with physical goods (including the goods required to support real-world services, experiences, and transformations) you can design/prototype/test, design/prototype/test, design/prototype/test until the forecasts come home before spending one dime on expensive machine tooling and full-scale physical production.

∞ *Bits enable the development of offerings otherwise flat-out impossible.* Long before virtual reality was a glint in Jaron Lanier's eye, in 1972 the first digital fly-by-wire (DFBW) system replaced conventional mechanical flight controls with electronic flight controls coupled to a computer. This new technology domain opened the door for a modern generation of inherently unstable military aircraft, unflyable by conventional controls but incredibly maneuverable when guided by DFBW controls.[7] Think bicycle versus tricycle: a bike is more unstable than a trike, but it is greatly more maneuverable.[8]

∞ *Bits are easily modified, combined, improved, and customized.* Who among us has not come to expect a never-ending stream of updates of, upgrades to, and personalizing of the software tools we use, often at no or minimal incremental cost? Google has taken great advantage of this characteristic. Google e-mail has been a constant stream of delightful surprises that make it more feature-rich as time goes on without users ever having to lift a finger to perform an upgrade. The same holds true for the Google Chrome browser and thousands of other offerings from hundreds of other companies. Goodbye out-of-date software—and so long to being treated exactly the same as everyone else, as technology increasingly customizes itself to our every desire.

∞ *Bits are abundant.* Once you produce something digitally, you in effect have an infinite supply. There is no physical limit to how many copies you make or who can have or experience the digital offering as is the case with material offerings made of atoms and all of the associate production and logistics issues. You can share bits-based offerings, again at little or no cost, not just to anyone but to *everyone* in the world, not just theoretically but practically.[9]

Together, these characteristics make digital technology the *technology of experiences.* As former Intel chairman Andrew Grove foresaw back in a mid-1990s speech at the Comdex computer show, "We need to look at our business as more than simply the building and selling of personal computers [that is, as goods]. Our business is the delivery of information [that is, services] and lifelike interactive experiences."[10] That vision has certainly become the case in the past fifteen years, for digital technology today enables wholly new-to-the-world possibilities for the staging of such experiences by an ever-broadening array of methods. As just one example, I (Kim) conduct extensive online research, engage in raging Twitter discussions, Facebook, LinkedIn, iPhone, and iPad (all verbs) to my heart's content, attend WebEx meetings, participate in Ning communities, and even conduct virtual consulting engagements with a combination of Skype and GoToMeeting.

Or consider MyFord Touch. Its touch screen enables you to control your entire environment, including customizing your dashboard, while voice recognition enables on-the-fly control, not only of the car, but of your mobile phone and digital music player as well. You can browse your phonebook and make calls with the sound of your voice, get turn-by-turn directions, contact 911 emergency in the event of an accident, access a vehicle health report letting you know if your car needs servicing (with the option to schedule that service immediately), do business searches or get traffic, sports, and weather reports—all at your fingertips, or, should we say, the tip of your tongue. As the great integrator, digital technology boosts the prospects of new discovery and invention, and hence the possibilities for new value creation, onto an even steeper upward trajectory.

All domains of technology, including computing, communication, entertainment, manufacturing, transportation, and genetic engineering, converge as their foundations each become digitized. Innovations increasingly make even matter itself programmable, and for those goods that resist digitization, companies digitize information *about* them so they can—often in collaboration with customers—virtually design and then after production track, monitor, and mirror them online.

Plain and simple, zeros and ones talk to zeros and ones. This provides a common language for the exchange of information and thus the integration between any forms of technology expressible in digital form. The ongoing digitization of broad swaths of technology, with no limit in sight, greatly extends the information revolution that began with the computer. The upshot: digital technology turbocharges innovation, becoming a super-catalyst for creating new value, for its ability to meet the needs of humanity is undisputed, unparalleled, unbounded—and *still* largely unexplored.

Thinking Long and Hard

In order to create that value, you must go on your own journey of exploration to the digital frontier, where infinite possibility awaits. This book presents a new way of thinking about the opportunities for creating new, wondrous, immersive, and fully engaging experiences that effectively fuse the real and the virtual. We illustrate it with copious examples throughout, although we (Joe and Kim) confess that in these fast-moving times we fully expect many to be out-of-date by publication—some maybe even out of business, as is endemic with any arena as fast-moving as this— with many even better examples brought to market after the book was written. So while the exemplars you see here may not be the latest and greatest at the time of your reading, they do well represent this book's concepts at the time of its writing. We also offer some thought experiments, numerous guiding principles, and, at the book's core, a novel framework—a three-dimensional sense-making tool—for discovering, depicting, and designing new offerings.

We won't sugarcoat it: this model is complex. You may have difficulty grasping it at first and remembering all of its facets. You will definitely have to think long and hard about what it means and, in particular, how to apply it. I (Joe) had a statistics professor at MIT, Arnold Barnett, who whenever the mathematical going got rough would say, "Fasten your seatbelts!" Well, here you're going to have to fasten your seatbelts just a few pages into Chapter 1, "Cosmos Incogniti," and keep them tight for most of the rest of the book.

But if you do so, and stick with it, you will be amply rewarded. For you will then be oriented to the framework central to employing digital technology in order to fulfill what customers seek in today's Experience Economy. You will be guided in learning multiple methods for generating ideas for new offerings that make sense for your company in particular, as well as techniques for mapping experiences that engage and compel. You will then not only have staked out your own region on the digital frontier, but you will be ready to advance your business in capturing the value there for the taking.

And along the way, you will further appreciate the greater implications for you, your business, and ultimately for society as we explore and then exploit these new possibilities—first in our imaginations, then with our technology, and finally through our direct experience.

Infinite possibility awaits those willing, able, and prepared to make the journey.

1

Cosmos Incogniti

INTRODUCING THE MULTIVERSE

Recall the maps of old where less-than-intrepid mapmakers marked unexplored territory with the words *terra incognita*: unknown land. This boundary, usually indistinct, marked the known frontier and separated it from the unexplored—that which was beyond our knowledge. Recall also that apprehensive phrase "Here be dragons" accompanied by drawings of fearsome beasts thought perhaps to inhabit such territories, providing a clear warning (or at least an expression of doubt and fear) of what lies beyond. It is hard to imagine such a need today, so thoroughly have we explored the earth and mapped it out (save perhaps the deep, dark depths of the sea, where—who knows?—fearsome creatures may still prowl).

A frontier remains, however. The digital frontier. Comprised of zeros and of ones, it leads us—unlike the earthbound frontier of old—to places entirely of our own making. It lies at the boundary of our imagination, where beyond it stretches out entire worlds not just to be explored but to be created! Think of what lies beyond the digital frontier as (if you'll excuse a slight abuse of linguistics) "*cosmos incogniti,*" a phrase we believe captures the essence of the possibilities that exist at the intersection of technology and the fertile ground of the mind's eye: "worlds unknown."

Should a modern-day cartographer label *cosmos incogniti* with an accompanying descriptor, surely it would be "Here be opportunity!" For at the digital frontier lay not dragons of doubt but new and wondrous offerings that create customer value by fusing the real and the virtual.

But what tool would such a cartographer use to chart these new worlds and indicate in which direction people could find such opportunities? A simple map would be grossly inadequate to capture the possibilities.

A single globe could never represent the fact that digital technology not only enables new opportunities, new offerings, and new value but can do so by creating entire new three-dimensional worlds, virtual though they may be—worlds of exploration, conquest, artistry, and just plain new fun. And even then such worlds represent just a small fraction of possibility. For again the digital frontier opens not to fixed country you may discover and settle but to original offerings you must imagine and create. It differs also in the number of explorers vying for such opportunities. These explorers number not in the handfuls but in the thousands and tens of thousands—companies rapidly pushing forward the boundary of the frontier as they innovate new offerings that customers value. There are no limits to a frontier such as this, for there are no limits to our imagination. Before us lies infinite possibility—if only we had a tool to adequately chart it.

That is the aim of this book. We present a new tool geared to the task of exploring the *cosmos incogniti* of our imagination. This guiding tool, or framework, is not as easily read as a map, nor as representational as a globe. It does not provide you with a detailed description of the lay of the land, nor a precise set of coordinates from which to set off. How can it with a boundary as fluid as the imagination, with unexplored territory as vast as human creativity? But like a map in the hands of explorers of old, this framework illustrates what we know today while pointing to the unknown worlds of opportunity, in order to give form, content, and intentionality to your explorations. Its vital foundation and dynamic architecture provoke inexhaustible discovery and idea generation. And its terminology provides you with a vocabulary for understanding the opportunities and for communicating them with colleagues, collaborators, and customers.

We recognize that readers may be veteran explorers well versed in digital technology or beginners seeking new ways of creating value. Therefore, we travel in this chapter at a pace that gives all explorers a chance to adapt to the atmosphere, to grow step-by-step into an understanding of the language, the meaning of the core concepts, the robustness of its dimensions, and the implications of the framework as a whole. We will deepen our understanding in successive chapters that dive into the framework to discover its fullness, and then we will provide you with approaches for applying the framework to your own company, in your own circumstances, for your own customers, so that you can chart the meaningful, substantive ways of creating value for your own business.

We stand on a platform poised to launch into an exploration of *cosmos incogniti*. It promises to breathe into existence extraordinary offerings once imagined only as fiction but now truly at our fingertips. Possibility abounds. Territory may stretch before us without limit, but value lies within our reach. Here be opportunity!

The Known Universe

To introduce the framework that explicates the unknown worlds lying beyond the digital frontier, let us first understand the nature of *cosmos cognitus*, the universe we know and in which all reality exists— particularly as it applies to and impacts on business. To do that, let us revisit Stan Davis' classic business book *Future Perfect* (as applicable today as when he wrote it over two decades ago). Davis expressed the inspiration for his thinking this way: "A basic progression governs the evolution of management in all market economies: fundamental properties of the *universe* are transformed into *scientific* understanding, then developed into new *technologies*, which are applied to create products and services for *business*, which then ultimately define our models of *organization*."[1] He goes on to write:

> These new models first get articulated in our scientific and technological understanding of how the universe works. My intention in this book is to give new meaning to time, space, and matter in shaping tomorrow's business and organization. In the industrial economy managers considered time, space, and matter as *constraints*, whereas in the new economy they will come to think of them as *resources*. This will require profound transformations in the way we think about time, space, and matter. Just as the scientific shift from the mechanistic age of Newton to the holistic age of Einstein affected notions of what was meant by time, space, and matter, these new notions in turn will affect the managerial transformation from an industrial mindset to a fundamentally new one.[2]

That new economy, the Experience Economy, is now here. As we create new experience offerings, we can see more clearly the way in which the universal dimensions of time, space, and matter shape the opportunities businesses have today.

These three dimensions comprise the known universe and come together as a true trinity to fashion the entirety of physical reality. As represented in Figure 1.1, all experience consists of objects made of

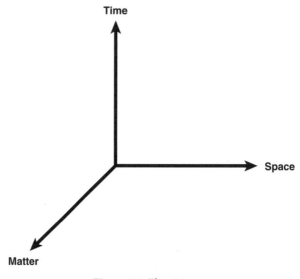

Figure 1.1 The universe

matter (physical entities, including the humans doing the experiencing and the sensory stimuli they experience) that move in time (the measure of change and therefore of experiencing) and across space (the background source and context of everything that is experienced).

One of the "profound transformations" Davis introduces in how we think about these dimensions is "**No-Matter,**" the title of a chapter in which he discusses how "in the new economy, the value added will come increasingly from intangibles . . . whose importance does not lie in their material existence."[3] Think of how much of the value of economic offerings has shifted over the past century from the tangible (goods) to the intangible (services) and on to the ephemeral (experiences). Further, think of how the design, production, marketing, and distribution of each kind of offering (commodities included) have all become more and more digitized over the past few decades, so that today there is scarcely a company of any size almost anywhere in the world that does not use computers at some stage of its processes, if not at the very heart of everything it does. If you could weigh the material component of all offerings, think how much higher the ratio of GDP to the mass required to produce it is today than in our industrial past.[4] To use the distinction made famous by Nicholas Negroponte, the founding director of the MIT Media Lab, in his book *Being Digital,* Matter and No-Matter are about *atoms* and *bits,*[5] about that which has materiality and resides in the physical world and that which has no materiality and resides within the zeros and ones of digital technology.

If No-Matter exists, it follows there must be **No-Space,** where experiences are not *real* but *virtual*; they do not take place in the physical world but happen virtually, in a place (or world) that does not really exist. The primary activity instead happens on (or in) a screen of some sort—movie, TV, PC, tablet, PDA, smartphone, watch, headset, goggles, or glasses, as well as windshield, wall, or anything else on which an image could be projected (including the retina itself once projectors become small enough).[6] Although virtual experiences still happen inside of us, in our mind's eye, the place conjured within the mind is not the same one in which our physical body resides.

And if there is No-Matter and No-Space, then there must be **No-Time,** where the nature of the experience is no longer tied to actual time—the moment-by-moment unspooling of synchronous events in the linear, sequential order of time as it exists in the real world. Rather, it becomes autonomous, independent of actual time, whether by being nonlinear, asynchronous, nonchronological, or transient, by shifting into the past or future, by slowing down, speeding up, or otherwise playing with one's awareness of time, or by any other way in which an experience creates a distinct, disparate sense of time (or timelessness) that does not truly exist.

Each dimension, in other words, has a positive side and a negative side (not in any moral sense, of course, but in the mathematical or logical sense), each one the opposite of the other. The original axes of Time, Space, and Matter all extend through the origin (the point in the middle of Figure 1.1 where they all intersect) to open up new ways of experiencing—and therefore of creating value in your business. As seen in Figure 1.2, which we have reoriented graphically to emphasize the new possibilities inherent in our logical extensions, the three fundamental dimensions of the universe decompose into six variables—Time and No-Time, Space and No-Space, Matter and No-Matter. These together comprise a $2 \times 2 \times 2$ matrix, with each pairing two sides of the same coin (or two variables lying along the same dimension in this case). Since $2 \times 2 \times 2 = 8$, this matrix delineates eight distinct universes, or *realms of experiences* (within which lie many worlds, or *cosmos,* to be discovered). Because "Octoverse" seems awfully clunky (not to mention conjuring connotations of the fearsome creatures prowling the depths of the sea on the maps of old), let's borrow a term from the discipline of cosmology that inspired this framework and call it the *Multiverse.*[7]

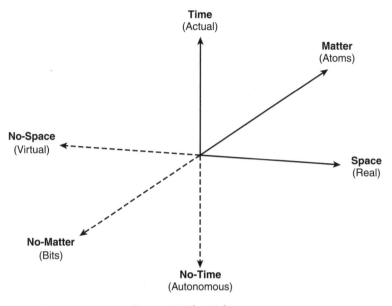

Figure 1.2 The Multiverse

The Unfamiliar Multiverse

This seems the best title for it, as this framework encompasses the multiple ways for *when* [Time ↔ No-Time] experiences happen, *where* [Space ↔ No-Space] they occur, and *what* [Matter ↔ No-Matter] they act on. The known universe of physical experiences [Time – Space – Matter] is just one of the octants within the Multiverse. Reality, as it seems most appropriate to call it, is of course the realm with which we are most familiar and within which most innovation still occurs. We will not ignore Reality, but we will focus on the seven other realms vitalized by the advent of digital technology. These realms are less known, not as well understood, more difficult to apply, and therefore abounding with possibility.

Infinite possibility, as a matter of fact, for the Multiverse furnishes the tool we need to explore the *cosmos incogniti* of our imagination. It helps us make sense of our explorations by showing us how to create offerings on the digital frontier that customers value.

Figure 1.3 visually depicts this framework, revealing the complete Multiverse and labeling each octant. Let us delineate the exact nature of each, realm by realm in logical sequence, to ensure every reader understands what is going on in this admittedly somewhat complex 2×2×2 framework:

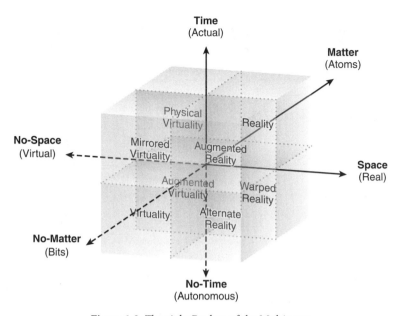

Figure 1.3 The eight Realms of the Multiverse

VARIABLES			REALM
1. Time	Space	Matter	Reality
2. Time	Space	No-Matter	Augmented Reality
3. Time	No-Space	Matter	Physical Virtuality
4. Time	No-Space	No-Matter	Mirrored Virtuality
5. No-Time	Space	Matter	Warped Reality
6. No-Time	Space	No-Matter	Alternate Reality
7. No-Time	No-Space	Matter	Augmented Virtuality
8. No-Time	No-Space	No-Matter	Virtuality

Each and every combination of the variables yields a distinct realm. Some are familiar, some intriguing, and some downright strange. But all ready to be explored.

Although we will more fully describe each experience realm in the succeeding chapters, here we wish only to give you a short preview of where we're heading. To highlight the distinctions between realms, we'll begin with the anchors of Reality and Virtuality, and then go on to introduce successive realms followed by their polar opposites. Note how in each case here we associate each realm with a particular visual icon (as shown in Figure 1.4) that we believe best captures its essence.

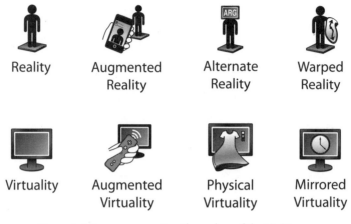

| Reality | Augmented Reality | Alternate Reality | Warped Reality |

| Virtuality | Augmented Virtuality | Physical Virtuality | Mirrored Virtuality |

Figure 1.4 Icons representing the realms of the Multiverse

We use these icons throughout the book, albeit sparingly, to make it easy for you to remember quickly and easily what each realm is about (while recognizing, too, that every realm encompasses experiences far beyond what can be represented by these small icons).

A Quick Tour of the Multiverse

Reality, of course, consists of the variables [Time – Space – Matter] or, as an equivalent way of looking at it, [actual, real, atoms]. Reality requires the least explanation of all the realms, for we experience it through the age-old medium of real life, where the sheer physicality of the experience reigns supreme. Think of such quintessential experiences as taking a walk in the woods, dining with family or friends, watching a sunset from a balcony, going to a raucous rock concert, skiing down a mountain, or playing a round of golf. And then think in each case of how the experience is situated in a particular point in time, set apart from what comes before and what happens after; how the specific place (in space) impacts the experience and affects its very nature; and what physical objects support and enhance the experience. Even as you explore the other seven realms for the new opportunities they provide, never forget the richness of Reality.

Virtuality lies exactly opposite Reality in the realm of [No-Time – No-Space – No-Matter], consisting of [autonomous – virtual – bits]. Quintessential Virtuality experiences—also now very familiar to nearly all of us—include playing computer games, exploring virtual worlds, probing real-world simulations, connecting via social media, or even just surfing the World Wide Web. They are not bound to a particular time or place, with the physical aspect of all activity receding away to a vanishing point. Yes, of course, anyone having a Virtuality experience resides in some physical place, at a particular point in time, using a material keyboard and mouse (or other interaction devices), but these are all ir-relevant—*im*material to the experience unfolding within the mind in reaction to the digital information displayed in front of the eyes (as well as sound waves hitting the ears).[8] So although all Virtuality experiences really sit atop Reality, for the purposes of exploring the digital frontier we will generally ignore this aspect of it to concentrate on using No-Time, No-Space, and No-Matter as resources for creating customer value.

These two realms, then, anchor the Multiverse. Reality is grounded firmly in our physical universe of [Time – Space – Matter], with Virtuality residing ethereally in the immaterial realm of [No-Time – No-Space – No-Matter]. Each could be labeled any number of ways. Reality could be called the Known Universe, the Real World, the Physical World, or a number of other commonplace names, whereas Virtuality could similarly be called the Virtual World (or Worlds), Virtual Reality, the Metaverse, and so forth. We decided the parallelism of the chosen words works best, for then the name of each of the other octants can relate directly to the two anchors. The names of each realm on the right half of the framework—the four revolving around the real Space axis and thereby rooted in physical Reality—therefore all denote their Reality-based nature, whereas the names of each realm on the left half of the framework— the four revolving around the virtual No-Space axis, embedded in immaterial Virtuality—denote their Virtuality-based nature.

So beyond these two anchors lay the six other realms, each one enhancing, extending, or amending either our Reality- or Virtuality-based experiences. These six are less well known, less thought about and explored—and therefore perhaps hold out greater possibility for value creation.

Of these, surely the most familiar is **Augmented Reality** [Time – Space – No-Matter], a term of increasing currency, where companies employ digital technology (the bits of No-Matter) to enhance our experience of the physical world. The profuse number of applications in this realm where [actual, real, bits] hold sway shows up in everything from day-to-day living, travel, and recreation to medical procedures, manufacturing, and the military. The most obvious example, however, is surely a GPS navigation system (such as those made by TomTom or

Garmin), which overlays the physical scene outside your windshield with a digital representation of it on your car dashboard. It enhances— or augments—your experience of the real world by making sense of it, providing directions to help you find your way, and even relieving the stress of a trip in unfamiliar environs.

If bits can augment Reality, then logically atoms should be able to augment Virtuality. This is exactly what happens in the opposite realm of **Augmented Virtuality** [No-Time – No-Space – Matter], which effectively flips a Virtuality experience from No-Matter to Matter, from bits to atoms. That means we're taking something material and tactile and using it to augment an otherwise virtual offering, resulting in an [autonomous, virtual, atoms] experience. Although high-tech examples exist, such as the haptic technology of sensor gloves that can manipulate virtual objects on screen, the clearest example here is the simplest: Nintendo's Wii, whose remote device detects movement in all directions to affect the digital play of on-screen games from tennis and golf to yoga and general fitness exercise. For the first time, players at home can get physically, materially engaged in computer games, removing the experience from one residing primarily between the fingers and the brain to one involving the whole body.

Alternate Reality [No-Time – Space – No-Matter] derives its name from alternate reality games, or ARGs. Such games have become increasingly prominent in the past decade in marketing circles as platforms for reaching the online gaming crowd, with examples including the *I Love Bees* promotion for Microsoft's *Halo 2* game, *The Dark Knight,* a marketing experience designed to generate demand for the Batman movie of the same name, and *The Lost Ring,* designed to promote the 2008 Beijing Olympics. Jane McGonigal, the "puppet master" for *I Love Bees,* defines an Alternate Reality Game as an "interactive drama played out online and in real-world spaces taking place over several weeks or months, in which dozens, hundreds, or thousands form collaborative social networks, and work together to solve a mystery or problem that would be impossible to solve alone."[9] In this realm of the Multiverse, [autonomous – real – bits] experiences take games (and increasingly other activities) of the sort that normally play out online and take them from No-Space to Space, making the physical world a technologically infused playground of hyperlinked activity. With implications far beyond marketing, this octant starts with Reality and superimposes an *alternate* view on top of it.

Where Alternate Reality takes an otherwise virtual experience and plays it out in the real world, its opposite, **Physical Virtuality,** takes real-world objects (atoms residing in actual time) and designs them virtually. Such a [Time – No-Space – Matter] experience occurs when virtually designed artifacts—created, viewed, usually customized, and generally sold online—take material shape. The most familiar include the mass customized T-shirts, coffee mugs, mousepads, and business cards available on sites like Zazzle and CafePress. The technology of 3D printing perhaps best captures the [actual – virtual – atoms] nature of Physical Virtuality. Here something designed virtually is printed, physical layer by physical layer in precise time sequence, to build up a material object from the experience. Originally used in industrial applications for prototyping or remote part creation, such companies as Shapeways and Ponoko have brought this to the masses, taking your own virtual design (or that of someone else offering designs for sale, which you can often further customize), printing it out physically, and shipping it to you.

The last realm on the real side of the Space dimension, **Warped Reality** [No-Time – Space – Matter], is named as much for how people use the term "warped" in conversation to describe something bent, twisted, or just plain weird as for Einstein's General Theory of Relativity (with gravity's warping of Space-Time) or for *Star Trek*'s warp drive. For Warped Reality differs from Reality only by flipping Time to No-Time. This realm of [autonomous, real, atoms] is not infused with the digital technology of No-Matter, nor does it reside in the virtual arena of No-Space. It just requires the offering to play with or manipulate time in some way that makes it clearly distinct and different from normal, workaday experience. Such reality-based time travel happens whenever experiences simulate another time and (physical) place, such as Renaissance Fairs and living history museums (Plimoth Plantation, Colonial Williamsburg, and the like) or transport us (in both senses of the word) into the past or even into the future (albeit a fictional future) such as at, yes, *Star Trek* conventions.

Though not exactly burning up the digital frontier, truly understanding Warped Reality will help you figure out how to embrace No-Time in the context of No-Space and/or No-Matter. Recall also those quintessential experiences of Reality: taking a walk in the woods, dining with family or friends, watching a sunset from a balcony, and so forth. Many such experiences alter our sense of time, slowing it down or speeding it up, heightening our awareness of the experience unfolding before us, which whenever it happens shifts the experience, even if subtly, from Reality to Warped Reality.[10] Think of it as Reality with a twist of time.

We arrive finally at **Mirrored Virtuality** [Time – No-Space – No-Matter], the exact opposite to Warped Reality: here Virtuality is tied to real time. This realm derives its name from the term "Mirror Worlds," coined by Yale computer scientist David Gelernter in 1992 to describe "software models of some chunk of reality, some piece of the real world going on outside your window."[11] Gerlenter's vision of what digital technology could bring about is now, if you pardon the expression, a reality, as more and more virtual experiences tether themselves to what is going in the real world, in real time. The best examples of such [actual, virtual, bits] models today can be found in myriad Google Maps mashups, such as HealthMap, a real-time view of infectious diseases around the globe, or the company's own Google Flu Trends, which beats the Center for Disease Control to the punch by analyzing searches for flu symptoms. The use of any sort of online tracking tool or any dashboard, whether in a car or plane or computer screen, qualifies as Mirrored Virtuality. For this realm offers a real-time view, a mirrored perspective, of what is going on out there, in the world.

Each one of these realms, in and of themselves, offers tremendous promise for creating customer value. In the succeeding chapters you will encounter them again, in more depth, to better understand the possibilities, learn about many more companies already operating within each realm, and then discern the principles that you can apply to your offerings, in your own situation. You will discover how embracing the realms of the Multiverse enables experiences impossible within the confines of Reality alone.

An Architecture of Experience

All the elements of the Multiverse—its three dimensions, six variables, and eight realms—fashion an architecture delineating all experiences. Its structure helps us perceive the distinct composition of the *when, where,* and *what* of an experience. This architectural perspective calls attention to the makeup and relationship of the experiential variables we discovered by extending Time, Space, and Matter to encompass their opposite. It also deepens our understanding of experience design by focusing on the qualitative nature of how these come together to form the three full dimensions of the Multiverse, as seen in Figure 1.5. Time and No-Time, being measures of change, mutually comprise a single dimension that defines what happens in an experience, or its *event.* Space and No-Space likewise jointly define the dimension of *place,* whether a real or virtual one. And Matter and No-Matter come together to define the *substance* of what makes up the experience.

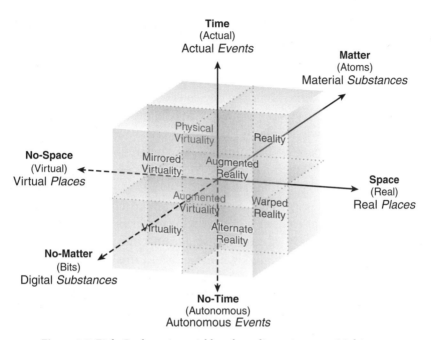

Figure 1.5 Eight Realms, six variables, three dimensions, one Multiverse

Think of the architecture of our tool of exploration as 8-6-3-1: eight realms flow from six variables that comprise three dimensions making up the one Multiverse. Although we will spend the most time developing the view from the perspective of the eight octants, we will examine the other views as well for additional ideas for new offerings, beginning here with a quick tour of what the three dimensions entail.

The Substance dimension speaks to the body of an experience, to all that a person encounters and how it is created. Designers develop experiences from *material substances* and *digital substances,* choosing from the variables of Matter and No-Matter. The choices made here thus *construct* the Substance dimension of the experience out of atoms or bits.

The Place dimension addresses the experience's venue, the setting of its activity made up of the arrangements of its substances. Designers develop experiences with *real places* and *virtual places,* choosing between the variables of Space and No-Space. The choices made here thus *form* the Place dimension out of real space and virtual space.

The Event dimension speaks to the activity of an experience, the order of what people do and encounter as they move from its beginning to its end. Designers develop experiences from *actual events* and *autonomous events,* choosing from the variables of Time and No-Time. The choices made here thus *enact* the Event dimension of the experience out of actual and autonomous time.

Notice that you need not limit your experience to one side or the other of the Substance dimension: you can construct an experience to incorporate both Matter and No-Matter, to be *both* material *and* digital concomitantly. Likewise, you can form an experience to encapsulate both Space and No-Space, to be *both* real *and* virtual in parallel. And you can even enact an experience to involve both Time and No-Time, to be *both* actual *and* autonomous simultaneously.[12]

Surely some of the greatest opportunities for creating customer value beyond the digital frontier will be discovered by operating on all the variables concurrently, effectively *fusing* realms into cohesive and compelling, rich and robust, individual and authentic *transversal* experiences never before envisioned, engendered, or encountered. For whereas the realms are introduced here as quite distinct entities with rather definite boundaries, our experiences rarely fit neatly into one of these eight boxes (as we shall see more clearly in Part IV, "Guiding"). These realms, with their distinguishing characteristics and clear labels, exist to help frame your thinking, not bind you to a rigid, constraining architecture. On the contrary, the boundaries within the Multiverse are permeable and its classifications elastic. We do not present this framework in order to have you argue over what box this or that experience belongs in, but to use it as a sense-making guide for exploring the digital frontier spreading out before you.

Therein lies the power of viewing the singular Multiverse as three dimensions with six variables that you can play with and vary independently. Viewing it solely through the lens of the eight realms tends to restrict the possibilities you explore, for naming an octant confers a linguistic bias on that particular combination of when the experience happens, where it occurs, and what it acts on. If, for example, you believe Augmented Reality not only lies within [Time – Space – No-Matter] but that these three variables *signify* what we mean by the term Augmented Reality, then you will never explore other ways of incorporating bits within an actual, real experience.

So, yes, fully understand the nature of Augmented Reality and each of the other realms as we examine them together in the successive chapters. But look at each example for the *enacting* of its event, the *forming* of its place, and the *constructing* of its substance. This qualitative perspective helps not only in decoding existing experiences but more importantly in depicting and staging new ones. Experience stagers must consciously pay attention to the verbs—to the *enacting, forming,* and *constructing*—to best create the nouns—the most engaging experiential events, places, and substances. Keep the full 8-6-3-1 experience architecture in mind—eight realms, six variables, and three dimensions within one Multiverse—as you read through the rich collection of examples throughout the rest of the book and ponder the infinite possibility available to experience stagers.

For as digital technology pushes the frontier of experience outward, opening up new galaxies begging for ambitious exploration, the Multiverse is the instrument by which you set the direction and chart the course. Its ongoing mission: to help you explore strange new dimensions, seek out new technologies and new experiences, and boldly go where no company has gone before. Therefore think of the Multiverse, with its distinct ways of harboring meaning to help frame your thinking, as more a flexible tool for taking you into the far reaches of your imagination than as a blunt instrument restricting where you can go and what you can dream.

And dream big. Recognize that the three dimensions of the Multiverse do not stop where we have drawn the boundaries of each box on the pages of this book. Those little arrows on both ends of the three dimensions mean the lines representing each variable extend out, further and further, reaching to infinity. With them go the eight realms, expanding ever outward, encompassing ever more possibility, creating deeper and more intense experiences through the innovations resulting from our imaginings.

And of that there is no end.

part II

REAL ORIENTATION

2

Reality

PRESENTING THE RICHEST
OF EXPERIENCES

Take a winter walk, as we have during the writing of this book, through the woods or along a park path on a sunny but chilly Minnesota morning. As you meander, you see your breath, and soon feel your heart beating in your chest as you zip your parka up as far as it goes. The crisp Arctic air stings your face before the low-hanging sun has the chance to warm your body. The wind resonates in your ears, the sound muffled a bit by the hat pulled tightly over your head. You walk a little faster against the wind, swinging your arms as you gradually feel a warming in your chest and limbs. You see an expanse of white snow with dry milkweed pods peeking through. You spy a hawk on a bare branch of a maple tree, then cardinals and blue jays darting from a linden tree to a sheltering spruce. You taste the peppermint balm protecting your lips, sniffle, and inhale a jolt of icy air. You smell wood fires burning in nearby homes and hear the songs of chickadees, the scraping of sharp skate blades against the ice on a nearby pond, and then the slap of a hockey stick against a puck. As you finish your stroll, you think of what a wonderful world it is.

Presenting the Richest of Experiences

If cold Minnesota mornings are not your cup of tea, stay inside and steep a cup, watching the flow of dark, leaf-infused liquid permeate the clear, steaming water. Or visit a cafe for a cup of coffee brewed from beans ground that very morning, observing all the rituals of preparation, production, and consumption. Maybe take your family out to dinner at your favorite restaurant and see how everyone's day went, and play a board game when you get home. Or go on a walk not in the wintry woods but on a summery beach to feel the warm, dry sand filter between your toes as you hear the steady motion of the waves and the happy cries of children. Or visit a store whose talents go beyond merchandising to experience staging, such as climbing a cliff face rising in the tower of a R.E.I. store, watching myriad fish dart by in an aquarium inside a Cabela's, dining with your daughter in the Cafe of an American Girl Place, or asking a genius to help you explore the newest capabilities of your iPhone in an Apple store. Or maybe you are a construction executive looking for a new piece of equipment; then ask Case Construction if you can head up to its Tomahawk Experience Center in the northwoods of Wisconsin to try out all its equipment in what is essentially a giant sandbox.

Perhaps you want to explore the world. (But don't do it alone! Bring along a loved one and/or make new friends as you go.) Have your tea poured for you through the spout of a three-foot-long pot in the confines of Jin Li Street in Chengdu, China. Visit the Caffè Florian in the Piazza San Marco at the heart of Venice, soaking in all the sights and sounds of that most old-world of Italian cities. Take your beach walk on the island of Mauritius before returning to your room at the One&Only Le Saint Géran. Observe fish without the glass of an intervening tank as you scuba dive during your cruise on Royal Caribbean's *Allure of the Seas.* Go mountain climbing in the Rockies, or skiing in the Alps, or golfing in Scotland, or any one of a million different ways you can experience the breadth of God's creation.

And imagine this: Throughout your experiences you enjoy stunning 3D visuals with complete stereo sound! Moreover, you encounter both natural and human-crafted artifacts that present incredible tactile sensations, excite the taste buds, and fill the nostrils with rich aromas.

Defined by its sheer physicality, Reality still presents the richest experiences of all the realms; its essence is to fully engage the five senses, enrapture the whole body, captivate the mind, involve the physical world, and bond you with your fellow members of humanity. Even the most ordinary of experiences—having dinner with family, making a cup of coffee, taking a walk—comes imbued with cultural references and hidden rituals worthy of the attention they so often lack. Extraordinary experiences such as those described above go a step further, commanding not only our attention but a response from deep within us while generating memories that last not just for days and weeks but months and years afterward.

Whatever the type, the common thread of such Reality-based experiences—or, rather, the three common threads weaving through the

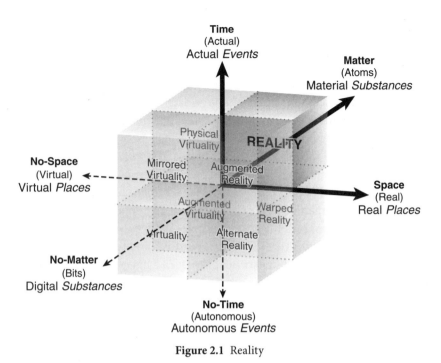

Figure 2.1 Reality

tapestry of our lives—are, as depicted in Figure 2.1, how each event unspools in actual time, the way it occupies a real place somewhere in the world, and how it brims with material substances, engaging our senses with the raw stuff of life itself. So do not consider this book a plea to abandon real-life experiences (business-book reading least among them!). No, we believe people should experience life more richly, savor it more fully, and live it more abundantly.

Think, though, of how each and every experience mentioned above is already infused with technology, from the pot of tea to the warm parka (perhaps filled with 3M Thinsulate), from a diminutive coffee grinder to a gargantuan ship representing the height of Finnish shipbuilding prowess, from aquariums that keep the water in to the mobile gates attempting (at least) to keep the water out of Venice. (And that doesn't even include that iPhone you took into the Apple store.) Life is no less real for already being filled with technology, for technology is how we humans navigate our lives.[1]

Fulfilling Human Purposes

We infuse life with technology, and have always done so. It could not be otherwise, for as noted economist W. Brian Arthur concisely defines it,

technology is "a means to fulfill a human purpose."[2] We have always devised better and better means by which to experience the world and thereby
fulfill our purposes, both individually and collectively. We have done so
through diverse technological domains, as Arthur calls them,[3] such as
clothing, containers, and ships (although each of these could also be broken down into more specific domains). Technologies create value by am-
plifying our innate human capabilities. Eyeglasses, microscopes, and
telescopes extend our sense of sight. Shovels, tractors, and saws increase
our capability to perform work. Postal services, telephones, and television
link us together beyond talking face to face. Protocols, laws, and management processes organize us for effective collective action.

Today, the tsunami of *digital* technology offers an ever-increasing
multitude of opportunities to improve our lives and fulfill our purposes
in wondrous new ways. It dwarfs all other forms of technical innovation,
for the innovations companies create from digital technology proffer
radically new capabilities in both degree and kind.

As this digital wave washes through the economy with permanent
order-of-magnitude changes in the value/price equation, in customer
expectations, and in company capabilities for accelerating innovation,
your company has scant time to learn how to ride this wave before being swept away. Figuring out how to employ digital technology within
your offerings, on your opportunities, and for your customers becomes
imperative. As you address this vast opportunity, keep this question in
mind: If technology is not used to make a human connection—a positive and enduring one—with and especially between your current and
prospective customers, what is the point? Never use technology for the
sake of technology (which goes for individuals as much as corporations).
Use it to connect with people on a human level and to enable them to
connect with others, with the greater world around them, and to the
dreams within them.

The Realms of the Real

Given this proviso to use technology to fulfill edifying human purposes,
and without ever forsaking the opportunities still abounding within Reality itself as a realm of experience, in the rest of this part of the book we
take a closer look at the other three octants within the Realms of the Real,
shown together in Figure 2.2. Each has its roots in Reality, all revolving
around the Space axis encompassing real places and therefore the realms
most played out in the real world itself. Think of it as one anchor of the

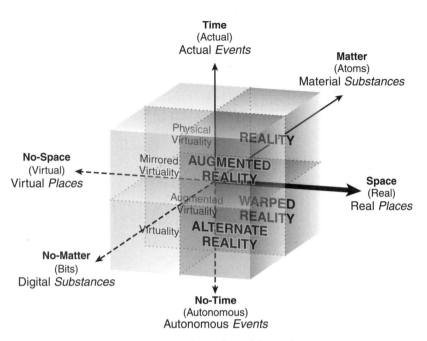

Figure 2.2 The Realms of the Real

Multiverse, Reality, stretching out to encompass aspects of the other anchor, Virtuality: shifting from Matter to No-Matter yields Augmented Reality, swapping Time for No-Time produces Warped Reality, and substituting *both* variables engenders Alternate Reality.

It would be just as accurate to say that Virtuality reaches out to *pull* a Reality-based experience in its direction by flipping the appropriate dimension from Reality-based to Virtuality-based: from atoms to bits for Augmented Reality, from actual to autonomous for Warped Reality, and again flipping both for Alternate Reality. Creating experiences in these four realms all involve staging experiences via forming real places. But while the next three realms all maintain the feel of the real about them, they each take on one or more facets of the virtual and thereby provide opportunities for discovering ways of creating customer value through the exploration of the *cosmos incogniti* lying beyond the digital frontier.

Augmented Reality

ENHANCING THE WORLD AROUND US

In August 2009, I (Joe) took the opportunity to attend the 2009 PGA Championship at Hazeltine National Golf Club in Chaska, Minnesota, with my wife, Julie. The fourth of golf's majors moves around to a different place every year, but it had also been at Hazeltine, not quite an hour from our home, in 2002. That year, journeyman Rich Beem withstood a furious Sunday charge down the back nine from a red-shirted Tiger Woods (who birdied each of the final four holes) to win his first tournament, and a major at that.

We were there at the 11th green when Beem hit a 5-wood to within 6 feet of the pin, making the putt for the only eagle on that hole for the entire 2002 tournament. But we could not be everywhere down the stretch; with Woods playing in the group ahead of Beem, we had to pick and choose which player to watch from what vantage point and then listen for the roar of the crowd from the other hole to guess what had happened. We did not, however, have the same issue at the 2009 Championship. It was not just that Woods, finishing second once again, played together with eventual winner, Y. E. Yang, in the last group, for we still had the problem of finding a spot from which to see the action amidst the throngs.

The solution to our problem of being there live but not being able to see everything going on? FanVision. Formerly called Kangaroo TV, it is a small but substantive device—about four by eight inches, with a TV screen at its widest point and narrowing down to form a handle with navigation keys, plus an ear jack for listening and shoulder strap for easy carrying—that packs a powerful experiential punch. Whether following the lead group or ensconced in a particularly good spot, we now could keep up with everything else going on in the tournament through the FanVision device. We could watch the live TV feed or just listen to the audio, catch up on the current leaderboard or examine the course layout, and even drill down to the scores and shots by any player we so chose. It was a completely different golf-watching experience; for the first time at any tournament, I did not feel like I was missing out on what was happening elsewhere on the course. I would hear a roar and in moments would know exactly who did what where. Also available for NASCAR, Formula 1, NFL, and other sports events, it's no wonder *Time* magazine placed FanVision on its list of best inventions of 2006.[1]

Enhancing the World around Us

You can see how the FanVision device, with its associated software and services, effectively enhances sports experiences, augmenting the reality of the live event. It fits squarely into the realm of Augmented Reality, where, as seen in Figure 3.1, the Reality-based experience shifts by one variable, from Matter to No-Matter, from constructing an experience purely physical to one that uses digital substances to enhance the world around us. There is such an explosion of Augmented Reality applications (often abbreviated AR, but we'll avoid that so as not to confuse it with Alternate Reality) that this chapter cannot help but touch on the possibilities. All the examples we discuss, though, share the essence of this realm: using bits to *augment* our experience of Reality, overlaying it with digital information constructed to enhance, extend, edit, or amend the way we experience the real world.

The quintessential example of Augmented Reality remains GPS car navigation devices (such as those made by TomTom or Garmin) that help you make your way to your destination. These are special-purpose gadgets, as is the FanVision. So is the Delivery Information Acquisition Device, or DIAD, which underpins the success of the United Parcel Service. UPS produced the first one in 1990 to automate scheduling, time-card reporting, and signature gathering, while today's fifth-generation device includes GPS tracking of all drivers and a camera for proof-of-delivery—with direct communications between driver and customer not far behind.[2]

Increasingly, though, people can augment their reality with whatever smartphone they carry. Our favorite example is Amsterdam-based Layar. The company—whose name combines "layer" + "AR"—blends digital data with views of the physical world through what the company refers to as a "Reality Browser." You view the real world through

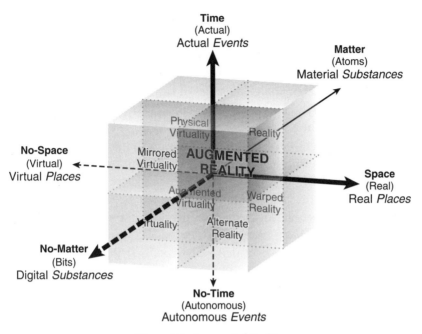

Figure 3.1 Augmented Reality

the built-in camera of your iPhone or Android handset, which then overlays a layer of computer-generated information on top of what you see, in actual time. You can access a layer to find a restaurant for lunch, for example, where as you pan around with your camera restaurants pop up whenever they are in your field of vision, with name, type of food, and the ability to access further information such as the menu. You can similarly look for apartments for rent, the nearest subway station, or the architectural history of buildings in front of you. As cofounder Maarten Lens-FitzGerald told us, Layar "shows you things you can't see," providing a "window on the world around you."

Layar has over 1,500 such content layers—with thousands more coming as developers increasingly use it as the platform for Augmented Reality. Many fit right into an urban lifestyle, while others are particular to a locale. For example, if you direct your mobile phone toward Museo Pablo Casals in San Juan, Puerto Rico, you can access admissions information to the museum or see video clips of Casals, the famous cellist. You can take a 42-stop tour of London dedicated to the Beatles (you never know what you'll see crossing Abbey Road). In many places you might also encounter a zeppelin or even a UFO in the sky above you, a 3D work of art on the grounds before you, or a new song released just in a particular spot for those "in the know."

While every Layar layer has to be individually developed, Google wants to bring the entire Web to users of its Android smartphone operating system through Google Goggles. It calls the function of this program "visual search," enabling people to just take a picture of whatever item on which they would like to know more—such as a building, a painting, or a store—and up pops information found via Google search. One obvious application: comparison shopping in stores, where a quick picture of a product in one store could bring up its price at all the other stores, real or virtual, on the planet. Christine Perey of Perey Research & Consulting says that Augmented Reality holds the promise of turning the world into one huge "interactive catalog."[3] Or how about a dictionary? Word Lens, from San Francisco–based Quest Visual, lets you look at Spanish text through your iPhone camera and replaces it with the word-by-word English translation (or vice versa)—even using the same color and font! Although it's nowhere near perfect, technology reviewer David Pogue of the *New York Times* calls it "software magic."[4]

Location-based Offerings

All such offerings, known generically as "location-based services," use the ability of cell phone towers to triangulate your personal location— or the more accurate GPS capabilities increasingly built into smartphones. Sam Altman, CEO of Loopt, whose offering even says who is near you at this very moment that you very well might want to meet, stresses that "while most technology isolates us behind computer screens and virtual worlds, location-based applications help us discover more, experience more, and connect with others in the real world. It's technology to save us from our technology."[5]

We increasingly see location-based *experiences* as well. "Jewel Collector" lets Layar users find virtual jewels scattered about to earn points and compete with friends. With Foursquare, players "check in" to various locations in their city and around the world, alerting friends (often via Twitter) to their whereabouts, tracking their movements, and uncovering new places to be and recommendations for what to do, eat, drink, or buy there. All the while players earn "check-ins" and, for particular venues at particular times or a set number of visits, badges that display on their Foursquare profile. Check in at a venue more frequently than anyone else, and you can even become "Mayor" of the place! As Nathan

Rice, our own social media strategist at Haberman, Inc., in Minneapolis and an avid Foursquarer, told us, "Foursquare helps me both connect with friends and get recommendations at each venue I visit. I have to admit, though, that my real motivation for using it is the gaming. I love building and maintaining my Mayorships, winning badges, and even uncovering the mystery of what some of the badges are."

Each such location-based experience augments our quotidian existence with not just an informational overlay but by superimposing experience elements onto our daily lives—and into our vacationing lives as well. Recall those old coin-operated viewers at the top of places such as the Empire State Building in New York ("Look! I can see the Statue of Liberty!") or in tourism locations such as Fisherman's Wharf in San Francisco ("Look! I can see Alcatraz!"). Well, YDreams of Lisbon offers an "augmented reality scenic viewer" at such places as the Pinhel Castle in central Portugal and the National Pantheon in Lisbon. You can spin it around to view the environs through its camera and then access further information, additional images, and video stories to enhance your learning ("Look! Do you know who that statue represents?").

Museums have for decades enhanced the visitor learning experience through audio devices that describe objects on display. They democratize the experience by providing a virtual expert for the masses, as if a curator were at your beck and call throughout the time you spend there. Now digital technology enables us to go beyond simple audio tours, with companies offering increasingly sophisticated (and immersive) augmented experiences. The Leeum, Samsung Museum of Art in Seoul rents a "digital guide"—a full-fledged PDA—that allows visitors to access not just audio but also pictures, video, and additional information on its collection. And the Museum of Natural History in Berlin employs a "Jurascope," developed by ART+COM and WALL AG, through which visitors can see animations of the dinosaur skeletons on exhibition come to life: first come the organs, which are overlaid by the muscles and then the skin, after which the animated dinosaur begins to move around ("Look! I can see what the dinosaur was really like!"). And while the Jurascope currently is limited to showing animations, the Digital Binocular Station from MindSpace Solutions of New Zealand can overlay the real objects themselves and bring them fully to life to interact with the viewer in 3D with immersive audio.

Sports teams also increasingly apply Augmented Reality to their in-stadium experience, going beyond special-purpose devices like the FanVision and connecting to the smartphones patrons already bring with them to the games. Those attending Pittsburgh Penguin games at the Consol Energy Center or Steeler games at Heinz Field, for example, can connect their phones to technology from YinzCam to watch, in real-time, the action from multiple camera angles, access up-to-the-minute statistics, or see instant replays automatically streamed to their seats.

Beyond Fun and Games

Augmented Reality can also be used for serious business—even though the previously mentioned businesses *are* all "serious" businesses,[6] this realm is fast becoming the basis for a number of sophisticated medical and industrial applications. For example, the VeinViewer, from Christie Medical Innovations of Memphis, takes an image of a patient's veins via near-infrared light and then superimposes that real-time digital image back onto the patient's skin so clinicians know exactly what to look for and where to find it. By seeing what they could not otherwise see, the technology takes the guesswork and unnecessary needle pricks out of drawing blood or starting IV drips. And medical device maker Medtronic provides a number of hardware, software, and service solutions to hospitals under the banner of "The Medtronic Navigation Experience" to "allow surgeons to precisely track their surgical instruments in relation to patient anatomy, even as that anatomy is shifting in real-time."[7] For such procedures as spinal fusion, this technology virtually extends the surgeon's vision into the opaque body itself and, more importantly, increases knowledge, ensures accuracy, and improves outcomes.

Such uses not only augment reality, but they effectively *amend* it as well. This occurs whenever the digital overlay changes what we do as a result of what we see. This may be particularly important in industrial applications, which can vary from a simple system that illuminates the right part to pick on an assembly line, and indicates the spot where it goes, to a head-mounted display that lets workers completely visualize the task ahead of them as it changes product by product. InterSense of Billerica, Massachusetts, calls its more advanced solution AuRAM, for Augmented Reality Advanced Manufacturing System, which precisely tracks the movement of everything on an assembly line to visually overlay virtual parts on top of physical products.[8]

The aerospace and automobile industries not only lead the way in applying such systems to their assembly lines but also in providing Augmented Reality to the users of their end products. Military and even commercial pilots have long used heads-up displays (whether via helmets or windshields) to access information about their aircraft and flight, and now the same sort of technology is coming to car drivers as well. Mercedes-Benz uses radar to detect vehicles in a driver's blind spots, for example, turning on a red light in the respective side mirror if a vehicle is present. Should the driver turn on his signal to indicate a lane change toward such a vehicle, the light flashes while an audible alarm goes off. Ford, meanwhile, places similar technology on the Taurus and adds a Collision Warning with Brake Support system that detects potential collisions ahead, flashing a red warning light directly on the windshield as it provides additional brake support.

Wired magazine parodied—or, rather, predicted—the direction of Augmented Reality in cars with one of its "Artifacts from the Future" features on the last page of its January 2008 issue.[9] Produced by Chris Baker, it showed the driver's eye view of the futuristic (and as yet fictional) "Hitachi 2400 Smart Windshield," showing not only the speedometer and navigation displayed on the windshield but the current weather, a videoconference call in progress, the turnoff for (naturally) the nearest Starbucks, and—our favorite—the location of a car in the next lane, highlighted in red, whose driver, one "Han, Jennifer // Age 23," is driving with an expired license and had a DUI conviction in 2012. (We only hope the police departments of the future can afford the same technology.)

And, really, we're not that far off. While not yet ready for prime drive time, General Motors is developing an "enhanced vision system" for later this decade that uses external cameras to see what is ahead, as well as internal sensors to ascertain the position of the driver's head and eyes, so it can superimpose visual information on the car windshield. It will highlight speed limit signs, draw the edge of the road under foggy conditions, point out animals near the car, and aid navigation not with a dash-mounted device that takes the driver's eyes off the road but with superimposed images on top of the physical road itself.[10] Can indicators for the turnoff for the nearest Starbucks really be very far behind?

Sensory Prosthetics

It is important, however, to not make the mistake of limiting this realm of the Multiverse to visual devices; *any* way of constructing digital technology to enhance reality qualifies, no matter what sense it engages. In the not-too-distant future when your new car is equipped with the sort of "enhanced vision system" described in the previous section, you likely will interact with it via your voice, much as a GPS navigation system already provides audio directions to you via its recorded voice. Certainly the visual will continue to lead, but already we see applications like Shazam, a smartphone app that you can hold up to "listen" to any musical track, which it can then identify for you (and make it easy to purchase).[11] Or RjDj, from Reality Jockey Ltd. based in Bizau, Austria, which provides "the soundtrack to your life"—where "YOU are inside the music," as its iTunes app description attests[12]—by incorporating whatever sounds happen around you (or by you) into its "reactive music" mix, played into your ears through your iPhone headphones. And then there is LookTel, from Santa Monica–based Ipplex, which lets visually impaired people point their smartphone camera at objects (such as money, medications, or merchandise) and have the app identify the object and state it out loud.

Or consider tactile augmentation. LeapFrog Enterprises builds its entire business around embedding digital technology into education toys to enhance learning via touch. Its latest Tag Reading System lets a child touch words on "Tag-enabled" books with a special digital "reader" to hear the word aloud or get its definition. The technology can read the entire book along with the child, play special sound effects for pictures or characters, or even launch learning games. People of any age can similarly use the Livescribe Echo digital smartpen to remember what they write down (and, with its microphone, hear) for recall later, and workers can apply Sweden-based Anoto Group's ExpeData Digital Writing Platform to record, transmit, and recall handwritten text, such as for invoice writing or package signing.

Researchers continue to push forward the boundary of such tactile augmentation. On the near horizon, the University of Tokyo's Ando-Shinoda Laboratory is working on "Touchable Holography," holograms that you can physically touch—at least that is the sensation created by the "Airborne Ultrasound Tactile Display." It uses pinpoint ultrasound projectors and hand-tracking sensors to create tactile sensations wherever a digital object is visually projected to be in the physical environment, creating, for example, the ability to "feel" holographic raindrops or the surface of any 3D shape.[13] At McGill University in Montreal, researchers "developed floor tiles that can simulate the look, sound, and feel of snow, grass, or pebbles underfoot."[14] And already out of the research lab is GaitAid, from Israeli-based MediGait, which helps those with diminished senses of touch and sight (such as many who suffer from Parkinson's disease) by superimposing a checkered pattern over the floor or ground via a headset and making a sound with every deliberate step. This additional sensory input helps patients normalize their gait and enables them to walk more effectively where they could not before.

Beyond such tactile enhancements lies kinesthetic augmentation. Consider the work of Hugh Herr, the head of the Biomechatronics group at the MIT Media Lab. After losing both legs in the aftermath of a mountain-climbing accident, Herr dedicated his life to developing new kinds of prosthetic limbs—"smart" prosthetics embedded with digital technology. For example, his microprocessor-controlled knee, commercialized by Reykjavik's Össur as the Rheo Knee, constantly senses the terrain and how its user walks to make adjustments that make the gait natural. His PowerFoot One, a powered ankle-foot prosthesis that Herr is bringing to market himself via iWalk, based in Cambridge, Massachusetts, has shown much promise in clinical trials: "Early results indicate that it significantly reduces wearers' metabolic costs while increasing their chosen walking speed. It may even bring the metabolic economy of movement above the levels experienced by people with intact limbs, the world's first limb prosthesis to do so."[15] As this indicates, Herr desires not just to provide amputees with capabilities of walking or grasping but actually to *improve* on "normal" for the physically challenged, giving them a "mobility platform" with greater capabilities—more strength, higher jumping ability, a longer reach, increased endurance—than they (and potentially anyone else) ever had before.[16] Like baseball pitchers having Tommy John surgery to "repair" uninjured ligaments[17] or using Lasik surgery to improve their eyes beyond normal to 20/15 (as Tiger Woods has done, raising some controversy[18]), one day people with no limb loss may even choose prosthetics to increase their natural capabilities.[19]

Another research center at the MIT Media Lab, the Fluid Interfaces Group headed by Pattie Maes, developed SixthSense to access the information in the real world we wish we had available at our fingertips—and in this case controlled *by* our fingertips. Developed by her student Panav Mistry, SixthSense consists of an off-the-shelf Webcam, a smartphone, a pico-projector, and a mirror to shoot images forward onto any surface, which becomes the display; a user wears the assemblage like a pendant around the neck. The device recognizes the movements of the user's hands via the webcam and color-coded finger-gloves or tape worn on the index finger and thumb of each hand (which Mistry plans on eventually eliminating). This enables a natural "gestural interface," where, for example, the four fingers forming a classic "frame" gesture make the device snap a photo, or holding up the left hand causes the projector to display a phone keypad on it, which the right hand can then dial. In a bookstore, the device could recognize a book the user selects and project information onto it, such as its Amazon.com rating or its price at competing stores in the area. A newspaper could trigger the device to search for relevant news video clips, and a person in the line of sight might prompt the display to show his contact details.[20]

Many have likened its gestural interface to the one used by Tom Cruise's character, John Anderton, in Steven Spielberg's *Minority Report* (2002).[21] The scientist who advised the *Minority Report* production, John Underkoffler of MIT's Tangible Media Group, founded LA-based Oblong Industries to develop the G-Speak Spatial Operating Environment, which he describes as "an interface that has no interface," adding, "You operate the world as you operate the real world, which is to say, with your hands."[22] G-Speak effectively unites the Space and No-Matter of Augmented Reality. As Keith Kelsen, founder and CEO of 5th Screen, explains, "What Oblong has been doing is essentially teaching the machine about space and its position in it, using what is essentially a new concept for an operating system. In this new world, the machine no longer thinks of the screen as a flat abstract collection of pixels but as a real object, in the real world, that exists at a particular location . . . and has a relationship to other things in the environment based on that location."[23]

The sense of smell is also a part of our environment, but olfactory augmentation may not yet make sense—DigiScents went belly up trying to develop the first Internet-enabled smell machine, the iSmell, and NTT did not make much of a (fragrant) splash when it demonstrated a similar prototype in Japan. At least Procter & Gamble made it into production for a few years before discontinuing its Febreze Scentstories machine, which "played" discs of scents that slowly changed over the course of an hour. But I (Joe) can still remember a decade later the odors of both good and bad wine emanating from their respective smell machines at Vinopolis in London—for no sense sparks memory more effectively than smell. As reality gets more and more enhanced with digital technology, olfactory augmentation will make increasing sense, although actually less so with Augmented Reality—where the real world remains right there in front of us—than with Virtuality, where over time it may become not only desirable but necessary to add aromatic elements to complete the experience (and thereby shift it over to Augmented Virtuality).

Throughout this tour of Augmented Reality we have seen how companies use digital technology to enhance the lives of people, quite often with rather specialized technology—from navigation devices to heads-up displays, from FanVisions to LeapFrogs, from Jurascopes to Vein-Viewers, and even from smart prosthetics to smell machines. Over time the technologies for augmenting reality have grown significantly more advanced (and less material).[24] Today companies are working on embedding tiny projectors onto people's normal glasses, providing information while still being able to see the real world in front of them. Researchers even hope to develop contact lenses that project images seemingly in front of the wearer's eyes.[25] Increasingly, however, dedicated devices are swiftly being replaced by the increased functionality available on smartphones. TomTom and Garmin, for example, face tough times competing against Google Maps Navigation, AroundMe, and other such apps available for free or next to nothing, without any special equipment on the dash.

Whatever the underlying technology, Augmented Reality supplies a flow (either constant or on demand) of sensory information and enhanced experience to the individual. So in a very real sense all of these devices are prosthetics, extending our sight and, increasingly, our other senses—and our mind as well. When viewed through the lens (pun intended) of digital prosthetics, this realm of experience also creates great potential for extending, even transforming, our very selves.

Few people, however, desire to realize *Star Trek*'s vision of the Borg, a race that assimilates both technology and other species into a Collective in pursuit of constant enhancement, if not perfection.[26] Resistance is not futile, for, as with all technologies, we maintain the personal choice to buy or not to buy, to use or not to use, to turn on and to turn off. Many prefer their sporting experiences undisturbed by the vital statistics of players and unmediated by the images of what is happening out of direct sight or current reality, whether forced on them by giant, flashing scoreboards or personally accessed by tiny, handy mobile phones. Some only want to avail themselves of the *old* possibility to just be.

So before choosing to play in Augmented Reality, you have to figure out how to provide the value many of your guests desire without perturbing the rest. And always keep the needs and wants of your guests—what the humans in the experience truly value—paramount over the technology. As pioneer Robert Rice of Raleigh-based Neogence put it to us, "It isn't about pages, servers, websites, or everything we have created over the last two decades. Augmented Reality is about WHO you are, WHERE you are, WHAT is around you, WHAT you are doing, and WHO is nearby."

Applying Augmented Reality

When you embrace this mindset, you can create great value by under-standing the essence of Augmented Reality: overlaying a reality-based experience with digital technology in order to enhance that experience, making it more informational, more effective, more engaging, more memorable. While many, if not most, of the examples cited here in this fast-moving realm will be superseded by the time we publish this phys-ical artifact of a book (or shortly thereafter), these principles will always apply:

∞ More so than with any other realm (outside of Reality its-self-contained-self), *use the real world as the background for the Aug-mented Reality experience.* So if you already have a reality-based experience—a store, an event, an office, a room, or any other phys-ical place—consider what information or immaterial experience you might overlay atop the physicality you already have. If you do not have such a place, no worries—the entire world can provide the background if you can figure out new ways of letting people interact with it digitally!

∞ The opposite is also holds true: *Use the real world as the foreground for the Augmented Reality experience.* Precisely because the real world is so important to this realm, do not let the technology take preeminence over the base reality.

∞ While long requiring special-purpose devices, increasingly you can *embrace the smartphone as the platform for augmenting real-ity.* Do you have an app for that?

∞ Whatever it may be, *view the augmentation device as a prosthetic extension of the body and/or mind.* In what ways, to what directions, for what purposes might you extend your customers' capabilities?

∞ In so doing, do not view this realm as purely one of informational overlays, but *always use digital technology to augment the experi-ence* as well.

∞ Moreover, *enhance real-world experiences not only visually but also along audio, tactile, and kinesthetic dimensions* (with smell and taste best left to Augmented Virtuality, if engaged at all).

∞ *Use Augmented Reality for tracking*—whether the location of a destination, friends, UPS packages, surgical instruments, assembly line parts, or anything else your customers find of value—*and other location-based experiences.* (Note that this realm shares tracking as a principle with its cousin Mirrored Virtuality, as both link directly to real time, the one in physical places and the other in virtual places.)

∞ *Enhance learning with Augmented Reality,* which is appropriate not only for museums and schools but for all forms of lifelong learning, including business skill training. What do your customers need to learn, and especially how might you help them do it on-demand, in real time?

∞ By its very nature, augmenting reality mediates that reality. Recognize that not all your customers will want that experience mediated, nor want to be bothered by those around them who are mediating their personal experience, so *tread carefully in augmenting reality for those that want it while not being a nuisance to those that do not.*

∞ In many situations you can also *use Augmented Reality to amend reality.* Beyond information and experience, how might you help your customers change their environments, revise their results, or even transform themselves?

∞ Finally, *understand very clearly that Augmented Reality is not about the technology, but about how that technology enhances people's experiences, lives, relationships, and selves.*

So, yes, think of all the fun ways you can apply Augmented Reality, but recognize too its potential for serious fun, even for transformation. If you have a reality-based business, there is no doubt whatsoever that you can augment that reality through digital substances in interesting and innovative ways. What are the right ways for you, and for your customers? For, as MIT scientist Herr declares, "The only limits are physical law and the boundaries of human imagination."[27]

4

Alternate Reality

CREATING AN ALTERNATE VIEW
OF THE REAL WORLD

In early August 2004, the alternate reality game *I Love Bees* gave its online players, over 600,000 in number, their first real-world mission. On a web page that had previously presented recipes for the fictional heroine's Saffron Honey Ice Cream and Bee-licious Chocolate Chip Cookies, a new set of tantalizing ingredients appeared: 210 unique pairs of Global Positioning System (GPS) coordinates; 210 corresponding time codes spaced four minutes apart and stretching across a twelve-hour period in the Pacific Daylight Savings Time zone; and a central timer counting down to a single future date: 08/24/2004.

There were no further instructions provided. The *I Love Bees* (*ILB*) players were given no goal, no rules, no choices, no resources to manage, no buttons to press, no objects to collect—just a series of very specific, physical locations and an impending cascade of actual, real-time moments. Taken together, what were these ingredients supposed to yield?

For two weeks following the initial appearance of the GPS data set on <http://www.ilovebees.com>, interpretation of its meaning varied greatly among the *ILB* players. There was no early consensus about what *ILB*'s designers wanted the players to *do* with these coordinates, times, and date. An explosion of creative experimentation with the data ensued. Some players plotted the GPS points on a United States map in the hopes of revealing a connect-the-dot message. Others projected the earthbound coordinates onto sky maps to see if they matched any known constellations. A particularly large group collected the names of the cities to which the 210 points mapped and then tried to create massive anagrams and acrostics from them. A smaller group decided to average the two numbers in each pair of coordinates and look for an underlying statistical pattern across the set.

Meanwhile, many players began visiting the locations nearest them and taking digital photos, uploading them to the *ILB* community online to see if a visual or functional commonality across the sites would emerge. Others without digital cameras carried out similar scouting activities and filed text-based reports, hoping to help uncover the secret message signified by the coordinates. Among this growing scouting group, numerous competing patterns emerged: The coordinates all pointed to Chinese restaurants, several players suggested—or mailboxes, or video game stores, or public libraries.

For a short while, the potential for plausible readings of the GPS coordinates seemed both inexhaustible and irresoluble. However, as the 8/24/2004 date loomed closer, and after tens of thousands of speculative posts on dozens of Web forums, a critical mass of players finally converged on a single interpretation: The GPS data set was not a puzzle, or a clue—it was a *command*. The designers were instructing players just to show up at the locations at the specified times and *wait for something to happen.*

And so, on August 24, swarms of "beekeepers" (a nickname many of the *ILB* players adopted) showed up at nearly all of the 210 locations, expectantly hovering in groups of a dozen or more. At the coordinates, the players clustered together laden with laptops, cameras, PDAs, cell phones, and anything else they thought to bring just in case, waiting to find out exactly what they were supposed to do. They explained to inquisitive passersby, "We're playing a game." The core mechanic of which appeared to be: Go exactly where you are told to go, and then wait for something to happen. Don't make meaningful decisions. Don't exercise strategy. Don't explore the space. Just go, and wait for further instructions.

This is a game?

Indeed, it is. For many gamers, the August 24th *I Love Bees* mission was their first introduction to a new mode of digital gaming, one that centers on real-world, live action, performance-based missions.[1]

Whether or not this new mode of digital gaming—alternate reality games, or ARGs, here ably described by Jane McGonigal, the world's foremost authority on them (and "puppet master" for *I Love Bees,* the ARG used to promote Microsoft's *Halo 2* videogame)—appeals personally to you or not, do recognize what a momentous experience it was for the players, who eventually did, as a group, figure out what in the heck was going on, and what it meant.

If you have not experienced an alternate reality game firsthand, it may not be the easiest experience to grasp. New media developer Asta Wellejus, of Copenhagen-based The Asta Experience, told us the best way she's found to describe them is like this: "An ordinary virtual game is like Alice going down the proverbial rabbit hole where she enters a virtual world totally unfamiliar to her experience in the real world. An ARG takes dynamite to the rabbit hole and blows it up, letting all that virtual activity spill out into the real world, and makes the distinction between reality and the game world disappear. The game is now alive." (Not coincidentally, ARG designers call the incident that begins the game the "rabbit hole.") Thus, computer-based games can now be taken out of the *terra nova* of Virtuality and played out on the *terra firma* of Reality.

Creating an Alternate View of the Real World

In terms of the Multiverse, Wellejus' description perfectly depicts the entire realm of Alternate Reality, which takes otherwise virtual experiences and plays them out in the real world. For although a Realm of the Real, as seen in Figure 4.1 it lies next to Virtuality, encompassing virtual experiences shifted from No-Space to Space, from a virtual to a real place. The resulting superimposition of the virtual onto the real creates an *alternate* view of the physical *reality*.

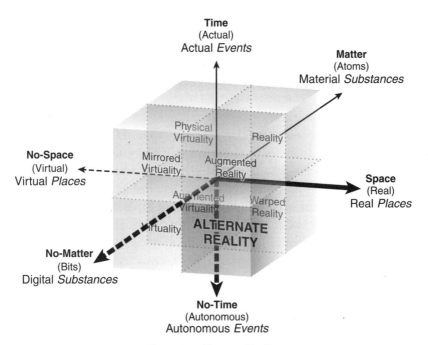

Figure 4.1 Alternate Reality

So the essence of Alternate Reality involves using Reality as a digital playground, changing the way people perceive, and interact in, the real world via a superimposed, virtual narrative freed from the bonds of actual time. It is enacted as a series of autonomous events, not just by the company but the participants themselves, who interlace it with their everyday lives as they collectively work to solve the mystery and bring about a resolution, their very actions affecting the direction and intensity of the nonlinear narrative. Although the *I Love Bees* command to be at particular locations on a specific date smacked of actual Time, players at each of the GPS-specified locations discovered payphones that all rang successively. Answering the calls yielded individual snippets of a five-hour serial radio broadcast chopped up and spread out, which then had to be pieced together to solve the puzzle in autonomous No-Time fashion.[2] As media expert Henry Jenkins notes, an ARG "depends on scrambling the pieces of a linear story and allowing us to reconstruct the plot through our acts of detection, speculation, exploration, and decryption."[3]

Because of this extreme level of involvement, participants take ARGs very seriously. This flows from the philosophy (or conceit) that, no matter what you may think, "This is not a game" (known by players as "TINAG").[4] ARGs are becoming more and more widespread, with the Alternate Reality Gaming Network, dedicated to sniffing out new this-is-not-a-game games and providing a central resource to playing them, listing eleven ongoing games at the time of this writing.[5] The first widespread ARG was *The Beast,* designed as a marketing experience for Steven Spielberg's movie *A.I.: Artificial Intelligence,* and to this day companies primarily employ ARGs to market offerings—Audi, for example, created *The Art of the Heist* to promote the launch of its A3; this ARG involved players tracking down actual A3s in the real world to secure clues.[6] But they also can be offerings unto themselves. *Perplex City* (say it three times fast), from London-based Mind Candy, offers cash prizes (£100,000 for its first contest) but makes money by selling cards that provide additional clues beyond what can be learned for free. Sean Stewart, the lead writer for *The Beast* and *I Love Bees* both, also writes novels, and using the knowledge gained from his work on ARGs now uses "websites, phone numbers, emails, and other 'fourth wall' techniques [that break the "wall" between performer and audience] to create uniquely interactive stories."[7]

Or consider the offering Walt Disney World uses to spice up its least exciting place for the younger set, Epcot. The *Kim Possible World Showcase Adventure* (named after the eponymous TV show teenager on the

Disney Channel who saves the world from evil villains when not going to school) puts youngsters in the role of detectives, who must join together to save the world themselves. The World Showcase in Epcot—a collection of pavilions demonstrating arts, crafts, and foods from around the world—provides the physical backdrop to the Alternate Reality experience, with kids given top-secret "Kimmunicators" (modified cell phones) that guide their journey, providing clues of where to go, who to talk to, what to encounter, and, finally, how to come together as Team Possible to save the world. While parents and others unaware enjoy learning about the world, those who play the adventure have a completely different experience in the same place and time, although in keeping with the autonomous nature of Alternate Reality, according to Disney the "Kimmunicators even recognize when a team has broken away from the action—even secret agents need ice cream breaks—and will alter your mission accordingly."[8]

Beyond ARGs

Of course, ARGs do not provide the only way of embracing Alternate Reality—they give the realm its name but remain only a subset of the possibilities here. Closely related are these other forms of gaming:

∞ *Pervasive games,* such as *Killer,* where you and your fellow players take on the roles of undercover assassins, have "one or more salient features that expand the contractual magic circle of play spatially, temporally, or socially," according to media culture expert Markus Montola.[9] He goes on to relate these first two features in ways immediately recognizable as Space and No-Time thinking, referring to spatial expansion as using the "whole world as [a] playground" and temporal expansion as going outside "the proper boundaries of time," and also acknowledging how digital technology, particularly that arising from Augmented Reality, is "a perfect way of adding game content to the physical world."[10]

∞ *Fantasy sports,* such as Rotisserie baseball, fantasy football, and so forth, are games in which players create their own teams of real-life players, but they distribute them throughout the fantasy league in ways that in no way resemble the actual teams and leagues. They then use computers to compile the statistics of the games played at various days and times to create their own, alternate universe of a game, and eventually an entire season, based on how their players did.

∞ *Scavenger hunts* pit individuals or groups against each other to find the right spots in the real world based on clues coming in from the virtual world. Boston-based SCVNGR, for example, describes its offering as "a geo-gaming platform that enables anyone to quickly and easily build location-based mobile games, tours, and interactive experiences that can be enjoyed from any mobile device."[11] Founder Seth Priebatsch says he wants "to build the game layer on top of the world."[12]

∞ *GPS games* are location-based games such as those provided by LocoMatrix of the United Kingdom, which claims that with its platform for "free-roaming games," downloaded on your GPS-enabled phone, "planet earth's a playground" (as the video on its home page attests).[13] Games, including chasing, racing, and strategy games, can be played solo or with friends at a park, on the beach, or in any open space. LocoMatrix emphasizes that its games are "not on your mobile" but played "with your mobile" and that it "takes gaming away from the screen and into the real world."[14]

∞ *RFID games* use radio-frequency identification chips rather than GPS to be location-aware. Netherlands-based Swinxs offers a self-contained gaming console with RFID wristbands that kids (generally younger than would participate in GPS games) can use indoors or outdoors to play such games as tag, relay, hide and seek, musical chairs, and even to take educational quizzes. As with LocoMatrix, the kids can even design their own games, in this case by connecting the console to a PC.

∞ *Geocaching* is another form of location-based game that Seattle-based Groundspeak describes as "a high-tech treasure hunting game played throughout the world by adventure seekers equipped with GPS devices" used "to locate hidden containers, called geocaches, outdoors and then share [their] experiences online."[15] The company, which popularized the activity, goes on to say on its official website that there are over 1.2 million geocaches around the world, with 4 to 5 million geocachers out looking for them.

∞ *Geoteaming* is an offshoot of geocaching used for business team-building. Its official website describes it this way: "Equipped with your cunning and the coolest high-tech toys—GPS receivers,

Pocket PCs, two-way radios, and digital cameras—you and your team strike out on a fun-filled mission to find hidden caches. It's a treasure hunt where the riches you take away are more than just prizes—they're transformational lessons that apply to how your team works in your company environment."[16]

Outside of gaming but in keeping with fun, consider GoCar Tours, which operates yellow go karts (tiny four-wheeled, two-seat vehicles) equipped with GPS-powered narration systems for tooling around tiny-car-friendly places in the United States as well as Lisbon and Barcelona. Its website description makes clear the No-Time, No-Matter nature of the real-world experience:

It's a tour guide . . . a talking car . . . a trusty co-pilot . . . and a local on wheels.
  GoCar is the first-ever GPS-guided storytelling car—and it's available to rent right now!
  Leave your guidebook behind and see the San Francisco, San Diego, and Miami most visitors never see. Hop into a GoCar and let this little yellow car take you on a guided tour of these fantastic cities.
  Your clever talking car navigates and shows you the way—but that's not all. As you enjoy the drive, it takes you to all the best sites and tells the stories that bring these cities to life.
  These cars are smart. An on-board computer and a GPS-system do the thinking so you can actually relax and take in the beautiful cities.
  The GoCar takes you to spectacular places few visitors get to see. It's like having a local show you around. And this little car can go where the tour buses can't.
  Best of all, the adventure happens at your pace. You can stop for photos, take detours, grab a coffee or break for lunch. (You'll actually be able to park!) Or you can blaze your own trail and explore the city streets, neighborhoods and parks on your own.[17]

With GoCars, people in effect randomly access any site they wish in any order and at any pace, a decidedly nonlinear activity relative to tour buses and other such constrained modes of visiting a destination.

Real-World Playgrounds

Notice how in almost every example inhabiting this realm people learn about something, whether it is the route of their traveling, how to traverse the landscape, clues that help solve a puzzle, where caches are located, or information about the other members of a team. Our favorite

Alternate Reality offering gears itself specifically to the task of helping kids learn—with the great added benefit of getting them exercise—using actual schoolyard playgrounds as its real-world location of virtual activity. Lappset Group Oy, a manufacturer of playground equipment based in Rovaniemi, Finland, decided to add intelligence to its offerings via its SmartUs line of interactive playgrounds. Kids carry around RFID-enabled iCards recognized by the central console—the iStation—and various iPosts placed around the schoolyard. Kids might decide to play an adding game, for example, where the iStation tells them to add up to a particular number, say, 27. They then start running to all the iPosts to see what numbers they represent via their iCards. One might be +7, another -3, a third +4, and so forth. So they have to keep running to the posts, which change the totals on the cards whenever they're read, until they execute a sequence that adds up to 27. The first kid to do so wins the game, and then off they go to play another, whether based in math, geography, history, or another subject. The iStation loads results into the Scorecard so kids can keep track of their results for long-term comparisons, determining their progress, and of course bragging rights.

They can also play other games using the iGrid, a jump mat placed in front of the iStation where each point in the grid can have different meanings in different games. Kids can even define their own learning games in the classroom, upload them to the iStation, and then play them with their friends. In this way SmartUs fuses gaming and digital technology with physical playgrounds and equipment to create a new generation of playful, active learning environments. While participants—not only children but often their parents on weekends, with other setups geared to keeping elderly adults as active (and as lean) as possible—run and jump and climb, they also solve puzzles, search for clues, and find solutions that enhance their learning, all in an atmosphere of compelling and competitive interactive play with all of its aspects of No-Time—enacting nonlinear sequences, starting and stopping, and so forth. Why, even recess is an autonomous respite from the otherwise linear sequencing of the school day! More than 70 schools across Europe now have Lappset digital equipment—not including its new Lappset Mobile Playground aimed at teens—and as its Managing Director, Juha Laakkonen, told us, "With SmartUs, schoolyards become a new classroom and a more diverse teaching facility—places where play, exercise, and learning all come together."

Consider another playground of sorts for kids and adults, the DigiWall from Digiwall Technology AB of Piteå, Sweden. It is a digitized rock-climbing wall, which the company calls a "gigantic computer game in the form of a climbing wall"[18] and sells to amusement parks and other attractions. Each hold in the wall is connected to a computer and comes with lighting and audio effects. This enables groups of people to use the DigiWall to play games, from seeing how many holds they can tap as they light up to a memory game in which they have to find matching holds that emit the same sound. Players can even play Pong with each other as the holds light up in sequence to simulate a moving ball, and when not in use the DigiWall can be programmed to play a light-and-music show for passersby.

As with SmartUs, DigiWall takes a reality-based experience, a climbing wall, and constructs digital substances to amp up the experience and thereby make players more active. They also both share the No-Time aspect inherent in games, which can be started and stopped, reined in or extended, and even frozen during a time out. They generally have a degree of autonomy that other, more natural and less rule-bound forms of physical space do not. Tom Chatfield points out "the sheer, changeless otherness of gaming, and its strange relationship with passing time" in his book *Fun Inc.* "To enter into the world of a game is to visit somewhere unfallen and ageless, where what you do and experience seems to occupy a special, separate kind of temporality; and where the passage of time in your own life leaves no mark."[19]

From Actual to Autonomous Events

Realize, too, that this shift from actual to autonomous events distinguishes Alternate Reality from the adjacent realm of Augmented Reality, which both share the variables of digital substance and physical place. That means that if you can take the technology used to augment reality and then add a dimension of playing with time in some way, you can use that very same technology to alter people's view of the reality before them! While Locomatrix, for example, refers to its technology as Augmented Reality, its No-Time games really belong in Alternate Reality. Sydney-based MUVEDesign, founded by virtual design expert Gary Hayes, is releasing a smartphone-based game called *Time Treasure* in 2011, which it describes as a "location based augmented reality story game" that, due to its "ten layers of time from 2050 back to 5000BC,"[20] also plants it firmly in this alternate realm. People can also use "Reality Browser" Layar to "see" into the past or future, with layers to perceive what the Coliseum looked like in ancient times from your position in present-day Rome, for example, and to envision what the Market Hall in Rotterdam will look like when completed as you stand before the construction site.

Similarly, the Jurascope that *ART+COM* developed to animate dinosaurs in a museum becomes a "timescope" when used to simulate traveling back in time. In Berlin, where very few remnants of the Berlin Wall remain today after absolutely defining the divided city for so many decades, an installation enables people to digitally reconstruct where it was located and what it looked like. They can even select among various dates to see how the Wall changed over time, with the timescope "superimposing historical photos and films at exactly the location where they had been shot."[21] Similarly, the timescope also allows people to peer into the future by, for example, seeing how a building will change as it undergoes construction.

Note a key difference between these two implementations: with the timescope users must remain stationary, whereas with Layar they can move around. Mobility proves key to most Alternate Reality offerings (even when confined to a playground or a location such as Epcot's World Showcase), for they exploit the technological capabilities of smartphones—cameras, video displays, accelerometers, compasses (magnetometers), GPS sensors, and Wi-Fi triangulation (where GPS doesn't work well, such as in urban centers). That means the entire world comes into play, such as with the Gigaputt game from Brooklyn-based Gigantic Mechanic, which defines a virtual golf course from wherever you physically stand, letting you and up to three other buddies play it by using your accelerometer-equipped smartphone as the club handle. Gigaputt measures your swing and plots the resulting path of the ball across your neighborhood, urban streets, a park, or wherever you happen to want to play. As journalist Peter Wayner notes in the *New York Times*, "Everything in the game will unfold in the imagination of the players who might look a bit mad to everyone else on the street. . . . With these new tools, designers are building mystical realms, orienteering courses, immersive fictions, and parallel universes in a way that may or may not have anything to do with the world around them."[22]

Affecting the Real World

What if companies squarely aimed Alternate Reality experiences at the world with the purpose of actually changing the real world in which they play out? Doing exactly that, on a regular basis, is the mission of our able ARG guide, Jane McGonigal. Her talk at the 2010 TED conference, "Gaming Can Make a Better World,"[23] outlined how she wants to bring the skills, capabilities, and, most importantly, the time of gamers to bear on the problems of the world. She put her own skills where her mouth is by helping design a 2007 ARG called *World Without Oil* for San Francisco–based Independent Television Service (ITVS). Its aim: to see how society might react to and solve—just like the usual fictional ARG puzzles—a global oil shortage.[24] *Superstruct,* a 2008 endeavor created in her role as director of game research and development at the Institute for the Future in Palo Alto, asked players to imagine the world in 2019, what tribulations they would face, and then what they might do to solve those issues, for "this is about more than just envisioning the future. It's about making the future."[25]

McGonigal went even further in a *Harvard Business Review* opinion piece by asserting to business executives that Alternate Reality should become "the New Business Reality":

> Although commercial ARGs are, in relative terms, a niche entertainment genre involving several million players worldwide, their enterprise counterpart could eventually become a significant platform for real-world business—in essence, the new operating system.
>
> Why? ARGs train people in hard-to-master skills that make collaboration more productive and satisfying. . . . Using these skills, players amplify and augment one another's knowledge, talents, and capabilities. Because ARGs draw on the same collective-intelligence infrastructure that employees use for "official" business, games will map directly to a familiar reality—no translation required.[26]

We should indeed see more of business played out in Alternate Reality, whether in forecasting, strategy, or even innovation exploration. "In all these cases," McGonigal suggests, "business leaders will become the vital puppet masters, guiding collaboration, introducing complicating variables, and helping focus players' attention in promising new directions," resulting in "an ARG-based operating system that amps up collaboration in the service of strategy."[27]

So Alternate Reality can also mean exploring alternate possibilities for the future of the real world and determining the best path in which to go.[28] Then the "this is not a game" activity really will not be a game.

Applying Alternate Reality

Whether used as a marketing experience, a playful offering, an active learning experience, a strategic tool, or as one of myriad other possibilities that have yet to be innovated, Alternate Reality takes a virtual experience and shifts it over to the real world, making participants physically active in solving puzzles or discovering solutions. Its essence lies in constructing a digital experience and superimposing it onto a real place to create an alternate view of the physical reality. It blends the richness and sensations of the real with the power and complexity of the digital to challenge and involve participants in play environments where they learn almost every step of the way. Follow these principles to determine what role it can play in your business:

∞ As with Augmented Reality, *use the real world as the background for the experience*—but keep it in the background, only rising to the fore when focused on the real world itself, as in McGonigal's plea. It is a Reality-based experience that flips not one but two variables—Matter to No-Matter and Time to No-Time—to yield new creative possibilities.

∞ With Alternate Reality, as its name implies, *create an alternate view of physical reality.* So what physical reality do you own or can you make into a digital playground? And what alternate views of that reality would create value for your customers?

∞ If you already are in the playground business, think about how to *use your playground* (by you or by others) *for an Alternate Reality experience.* Here think broadly, including in the definition of playground not only literal playground equipment like Lappset makes or the schools and parks it sells to, but also amusement and theme parks, golf courses, tour operators, tourism areas, urban districts, stadiums, and any other such physical places; even experientially active restaurants such as ESPN Zone or Dave & Buster's plus outdoor-based retailers such as REI, Cabela's, or Bass Pro Shops could take advantage of this realm. Such business venues as educational and learning places, conference centers, trade shows, and executive briefing centers should also closely examine this realm to create innovative offerings.

∞ Manufacturers of toys and other offerings for kids—think LEGO, Mattel, Fisher-Price, Topps—should look to *make playful goods the basis for playful Alternate Reality experiences.* If Walt Disney can do a Kim Possible experience at Epcot, how about Mattel's American Girl making an Alternate Reality offering in each of the physical places (and past times) in which the stories of all of its historical dolls are set? Recognize, too, that you don't have to make toys to have playful products—think of all of Apple's offerings—and perhaps many B2B goods qualify as great bases for this realm, too, ranging from personal computers to construction equipment (such as at the Case Tomahawk Experience Center mentioned in Chapter 2).[29]

∞ If you already use (or develop) Augmented Reality offerings, figure out how to *manipulate time to shift from Augmented to Alternate Reality.* This might include looking to the future or past, nonlinear narratives, and random or unconstrained access to content.

∞ *Look to mobile technology—cellphones, GPS sensors, cameras, compasses, accelerometers, and so forth—as the means to get customers out into the real world.* Geocaching and geoteaming have already been innovated; what other "geo-activity" might you come up with?

∞ One commonality among all Alternate Reality offerings: *get people up and active in the real world.* It's a great way to get people to exercise their bodies while exerting their minds.

∞ Another commonality at least most share: *help people learn about the greater world around them.*[30] What value can you create by helping customers learn about your offerings, about societal issues, history, places, and subjects, or even about themselves? An alternate view of reality can in fact make that reality more accessible.

∞ Finally, *apply this realm internally,* just as McGonigal suggests, *to your strategy or innovation process, and even to education and employee development.* Over the long term, that could be one of the most impactful ways of creating value for your company.

So, here, think of all the lively ways you can apply Alternate Reality, but recognize its potential for serious play and learning, including for strategy and innovation, even for transformation. So how can you get your customers out in the real world, in your place or their place or public places, in ways that they value?

5

Warped Reality

PLAYING WITH TIME

Several years ago a friend of ours took his son, a Civil War buff, to Civil War Adventure Camp at Pamplin Historical Park near Petersburg, Virginia. The first thing they and their fellow reenactors did was to remove their clothing—except their socks and underwear, thankfully—and all other encumbrances of modern life (no cameras or cellphones, which would only remind the guests of the present time) and put on wool Civil War garb.

This was done in a barn structure that served as a place in which guests also discarded their normal, workaday lives in order to welcome the Civil War experience with its period attire and mindset. Having shed the present and embraced the past, all the reenactors then marched down the hill to camp where, once split into North and South units, they spent the evening learning how to do formations, practicing marching drills, signaling with flags (for day) and fire (for night), guarding the perimeter of the camp, and finally sleeping outdoors, with all meals served in the same tin cup. The next day—it was the middle of summer, so those wool uniforms were authentically hot and sweaty—consisted of skirmishes and maneuvering between the two sides. While they did get to shoot muskets and even a cannon, the only unrealistic detail was the wooden rifles they carried for safety reasons (well, they still did have their own socks and underwear). Our friend told us it was an amazingly well-orchestrated experience, a "total throwback in time" that was "not mediated in any modern way." His then nine-year-old son, meanwhile, described it simply as "the best day of my life!"

Playing with Time

That was the best day of his then still-young life because the Civil War Adventure Camp warped reality for him, his father, and their fellow campers. It took them out of the present day, removing virtually all reminders of it, and shifted them back in time to a period that looms large in our nation's history and has been seared into our consciousness. It was a great experience for all of the participants, no doubt, but one devoid of digital technology—or any observable post-nineteenth-century technology for that matter. For to have used any digital tools or modern machinery would have destroyed the effect, taking them out of the past and bringing them back to present-day Reality.

As opposed to Augmented and Alternate Reality, this realm isn't about embracing digital technology or bringing virtual places into the real world. Rather, it takes an experience firmly grounded in Reality and shifts only one variable, moving the event from actual to autonomous time, as illustrated in Figure 5.1. The essence of this realm is simply playing with time in any way possible. So people leave actual time behind, departing Reality for another realm—a realm not only of Space and

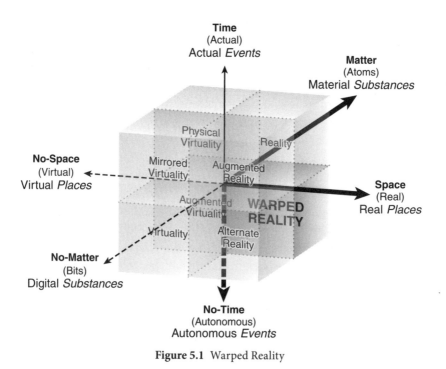

Figure 5.1 Warped Reality

Matter but of No-Time, A journey into a wondrous cosmos whose boundaries are that of imagination. That's a signpost up ahead. Your next stop:
Warped Reality.

So, yes, on the face of it, Warped is weird, a twilight zone of a realm. Do
not give up on it, however, because done well you can create great customer value by taking a real-world experience and warping it—by serving Reality and adding a twist of time. Moreover, this realm has much
to teach us about enacting autonomous events that applies to each of the
other No-Time realms of Alternate Reality, Virtuality, and Augmented
Virtuality.

Few things capture the imagination more than the notion of traveling
through time. Warped Reality is not, however, about TV shows, books,
or movies that play out solely *in* our mind. Rather, it is about happen-
ings in the physical world of space and matter that play *with* our mind,
and in particular its perception of time. This makes time—or, to be more
precise, No-Time—a lead character in the drama. Experience produc-
ers can treat time not as a fixed dimension but as an independent variable. In doing so, the adventure and intrigue explode, stretching the
horizon of possibility far beyond the conventional bounds of storytelling.

Getting into Flow

One need not travel in time to play with time. A key aspect pertaining
not only to Warped Reality but to each of the No-Time realms, we believe,
is Mihaly Csikszentmihalyi's concept of *flow*. The Hungarian psychologist's research led him to the conclusion that we as human beings are
most happy in flow, an optimal experience that evenly balances our skills
with the challenges we face at a high level. This can occur in myriad ways,
from mountain climbing to ballet dancing, from surgery to schoolwork,
from playing music to playing games. Surely you have encountered a
flow experience yourself in some endeavor you faced with passion and
persistence.

Encountering too high a challenge for your skill level, however, leads
to worry or anxiety, and too high a skill level for the challenge leads to
boredom or relaxation. Csikszentmihalyi found that a key component of
such an optimal experience involves changes in the perception of time.
"One of the most common descriptions of optimal experience," he explains, "is that time no longer seems to pass the way it ordinarily does.
The objective, external duration we measure with reference to outside
events like night and day, or the orderly progression of clocks, is rendered

irrelevant by the rhythms dictated by the activity. . . . During the flow experience the sense of time bears little relation to the passage of time as measured by the absolute convention of the clock."[1] He adds that "freedom from the tyranny of time does add to the exhilaration we feel during a state of complete involvement."[2]

Freedom from the tyranny of time. Let that phrase sit on your head for awhile, as a friend of ours likes to say.

Flow experiences free us from the tyranny of time. They let us escape the routine, shed the mundane, and throw off the dictums of this hidebound world. They exhilarate our emotions, excite our senses, energize our bodies, and elate our minds. And whenever the challenges we face slightly exceed our skills, they instigate a virtuous circle as we stretch and grow and enhance those skills, which incites us to seek out greater challenges, which yields further enhancements to our skills, and so on. Short of the time travel we encounter only in books, TV shows, and movies, getting into flow may be the best way to embrace No-Time and thereby warp reality.

Shifting into the Past

The easiest way to warp our *perception* of time may be to shift us into another time period, usually the past (as we tend to know just a bit more about it than the future). The quintessential examples out there in the real world are historical reenactments such as the Civil War Adventure Camp discussed earlier and festivals such as the numerous Renaissance Faires the world over. *Wikipedia* lists 188 reenactment groups from around the globe, including those that recreate the 1815 Battle of Waterloo in Belgium, the 1627 Siege of Groenlo in The Netherlands, and reaching way back, the Spartan Society in the UK commemorating combat in that ancient Greek city-state.[3]

Similar in concept but different in focus are LARPs, or live action role-playing games, which are less about reenacting what actually happened than seeing how people would act (of their own volition) in certain circumstances. Although many LARPs feature real-life situations, this experience genre springs from fantasy literature (such as *Lord of the Rings*) and related tabletop games (such as *Dungeons & Dragons*), which means they shift into times seemingly past but never were.[4] (LARPs influenced alternate reality games, which add in a heavy dose of digital technology to shift from Warped to Alternate Reality.)

Whereas LARPs and reenactments do not really appeal to the masses, anyone can enjoy living history museums like Plimoth Plantation and Colonial Williamsburg. Each of these portray life in colonial times, the former the Plymouth Colony in Massachusetts set in the year 1627 and the latter highlighting the period from 1699 to 1780 when Williamsburg was the capital of the Colony of Virginia. The workers—actors on their colonial stage—wear garb appropriate to the time, speak in the language current at the time, and work and act in ways that colonists worked and acted at the time (hence the term "living history"). In keeping with the theme, they do not even acknowledge modern inventions or events, all to help guests learn about colonial life.

Many cities and areas furnish naturally aged places with a patina of history suitable for transporting to the past. Regulations against motor transport on Mackinac Island in Lake Michigan convey visitors more than a century into the past. Or think of Venice. A visit to this City of Dreams transports you into a meticulously preserved past that puts you in the mood for historical erudition, personal reminiscences, and perhaps even romance.

Experiences can also evoke the past by using rules from earlier periods. For example, at Oakhurst Links in White Sulphur Springs, West Virginia, golfers must use nineteenth-century equipment and follow the rules in play at the club's founding in 1884. That means hickory clubs and guttie balls, sand tees and sheep-grazed fairways.[5] Or consider the Vintage Base Ball Association, which encourages players (or "ballists") to wear old-time replica uniforms and to play the game the old-fashioned way, with such nineteenth-century rules as a ball caught on one bounce (called one "round") being an out, and a hit being fair or foul based on where it first touches the ground. It also strictly maintains such customs as no gloves, no fences, and the utmost in sportsmanship (including helping out the umpires on calls and cheering the opponents).

Many people commemorate all these experiences via scrapbooking, a wonderful way to remember and cement our memories of the past—and a big business as well, with many companies helping consumers preserve their photographs and other memory-laden materials in increasingly sophisticated books. More and more people embrace digital scrapbooking—using computers to scan pictures, arrange layouts, and print pages—which would, of course, move the activity one realm over, from Warped to Alternate Reality (with the alternate view as one of shifting the real experience in time as well as in intensity). Everyone, however, imbues particular things with memories of past times. Whether they be everyday objects, such as a particular coffee cup your mother gave you, or special items of memorabilia, such as a ticket to the first concert you went with your soon-to-be spouse, these items become "time machines" that can instantly convey you into the past.

Shifting into the Future

By their very nature most museums also take us into the past, preserving artifacts, whether photographs, paintings, sculptures, tools, or other man-made relics, or objects of the natural world, such as fossils or the flora and fauna of quickly shrinking present-day habitats. It is of course easier to shift people backward into the known past, but some museums do focus on the future, at least on occasion, such as the Chicago Museum of Science and Industry's Fast Forward exhibit on how the inventions of today shape our lives in the future. Even then—as with Walt Disney World's out-of-date-as-soon-as-it-opened Tomorrowland—the exhibit is more about how yesterday's inventions will make the future we experience tomorrow than it is on the unwritten future itself.

And since the actual future remains unwritten, some turn to fictional futures to engage and even enlighten. *Star Trek: The Experience* was an admission-feed experience at the Las Vegas Hilton centered on simulation rides that placed guests into an episode of *Star Trek: The Next Generation,* which, naturally, transported present-day visitors into the future setting of the show. While the technology-infused rides reside squarely in the Virtuality realm, part of its ten-year mission (it closed in 2008) included a low-tech History of the Future Museum. Functionally a pre-show queue for the rides, this museum housed many Star Trek artifacts and provided a consolidated timeline that weaved together all the various TV shows and movies in one physical place. It enacted a Warped Reality shrine, almost, for Trekkies while simultaneously giving enough information to non-Trekkies that they knew enough to enjoy the ride. (Although for the non-Trekkies, it really was Warped Unreality.)

Companies hire consultants to help take them into the future, but it is generally a process fraught with peril. Doblin, a Chicago-based innovation strategy firm now part of Monitor Group, helps overcome these issues through what it calls "business concept illustration"—or "end-to-end prototyping of an entire business," as the company's co-founder and president, Larry Keeley, put it to us. Doblin's Peter Laundy says such an illustration (either in the form of printed communications or an experience vignette) "depicts an attractive, entirely plausible future business that could be profitably pursued by a company that has a requisite appetite and commitment."[6] As opposed to scenario planning and other future-oriented exercises, Doblin's approach envisions the business itself, rather than the business climate, and Keeley pointed out that businesses that go through this process "routinely transform themselves."

The same can be said for Starizon Studio, a transformational consulting company that turns businesses into premier experience stagers (and includes Joe as a partner) at its experience design place in Keystone, Colorado. Founder Gary Adamson devised Starizon's design process to enable the client first to experience what it would be like to live and work in a world where the strategy has been achieved and then to actually create that future world. Through a theme, declaration, and experience map that broadly lays out that future experience, the client (or "explorer") team journeys not just to Keystone but to its own future, commits to making it happen, and then travels back in time (and to its own place of business) to realize that future. The explorer team acts *as if* that future will happen, as if it were real , and then makes it so.

Think of it as the future equivalent to reenactment: *preenactment*. We thought we coined that word on these very pages, but we Googled it and discovered 7,260 pages of prior mentions, including some to the Historical Preenactment Society (based on a comic book but now, so to speak, real).[7] Think about it, though—how often and in how many ways do we prepare for the future? That is the essence of training, whether preparing to work on an assembly line, lead a mission in Afghanistan, or give a presentation in front of a huge audience. We preenact the future by acting *as if* we were in that future. But beyond shifting into the past, glimpsing the future, and preenacting what one day you hope to be, also look for value in just being timeless—taking actual time as a significant factor out of the equation altogether.

Being Timeless

The Vintage Base Ball Association notes that "modern spectators would still recognize [the] vintage version as base ball,"[8] for as historian Doris Kearns Goodwin points out, baseball "is the most timeless of all sports."[9] A statement understood and embraced by all of its devout fans, baseball preserves this sense of timelessness to this day for a number of reasons, but foremost among them: there is no clock. Teams can never "run out the clock," for baseball is not governed by time. If a game is tied at the end of regulation nine innings, it goes into extra innings, and theoretically at least, could go on forever—witness the most recent twenty-inning game on April 17, 2010, in which the New York Mets and St. Louis Cardinals remained scoreless through eighteen of those innings. The Mets finally won the hard-fought battle in the 20th after six hours and fifty-three minutes.

Populous, formerly known as HOK Sport+Venue+Event, incorporates this sense of timelessness into the stadiums it builds for major and minor league teams by making a walk in or through its stadiums seem like a stroll into the very past that birthed and nurtured the game. Visit Camden Yards in Baltimore, opened in 1992, and if not for the clothing of the patrons, you could be in any era—perhaps half-expecting to see Jim Palmer on the mound, Brooks Robinson anchoring third base, and Boog Powell at first rather than at his BBQ place in front of the warehouse beyond right field.

Other sports do not share this same quality of timelessness (although some might point to cricket). Consider basketball and (American) football. The clock rules both of them—but in a way that also shifts the live experience from Reality to Warped Reality, albeit quite differently than with baseball. (The same is true for hockey and soccer, but we will limit our remarks to those sports with which we are more familiar.) In each case, both pro sports divide games into halves and then quarters, each ruled by their own set time limits (twelve minutes in basketball, fifteen in football). But it's not twelve or fifteen minutes of actual time—it's twelve or fifteen minutes of *game time,* which can be stopped and started independently of actual time. In basketball, a team has to shoot within twenty-four seconds of getting the ball, and the game clock stops whenever a foul is called or the ball goes out of bounds; in football, plays have to be run within forty seconds of the referee placing the ball on the ground, and the clock stops whenever a penalty is called, a pass is incomplete, or the player with the ball goes out of bounds (not to mention when the TV broadcaster wants to show some game-stopping commercials). Scoring does not stop the clock in basketball, but it does in football (although with extra points, no game time elapses). In both, sports coaches and players can call a timeout specifically to stop the clock and manage it to their advantage. Witness how the last few minutes of game time in close contests take much, much more actual time than the rest of the game.

Recall how in describing Warped Reality's adjacent realm, Alternate Reality, we remarked on the inherent No-Time aspect of games. As our discussion of football and basketball exemplifies, almost all games (whether physical or virtual) can be started and stopped, reined in or extended, and frozen during a time out; mistakes can be replayed. They enact a degree of autonomy that most experiences simply do not.

Although casinos like to call gambling "gaming" to reduce certain disreputable connotations, gambling really does not have this same level of autonomy. (Do not try for a do-over at the roulette wheel.) But gambling can become so engrossing that you lose your sense of time and spend far more hours at the table than you expected or imagined, and of course is designed to be that way, with no clocks on the walls, no windows to let in signs of nature's passing, and with the same cheery faces from dealers, drink servers, and other employees twenty-four hours a day. As Christopher Caldwell, senior editor at the *Weekly Standard,* put it in an editorial citing the work of MIT anthropologist Natasha Dow Schüll, problem gamblers in particular often " 'disappear' into the games they are playing or 'exit from time.' "[10] Casinos keep patrons from noticing the passage of time for good reason. Nonetheless, they provide an engaging, and obviously highly valued, experience for the masses.

Another such clockless (but not windowless) experience: theme parks. Like casinos and the best of experience offerings, theme park operators want you to forget about the outside world so you can enjoy totally the time you and your family spend in the places they have made. Many, such as Main Street USA at Disneyland and Walt Disney World, harken back to a bygone era (whether or not it ever actually existed), and old rides such as carousels, wooden roller coasters, and even "It's a Small World" become old friends that harken back to our own bygone era when we were young. Santa Park in Rovaniemi, Finland (Lapland, as we have learned, is the *real* home to Santa Claus!) has as its theme "Everlasting Christmas," so no matter what time of the year you visit, as you walk down into the underground place your surroundings—the sights, the sounds, the smells, the tastes, the activities—transport you to Santa's home cavern on Christmas Day, captured "as a moment, a feeling, that lasts and is available for the entire Christmas season," says the owner, Ilkka Länkinen. The Santapreneur (he also reopens Santa Park in the summer and runs the Joulukka experience in Rovaniemi, Santa's Summer House in Helsinki, and other such experiences) further told us that he "makes the experience more real" by "eliminating any sign or thought of the world above."

Think back too to the Civil War Adventure Camp story that opened this chapter. Remember the barn? It was a particular experience design element that served as a *liminal* place between the Reality of real life and the Warped Reality of the Adventure Camp—a place constructed to be neither one nor the other, but rather a threshold between the two worlds. Even more importantly, it was a liminal *time,* one betwixt and between the present and the past, a timeless moment. We learned of this notion of liminality from Miami University Professor Sally Harrison-Pepper's absolutely wonderful *Drawing a Circle in the Square.* A study of street performers, she describes how "Washington Square becomes a place of suspended time and space, an area chosen for escape or for freedom—perhaps a liminal realm in the mist of New York City."[11] Harrison-Pepper further cites cultural anthropologist Victor Turner defining liminality as "a state or process which is betwixt-and-between the normal, day-to-day cultural and social states or processes." Turner elaborates: "It is a time of enchantment when anything *might,* even should, happen. . . . Liminality is full of potency and potentiality. It may also be full of experiment and play."[12]

We saw this liminality also in Starizon Studio's experience design place in Keystone, where taking explorer teams out of their normal, day-to-day working environment enabled them to think anew about what might, even should, happen in their business. Enacting such a liminal time, betwixt and between the client's past and its future, is just as important, if not more so, than constructing the liminal place.

Liminality is an underutilized element of experience design that applies not just to Warped Reality but to all the realms of the Multiverse. So at least some senses of the term "timeless" need not require ages to accrue, as with baseball, but can be created through exceptional experience design. Even the quintessential experiences of Reality, such as family dinners, beach walks, or sunset scenes, come encoded with memories of moments from our own past, and in so doing may alter our personal sense of time.

Slowing Down, Speeding Up

That sense of stopping time itself, or at least slowing it down, can also be designed. I (Joe) have that sensation whenever I visit P. G. C. Hajenius in Amsterdam for cigars. The setting of the almost one-hundred-year-old location, the conversation with general manager Jan Kees De Nijs, who often stops his work time to join customers for a cigar, the curl of the smoke as I leisurely release it from my mouth to rise ever so slowly overhead—all contribute to such a break from the hustle and bustle of my daily to-dos that it becomes akin to stopping time. Anthropology

Professor Thomas Hylland Eriksen, echoing Csikszentmihalyi, says that in today's fast-paced times we face a "tyranny of the moment":

> The unhindered and massive flow of information in our time is about to fill all the gaps, leading as a consequence to a situation where everything threatens to become a hysterical series of saturated moments, without a "before" and "after," a "here" and "there" to separate them. Indeed, even "here and now" is threatened since the next moment comes so quickly that it becomes difficult to live in the present. We live with our gaze firmly fixed on a point about two seconds into the future.[13]

Eriksen's solution is for people to deliberately and regularly seek out what he calls "slow time," unhurried and thoughtful periods that resist the "stacking" of modern life, "the strange fact that more and more of everything is stacked on top of each other rather than being placed in linear sequences."[14]

More and more people will seek such slow time in their daily lives, whether through a cup of coffee or tea made at home, at work, or at that most ubiquitous of third places betwixt and between the two, Starbucks; through a stroll outside; through a game of Solitaire on the computer; or myriad other ways we as humans look for respites and reprieves. Specifically to reduce stress in and slow down the lives of its patients (and their family members), Mid-Columbia Medical Center in The Dalles, Oregon, placed a labyrinth outside its Celilo Cancer Center. Not to be confused with a puzzling maze, walking the solitary path of a labyrinth with an attitude of contemplation naturally decreases our pace, decelerates our heart rate, and deliberates our thinking. It slows down time.

Companies can also speed up time, creating the perception that experience time is moving faster than actual time, as is often the case with flow experiences. It turns out that, according to a set of researchers headed by Aaron Sackett of the University of St. Thomas in St. Paul, "felt time distortion operates as a metacognitive cue that people implicitly attribute to their enjoyment of an experience," which they helpfully translate for us laymen: "time flew, so the experience must have been fun"![15] Sackett elsewhere indicated to a reporter that to do this, you first must minimize "people's access to accurate time cues"—that is, get rid of clocks and anything else that signals the tyranny of time. "Next, alter their subjective time perception. . . . For example, physiological arousal speeds time perception so a free coffee at the start of a long queue could work. . . . Finally, you need the surprise moment, when people are alerted to the true passage of time. That provokes in people the sensation of time having flown, followed by the gratifying inference that they must therefore have been enjoying themselves."[16] So you actually do want clocks around—but only *after* the experience so the surprisingly long amount of elapsed time convinces guests that the experience was even more engaging than they thought at first blush.

The Walt Disney Company is a master at another perception-changing way of freeing us from the tyranny of time: rethinking what is and is not part of the experience. This was pointed out to us in a conversation with University of Virginia Darden student Tyler Carbone. Places like the Department of Motor Vehicles (DMV) in so many states create "an utterly miserable experience" because waiting is presented as part and parcel of the experience and takes so very long. Tyler contrasts waiting at the DMV, where "it takes a long time and *feels like* it takes a long time," with waiting for an attraction at Walt Disney World, where "it takes a long time but feels like a short time." Disney uses a number of elements to make it so: stating a wait time always longer than the actual wait, snaking lines so you can people watch, and turning the queuing into a pre-show for the live experience that engages all by itself. And, of course, there are no clocks to remind you how long it's taking to get on to the ride!

Hyperlinking Time

Experiences of course can be broken up into more segments than show and pre-show. What if you could randomly access interstices of real-world experiences normally played out in rote sequence? What if you could instantly jump around from, to, and within physical places equivalent to hyperlinking from, to, and within virtual places on the Web? The technology of teleportation only exists in science fiction (think of *Star Trek* transporters beaming Federation officers through space), but short of that, think of transportation vehicles—planes (particularly "per-seat" services like Dayjets), trains (particularly other-worldly subways), and automobiles (particularly random-access taxis) that cause you to interrupt your experience of one place and effectively move it to another place, where it continues apace. By once again changing guests' perceptions of what is and is not part of the experience, they can perceive it as taking a breather in time—not unlike an intermission within a play—before the experience starts up again, although here in a different place. Just as theatergoers easily pick up the dramatic action once intermission ends, so people pick up the narrative of the experience after being transported (if not yet teleported) in such a way. It's like Alternate Reality's example of GoCar Tours or even a DVR, which belongs in Virtuality—but you as the experience stager accomplish the feat without the use of digital technology.

For example, Mark Brady Kitchens of Simsbury, Connecticut, offers a "Shopping Cruise" where the eponymous designer himself picks you up at your home in a stretch limousine. He begins by taking you to breakfast at a local diner to discuss your needs, and then you're off exploring various kitchen stores, finding exactly the right cabinets, appliances, countertops, and so on. In between each segment of the Shopping Cruise experience, guests embark and disembark the limousine that provides interstitial respite from the dramatic tension of examining all the possibilities and making exactly the right choices.

Applying Warped Reality

Warped Reality experiences remain distinct from but connected to the real-world experiences on which they are based by virtue of the real places of Space and the physical substances of Matter. So many businesses, big and small, creating value within this realm should impress on you that enacting events stands as an equal to forming places and constructing substances in the staging of experiences. And as we trust we have amply shown, Warped Reality itself remains set apart from the others because it does not create customer value on the digital frontier. In fact, no digital technology is involved at all in purely warped experiences. It does, however, hold great potential for forming powerful experiences attuned to customer needs—even if, as with scrapbooking and much of gaming, those experiences generally become infused with digital technology and thereby shift over to other realms. Or *especially* if the experiences birthed in Warped Reality shift to another realm of virtual places and/or digital substances.

Although Warped Reality has value in and of itself, perhaps its greatest value lies in teaching us what shifting from the actual events of Time to the autonomous events of No-Time is all about. For the essence of this realm is simply playing with time. This then should more fully inform your work exploring the other realms on the digital frontier with which it shares this variable (Alternate Reality, Virtuality, and Augmented Virtuality). To begin the learning process, understand these principles of warping:

∞ To shift from Reality to Warped Reality you must *manipulate time in some way that makes it autonomous*—or at least so that we as guests perceive it to be autonomous—*from actual time* as we experience it moment by moment in the real world. How can you make your experience independent of actual time, *warping* your guests' sense of time in some way?

∞ A wonderful way to do so: *get into flow.* Embrace Csikszentmihalyi's concept of optimal experience by evenly balancing, at increasingly higher levels, the challenges you present with the skills of your guests. This requires that you customize the experience to individual customers, or make the experience itself customizable to them, as well as adaptive over time as individuals improve their skills.

∞ Perhaps the easiest way, however, is to *shift guests into the past.* Through design, costuming, speech, and acting—as well as removal of all reminders of the present day—transport them to a specific historical period.

∞ Even better, *make guests* not just observers but *full-fledge participants who reenact the past.* When they become not just immersed and engaged but involved and active, the experience creates much more value within them.

∞ *Provide ways for people to remember and cement their own past,* whether as an offering unto itself (as with scrapbooking) or as memorabilia for any experience.

∞ Of potentially greater value than focusing on the past, even if a bit tougher, is to *shift guests into the future.*

∞ Moreover, *get them to preenact their own personal or corporate future,* which makes the warped experience not just fun and informative but potentially transformative as well. This is a key area where mixing in a dollop or more of digital technology to shift it from Warped to Alternate Reality holds the potential for even greater value.

∞ *Find other ways to transport us through time,* whether musically, via period artifacts, or any other way you can devise that adds value to your economic offerings.

∞ You can also *evoke the past by using rules from earlier periods.* Is there some vintage version of your current experience that people would enjoy? (You could at least theoretically do so for an imagined or fictional future as well, such as when *Star Trek*'s three-dimensional chess was sold as a real game.) Recognize that you must encourage, cajole, and even force participants to accept the premise as well as the rules of the time being experienced lest they spoil it for themselves and everyone else.

∞ *Be timeless.* If you already have an experience with the patina of authenticity that comes with age, then be sure to take advantage of that to embrace your timelessness. But you can also design timelessness into your experience if you throw off the tyranny of time, not just by getting rid of clocks but by eliminating the need for clocks in the first place: make your experience so engrossing that your guests' perception of actual time falls away. Here, too, you must take care to remove all signs of the present time, sheltering guests from the distractions of the outside world lest they take guests out of the experience.[17]

∞ In whatever way you play with time, look to *design a liminal place between the Reality your guests are coming from and the Warped Reality of where you are taking them.* This place—whether a distinct structure or just an entryway—should be a threshold between the two worlds, serving as a liminal time as well, one betwixt and between the present and the past, a timeless moment.

∞ *Create experience time separate from actual time,* using clocks that can be stopped and started independently of how many seconds tick away in real life.

∞ There may be many ways to separate experience and actual time, but by far the easiest is to *make your experience into some sort of a game* (a subject we will return to in Chapter 13, "From Design to Deployment"). You can start and stop games, rein them in or extend them, freeze them with a time out, replay mistakes or prohibited moves—with more ways of gaming time out there to be discovered.

∞ *Stop time itself, or at least slow it down.* Provide a respite from the daily grind, whether with coffee in a third place or via other methods elsewhere. It always helps here to start with an experiential good—think of not just coffee and cigars but wine, cuisine, or anything else that excites the senses.

∞ Conversely (a frequent adverb when it comes to playing with time), *speed up time,* creating the perception that experience time is moving faster than actual time.

∞ Finally, *change guests' perceptions of what is and is not part of the experience.* Whether through pseudo-teleportation devices such as transportation vehicles, segmenting the experience into pre-show and show (and there's also post-show), dividing the experience into many different interstices, or providing some sort of out-of-the-ordinary access, shift the nature of the experience from the *linear* to the *nonlinear,* from the synchronous, time-sequenced, lasting, and static spooling of events to the asynchronous, un-sequenced, transient, and dynamic access of any single event, or of the hyperlinking of multiple events together.

As you can see, there are even more ways of warping reality than there are of augmenting or providing an alternate view of it. Warped Reality is a realm of possibility, not an afterthought to its digital cousins. Just as Time is a fundamental dimension of the Universe, so No-Time is a fundamental variable of the Multiverse. The right opportunity for you amid the infinite possibility of *cosmos incogniti,* therefore, may very well lie right here, right now. (Or in keeping with its fundamental variable, right here, right not-now.)

More likely, however, you will end up in one or more of the other realms, and if so, still explore the principles of warping for the ideas they could spark in creating value for your customers. When designing an experience—any experience—while you form its place and construct its substance, attend to the enacting of its events as well. For more than any other variable, No-Time stands for freedom. If you free yourself from the tyranny of time, you will free your mind to go beyond the boundaries of imagination and possibility.

part III

VIRTUAL ORIENTATION

6

Virtuality

CRAFTING THE MOST IMAGINATIVE
OF EXPERIENCES

```
.RUN ADV11

WELCOME TO ADVENTURE!! WOULD YOU LIKE INSTRUCTIONS?

YES
SOMEWHERE NEARBY IS COLOSSAL CAVE, WHERE OTHERS HAVE FOUND
FORTUNES IN TREASURE AND GOLD, THOUGH IT IS RUMORED
THAT SOME WHO ENTER ARE NEVER SEEN AGAIN. MAGIC IS SAID
TO WORK IN THE CAVE. I WILL BE YOUR EYES AND HANDS. DIRECT
ME WITH COMMANDS OF 1 OR 2 WORDS.
(ERRORS, SUGGESTIONS, COMPLAINTS TO CROWTHER)
(IF STUCK TYPE HELP FOR SOME HINTS)

YOU ARE STANDING AT THE END OF A ROAD BEFORE A SMALL BRICK
BUILDING. AROUND YOU IS A FOREST. A SMALL
STREAM FLOWS OUT OF THE BUILDING AND DOWN A GULLY.

GO IN
YOU ARE INSIDE A BUILDING, A WELL HOUSE FOR A LARGE SPRING.

THERE ARE SOME KEYS ON THE GROUND HERE.

THERE IS A SHINY BRASS LAMP NEARBY.

THERE IS FOOD HERE.

THERE IS A BOTTLE OF WATER HERE.
```

Thus begins the very first computer adventure game in the world, *Colossal Cave Adventure,* created by Will Crowther in 1976.[1] As crude as such a text-based game seems today, notice its salient attributes that continue through to the most wondrous of computer adventures today (which all owe this first game a great deal of debt):

∞ It creates a world in which the game action occurs, a world that does not exist in reality (although Crowther did model the environs after Bedquilt Cave, part of the Mammoth Cave system in Kentucky).

∞ That world does, however, have a real sense of place. (Where generic space is amorphous, place has presence.) A player can embrace and learn that place as if it were real, feeling as if he were there.

∞ It is immersive. While playing the game, everything else—the real room in which the player resides, the sights and sounds there, potentially even the monitor and keyboard on which it is played —recedes into the background and effectively disappears.

∞ It supplies a story, a narrative that sets the action in motion and creates drama.

∞ It grants agency. More than mere interactivity, the player has control and his actions have meaning, at least within the bounds set up by the game, making for a nonlinear narrative.[2]

∞ The player himself is represented in the game world in some way, even if only by the reference to "You."

∞ The real experience of playing the game happens inside the player, in his own mind.

Think of any kind of game (not just adventure games, but battles, conquests, puzzles, and any other genre you can think of) played on any kind of digital computer system—*Pong* on an Atari, *Doom* on a PC, *Pac-Man* on an arcade machine, *SuperMario Bros.* on a Nintendo DS, *Halo* on an Xbox, *Tetris* on an iPhone, and on and on we could go—and these foundational characteristics all seem to be present: world creation, a sense of place, a feeling of immersion, narrative, agency, individual representation, and a real experience.

Crafting the Most Imaginative of Experiences

Moreover, these characteristics apply not just to computer adventures but to all of Virtuality.[3] Rendering an experience inside of a digital computer means creating a world that does not really exist, but a world that does feel real enough to have a sense of place (even if it does not look like the real world in any way). The essence of Virtuality lies in how it immerses the mind, although generally not the body, in ways that free us from the constraints of Time, Space, and Matter. The individual sees himself inside the created world, interacting with and within it (even if the user/player/experiencer/person cannot change that place in any way, as with a work of art) in a way that creates a real experience within him.

This last characteristic applies to all experiences everywhere, whether formed in a real or virtual place. Experiences happen inside of us, as our reaction to the stimuli staged outside of us, whether the substance of that stimuli be material or digital. Experiences are memorable events that engage each person in an inherently personal way, whether the events enacted are actual or autonomous to our everyday lives and surroundings. So don't make the mistake of thinking an experience must be based in Reality to be real! The research of Byron Reeves and Clifford Nass shows that "individuals' interactions with computers, television, and new media are *fundamentally social and natural,* just like interactions in real life."[4]

Of course, as we stressed in Chapter 2, "Reality," the richest of experiences still resides in real life, and we believe always will. For although the essence of the realm of Reality is its sheer physicality—immersion in God's creation, not the creations of Man—Virtuality, conceived in imagination and birthed in immateriality, enables experiences otherwise impossible in Reality.

Virtuality is not constrained by physical places, existing not in the real world but in the ethereal world of the Internet, or cyberspace. This now-old term derives from cybernetics, the study of communication or control, based on the Greek word *cyber,* meaning "to steer." In the No-Space of cyberspace, however, it is not the body that steers but the mind, through its manipulation of No-Matter. For Virtuality is not limited by material things, being constructed of digital bits. Further, Virtuality is not bound by actual time, as it opens up to past times in the history of the world, invented times in possible futures of the world, or fictional times in *cosmos incogniti* that never were, are not, and never will be other than in our imagination. Even when a Virtuality experience remains tethered to the real world of the here and now—such as with social media—there remains an otherworldly sense of how time flows, taking advantage of the hyperlinked nature of the hypertext Internet to flit about in all possible sequences, multitasking to the max until time and space themselves recede and we seem to become more mind than body, more out there than in here, more immaterial than material.

The Greek-derived term *hyper,* in fact, means "over, above, or beyond," and its use serves notice that one is leaving Reality as we have always known it and entering a different kind of place, one over, above, or beyond. Think too of hyperspace, that fictional dimension where undiscovered laws of physics enable faster-than-light travel, which in turn enables travel through time. Such is possible only in Virtuality, the realm of [No-Time – No-Space – No-Matter] or [autonomous, virtual, bits], shown in Figure 6.1 where physicality recedes, mental activity ascends, and links to actual time fall away.

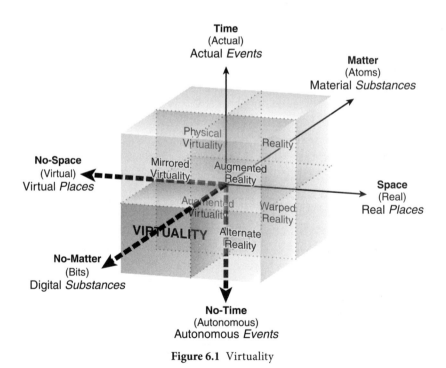

Figure 6.1 Virtuality

The Promise of Virtual Reality

Virtuality first captured the imagination in the form of *Virtual Reality,* a term popularized if not coined by Jaron Lanier, who was one of the pioneers of the head-mounted displays and data gloves associated with the concept. The goal was to replicate reality using digital technology, ideally with a verisimilitude so high that one could feel the technology melt away as the re-creation came to seem real, immersing the body, filling the senses, and engaging the mind. Research into Virtual Reality (VR) both inspired its loftiest depictions in fiction—the Holodeck of *Star Trek* (a completely realistic virtual simulation involving not only sights and sounds but smells, tastes, and tactile sensations) and the Matrix of *The Matrix* (where a complete simulation of reality was jacked straight into characters' brains), among others—and in turn was inspired by these portrayals to reach higher, further, and realer.

While that vision remains remote still decades later, the first known depiction of a virtual environment reaches back over two millennia: the Allegory of the Cave in Plato's *The Republic.*[5] In this well-known story the ancient Greek philosopher held that most people were like prisoners who lived in a cave all their lives, bound by chains, seeing only the shadows thrown on a wall by some unseen light source. These shadows came to comprise their reality, for they knew nothing else. The philosopher, on the other hand, is like a prisoner set free, who comes to understand the true nature of the shadows: that they merely represent what is real and true existing outside the Cave. For Plato, these shadows were the material things that we can sense in the world, and the real and true things were not things at all, but ideas and ideals from which all else was but mere shadow. Of course, the irony—and the lesson—here is not that what seems real (the shadows) is virtual, but that what Plato says is really real (the ideals) is actually virtual, existing only in the collective mind of humanity!

The Reality of Virtuality

And the mind is a wonderful thing. It turns out that we do not need full immersion of the VR kind to participate fully in imaginative virtual worlds; we only need a representation of a world we can believe in, good enough that we can act *as if* it were real.[6] Even a text-based environment, as we saw with *Colossal Cave Adventure,* suffices in this regard, although of course visual representations work even better by making explicit what the mind only imagines.[7] The first virtual experiences that could earn the appellation "world" were text-based Multi-User Dungeons, or MUDS, which brought the live action role-playing games (or LARPs, mentioned in Chapter 5, "Warped Reality") inside a computer where they could be played individually and accessed repeatedly, whenever desired. These moved from text descriptions to graphical representations over time, morphing into the awkwardly acronymed MMORPGs, massively multiplayer online role-playing games, such as *World of Warcraft, Ultima Online, Everquest, Call of Duty, Battlestar Galactica,* and *Eve Online.* These spawned open-ended places of exploration, creation, and conversation such as *Second Life, There, The Sims Online, Cyworld,* and *Habbo Hotel,* not to mention the intriguingly named *Real Life Plus.* And their progeny include virtual worlds designed especially for children, such as *Webkinz World, Build-A-Bearville, Club Penguin, Virtual Magic Kingdom, American Girl's Innerstar University,* and *LEGO Universe.* Video games, too, create virtual worlds with a sense of place and sensation of the real, whether played on an arcade platform, a personal computer, a computer-based console, a smartphone, or any other digital delivery device.

What they all have in common, again, are the attributes mentioned above: world creation, a sense of place, a feeling of immersion, narrative, agency, individual representation, and a real experience. In other words, we don't need the full promise of virtual reality to create Virtuality; we only need to create, in poet Samuel Taylor Coleridge's immortal phrase, "that willing suspension of disbelief."[8] In this view, people let what actually *is,* Reality, wash away to believe the representation, Virtuality. Coleridge, however, did not quite get it right. In *Hamlet on the Holodeck,* Georgia Tech professor Janet Murray rightly comments on Coleridge's famous expression:

> But this is too passive a formulation even for traditional media. When we enter into a fictional world, we do not merely "suspend" a critical faculty; we also exercise a creative faculty. We do not suspend disbelief so much as we actively *create belief.* Because of our desire to experience immersion, we focus our attention on the enveloping world and we use our intelligence to reinforce rather than to question the reality of the experience.[9]

Creating Virtuality, then, requires fashioning a representation people willingly, actively desire to believe. It is a matter of *creating belief.*[10]

J. R. R. Tolkien, who knew a thing or two about fabricating worlds in which people could immerse themselves through belief, called his craft "Enchantment" and outlined how to go about it: "What really happens is that the story-maker proves a successful 'sub-creator.' He makes a Secondary World which your mind can enter. Inside it, what he relates is 'true': It accords with the laws of that world. You therefore believe it, while you are, as it were, inside."[11]

And inside people go, tens of millions of them, with their numbers increasing every day. Such virtual worlds, *Second Life* in particular, became all the rage a few years ago as hundreds of companies followed, moving in-world to market their out-world merchandise. Few, however, bothered to truly understand the phenomenon or create anything but empty stores with no real experience. And so in the eyes of many it crashed and burned.[12] As is so typical with high technology, virtual worlds were overhyped on the short term (with many worlds sure to go under, perhaps even *Second Life* itself), but almost certainly underhyped on the long term.[13] Edward Castronova, the first economist to study the trend, predicts that eventually hundreds of millions of people, maybe a billion or more, will spend tens of hours every week inside virtual worlds, for "these two domains"—Reality and Virtuality in our terminology—"are in competition with one another." "An exodus is under way," he explains. "Time and attention"—the currency of experiences—"are migrating from the real world into the virtual world."[14]

This migration of time and attention to virtual worlds applies not just to full-fledged renderings like *Second Life,* it also applies, perhaps even more so, to much less realistic but more easily played casual or social games, such as *Tetris, Peggle, My Empire,* and *FarmVille.* The latter game, from San Francisco-based Zynga, lets Facebook users set up and manage a simulated farm, with, at the time of this writing, over 215 million annual players, 20 million of whom check in on their crops and livestock every day.[15] At the time of your reading, those numbers will certainly be much higher (and perhaps it will even be surpassed by its urban cousin, *CityVille*). As friend Dave Wright told Joe point-blank: "*FarmVille* has captured my wife."

A key reason for the level of engagement all of these virtual experiences epitomize is, once again, Mihaly Csikszentmihalyi's concept of flow. Although discussed in Chapter 5, "Warped Reality," in regard to that realm's aspect of No-Time, flow applies just as much to Virtuality experiences (of all stripes and realms).[16] For being "captured" need not be bodily; we only need some sort of *avatar,* some virtual representation of the real self that fulfills that fifth attribute of individual representation. An avatar serves as our virtual identity, representing who we are, whether via a mere camera view that says someone in particular is looking at the scene, a cartoon-like figure that performs actions, or a full-fledged virtual body that we may create, customize, clothe, and call pretty much anything we desire. In those virtual worlds with such extensive, customizable, and embodied avatars, if the creator proves an adept story-maker, then when our minds enter it, our avatars enable us to believe it, to see it as true. As anthropologist Tom Boellstorff says in his wonderful study *Coming of Age in Second Life,* "Avatars make virtual worlds real . . . they are a position from which the self encounters the virtual."[17]

The Virtuality of Reality

The virtual worlds our selves encounter need not be solely fictional, invented, or hypothetical. You also can fashion representations of the real world to let people experience places they may not be able to visit physically or in ways they cannot experience materially. Think of all the websites layered on top of Google Maps, such as Globe Genie, from MIT graduate student Joe McMichael, where hitting the "Teleport" button takes you to a random spot on the seven continents, albeit virtually.[18] Or even more experientially, consider Google Earth, a virtual globe where you can zip around and zoom in to any place in the world. Because Google's done all the hard work of stitching together satellite images and other information to create a virtual 3D representation of the physical world, Google Earth has become a platform for all sorts of Virtuality experiences, from election results, blue state by red state, to the location of items for sale on Craigslist, home by home. In autonomous fashion it also provides historical imagery, seeing sites from present time back to the first available images in 1930, as well as a time slider to see the effects of the earth's rotation over the past twenty-four hours as day and night shift across the globe.

NASA provides an open-source satellite view of the earth, World Wind, that people can browse and fly through, and Microsoft maintains its own offering called Virtual Earth. One of the latter's most intriguing aspects is Photosynth, which at the street level stitches together numerous digital photographs of the same place into one navigable image. The resulting "synth" converts 2D photographs into a 3D synthesis that recreates the original, real-world place as a mesmerizing mishmash of days, times, lighting, angles, and resolutions.

Far more accurate and even more fascinating, CyArk uses 3D laser technology to scan and build virtual models of cultural heritage sites around the world. The nonprofit organization, founded by civil engineer and inventor Ben Kacyra of Orinda, California, desires to preserve and share sites that might otherwise be lost forever to erosion or disasters. Its lasers collect millions of measurements per hour as they scan such sites as Mount Rushmore, the Mesa Verde cliff dwellings in Colorado, the Piazza del Duomo in Pisa, Italy, and ancient Nineveh in Kacyra's native country of Iraq. (All of CyArk's projects are nicely laid out in a Google Earth mashup on its website![19]) The vast collection of digital data should result in the most complete and precise 3D virtual models ever detailed, in effect enabling time travel, as Michael Kimmelman of the *New York Times* makes clear:

> Through scanning, the experts can conjure up what objects looked like ages ago, in effect turning the clock back on ancient sites. They can simulate the effects of climate change, urban encroachment or other natural or man-made disasters on those same sites, peering into the future.
>
> Given a proposal for a new building in a city like Edinburgh, they can also create virtual realities, almost microscopically accurate, so viewers might see what the building looks like from all angles in the place where it's intended to go, including the shadows it might cast at different time of day. . . .
>
> A virtual past that never dies.[20]

Less accurate than any of the previously mentioned examples but equally appealing, people also create simulations (or "sims") of real-world places inside of virtual worlds, especially in *Second Life* (or SL). These include re-creations of physical entities that exist in Real Life (or RL), such as buildings like the Eiffel Tower from Paris, Burj Al Arab hotel from Dubai, and the Arch from St. Louis; museums like the Exploratorium (the original museum of science, art, and human perception in San Francisco); and sims of cities like Seattle (complete with Space Needle), Berlin (after the wall came down), and New York (with numerous places recreated within SL, and where 9/11 commemorations now happen every year, demonstrating the ability to have authentic experiences in virtual places). Countries have even created virtual representations for diplomatic relations, with the Maldives placing the first known embassy inside SL.[21] And taking full advantage of the No-Time dimension of Virtuality, there are even reenactments of historical places, such as Tombstone, Arizona, in 1899 where you—that is, your avatar—must wear suitable nineteenth-century clothing, and ancient Rome, or Roma, where your avatar is supplied a toga on entering the Customs House.

IBM made a place inside *Second Life* that exists nowhere in the real world: IBM Land. Here its executives meet with clients and give presentations; even CEO Sam Palmisano has been known to meet with clients here, avatar to avatar, as it were. In IBM Land its consultants create models of clients' businesses to experiment (at very low cost) with process changes and assess the potential results. The company also created a Virtual Universe Community (VUC), which it uses to help clients conduct business inside virtual worlds, as well as for other business activities, including learning and training, teaming and collaboration, connecting and networking, scenario planning, and business process simulation. By using virtual worlds for conferences, brainstorming, and networking, IBM saves money and time while providing a platform that invites broad participation, with people from all over the world taking part at incredibly low costs compared to traveling to the same place at the same time.[22]

Simulation of Reality

IBM also created the *CityOne* game to help companies figure out how to use the offerings in its Smarter Planet initiative by trying them out in a "Real World Game" with "Real World Impact," as its tagline attests.[23] But the games and simulations IBM runs to help clients figure out how to improve their real-world businesses of course reside in Virtuality. Such simulations have long been around, particularly in the field of training, whether to prepare people for the manufacturing line, the cockpit, the operating room, a burning building, or the theater of battle. Digital technology now enables increasingly realistic, lifelike, and immersive experiences that can be replayed over and over, across myriad variations, until people become prepared to take on the tasks of real life. These all purposefully commoditize people's experience in order to change them, and thereby shift up the Progression of Economic Value (see Figure I.1 in the Introduction, "Innovation on the Digital Frontier"), to become the fifth and final economic offering: transformations. By having people go through simulations of real-world experiences over and over and over again, their reactions become second nature, creating the ability to react instinctually to fast-changing, often life-threatening, situations.

The military specializes in this field, for the greater the danger of those real-life tasks, the greater the need to prepare. In 1999 the United States Army helped found the USC Institute for Creative Technologies in Playa Vista, California, to develop digital technologies that would prepare soldiers for far-flung battlefields. The directive from Army chief scientist Mike Andrews: "Build us a holodeck."[24] In concert with colleagues from Hollywood, ICT's researchers continue to this day to get as close as they can to that vision, using interactive digital media to simulate such scenes as battlefields in Iraq, tunnels in Afghanistan, and the skies overhead both arenas. They also create simulations to prepare warriors to come back home, including one to help treat soldiers diagnosed with combat-related post-traumatic stress disorder (PTSD).[25]

The Army also effectively uses virtual simulations as recruiting experiences, including the highly effective *America's Army* online video game and its *Virtual Army Experience* that it moves around the country. Interestingly, in collaboration with Pandemic Studios, ICT produced a commercial offshoot of its work, the popular Xbox video game *Full Spectrum Warrior.* This is not the same-old first-person shooter game as with so many other bloody titles; rather, the institute calls its products "first-person thinkers,"[26] for it is all about making the right decisions at the right time. (And then you shoot.) Many object to such games, including the recruiting ones, but their impact extends far beyond the military. ICT now also produces "virtual humans, computer training simulations and immersive experiences for decision-making, cultural awareness, leadership and health."[27] One of the roles players take on in *America's Army* is a medic, with the simulation so realistic that one such player, Paxton Galvanek, was able to serve effectively as a first responder in a life-threatening car accident. As Colonel Casey Wardynski, America's Army Project director, now retired, noted, "Because of the training he received in America's Army's virtual classroom, Mr. Galvanek had mastered the basics of first aid and had the confidence to take appropriate action when others might do nothing. He took the initiative to assess the situation, prioritize actions, and apply the correct procedures. Paxton is a true hero. We are pleased to have played a role in providing the lifesaving training that he employed so successfully at the scene."[28]

Virtual simulations increasingly provide an advanced platform for training and learning. Pro sports teams now apply the same motion-capture technology used in 3D films to create simulations of individual players to teach them better mechanics, or even "to train against life-size animations whose movements are based on statistics of specific opponents"; the real player, wearing 3D goggles, "runs, jukes and throws" as the virtual players chase him.[29] Corporations increasingly use custom simulations and games to train their employees for the arena of business, or they take advantage of competitive games like *EVE Online, Lineage,* or *Star Wars Galaxies* to teach their employees leadership skills in fast-moving galactic arenas. As reported in a *Harvard Business Review* article, IBM found in a survey of its employees that such games were "surprisingly relevant to their day-to-day work"; three-quarters of the game players said they "could be applied to enhance leadership effectiveness," with half having "already improved their real-world leadership capabilities."[30]

In *Learning in 3D,* Karl Kapp and Tony O'Driscoll make the case for using, and provide a blueprint for, what they call "virtual immersive environments," or VIEs, across myriad learning situations. They believe such simulations will eventually be done as a matter of course: "The Immersive Internet will become a worldwide virtual platform that allows people to immediately exercise their skills and abilities around endeavors that matter most to them."[31]

Byron Reeves, the Stanford University communications professor mentioned earlier, extends this, with his colleague Leighton Read, to say that Virtuality should not just be used by workers to learn, but should apply to *work itself.* Echoing what Jane McGonigal said of alternate reality games, businesses should incorporate "the power of multiplayer games in the redesign of work, making work more engaging and making workers more productive."[32] This will happen because so much of work today lacks engagement, whereas "sophisticated online multiplayer games" require what businesses need: "extraordinary teamwork, elaborate data analysis and strategy, the recruitment, evaluation, and retention of top players in multiperson 'guilds,' the cooperation of people who have complementary roles that require coordinated action, player innovations that come from everyone, and decision making and leadership behavior that happens quickly and with transparent consequence."[33]

Virtuality in Everyday Life

Although an Immersive Internet, replacing 2D pages on the World Wide Web with 3D environments, may very well be on the way, and multi-player games within virtual worlds very likely will transform the work-place (more on that in Chapter 13, "From Design to Deployment"), the Web as we know it already comprises a place—ok, billions of individual but instantly interconnected and endlessly absorbing places—for Virtuality experiences. People spend prodigious amounts of time on social networking sites such as Facebook, MySpace, YouTube, Twitter, hi5, South Korea's CyWorld, and China's QQ, not to mention professional B2B sites such as LinkedIn and Chatter. They frequent social book-marking or news sites such as Del.icio.us, Digg, and reddit. They seek out blogs such as the *Huffington Post, Gizmodo, Boing Boing,* and *Townhall.* They participate in online communities such as chat rooms, in-stant messaging, forums, and wikis.[34] They play. They work. They live.

The Internet makes nearly everyone, everything, and everywhere almost immediately accessible to all of us virtually, eliminating geo-graphic barriers and time differences to engender myriad options for connecting, creating, and collaborating. When Frances Cairncross so presciently said in 1997's *The Death of Distance* that the communica-tions revolution would yield, well, the death of distance, she noted that it meant (even more so than the coming of the telegraph had meant to nineteenth-century England) "the annihilation of . . . time" as well.[35] For not having to travel means not having to spend time traveling. As the telegraph annihilated the distance and time of information, as the tele-phone annihilated the distance and time of voice, as radio and televi-sion annihilated the distance and time of entertainment, so the Internet annihilates the distance and time of *experience.*

No one has captured the No-Time, No-Space, No-Matter essence of the Web better than David Weinberger in his wonderful treatise *Small Pieces Loosely Joined*:

> Our real-world view of *space* says that it consists of homogenous mea-surable distances laid across an arbitrary geography indifferent to hu-man needs; the Web's geography, on the other hand, consists of links among pages each representing a spring of human interest. Real-world *time* consists of ticking clocks and the relentless schedules they enable; on the Web, time runs as intertwining threads and stories. . . . Our "re-alistic" view of *matter* says that it's the stuff that exists independent of us, and as such it is essentially apart from whatever meanings we cast over

it like shadows; the matter of the Web, on the other hand, consists of pages that we've built, full of intention and meaning.[36]

So we seamlessly weave manifestations of Virtuality into our daily lives: not only the World Wide Web via Google searches and hyperlinks, but with mobile phones incorporating the ability to instantly access digital text, images, and videos sent and received from across the globe. We carry out more and more aspects of our everyday lives online. We e-mail, access, talk, text, twitter, blog, bank, search, shop, sell, purchase, pay, play, plan, track, travel, fritter, relate, love, enjoy, escape, learn, be. We experience.

Thus have our daily activities been transformed, and in so doing have transformed us. The World Wide Web is the Wild, Wild West of Virtuality. It is a digital mash-up of times and places, telescoping location and distance along with past and future into an ever-on, always accessible here and now.

Virtuality Unbound

Of course, in reality, if you think about it, all we can ever live in is an ever-on, always accessible here and now. That is the nature of real life. What digital technology does (for good and ill, it must be said) is intensify that life, increase its reach, and, yes, telescope what is accessible to make nearly everything within reach, virtually.

There is, however, an older way of moving beyond what lies physically at our fingertips, a way that predates digital technology: our imagination.

Long before the Internet made all information accessible—every book that has ever been published, every paper that has ever been written, seemingly every thought that has ever been thunk—we could read books and imagine. In our mind's eye we could escape the humdrum of everyday life and see vistas unknown, travel to places unexplored, encounter dramas untold, and, with Plato, contemplate ideals unappreciated.[37] Before the telephone, we could listen to the stories of others—true stories as well as made-up ones—and picture them in our mind, maybe dream of being the protagonist, the hero saving the day. Before radio and TV and movies—all varieties of Virtuality themselves, with the primary experience happening on a screen—kids could break free of the boundaries of parental expectations and communal constraints through play, unadulterated fun where anything can happen and often does. Before the personal computer and the PlayStation, before Nintendo DS and the iPhone, we all could compete in games defined by rules of our own making, or join in with others on well-worn pastimes with rich histories.

In each case you can see Virtuality at work. No, not Virtuality enabled by digital technology, but Virtuality still conceived in imagination and birthed in immateriality, enabling experiences otherwise impossible in Reality.[38] Virtuality enacted by the autonomous events of No-Time, formed in the virtual places of No-Space, and constructed of the immaterial (if not digital) substances of No-Matter.[39]

As discussed in Chapter 2, "Reality," the key characteristic of Reality is its sheer physicality, involving not just the mind nor only the body but the physical world that lies outside of them. With Virtuality, where anything is possible, the opposite holds true: its primary characteristic is its utter immateriality, an experience unencumbered by the physical world and existing *only* in our mind. Sure, the body never really goes away, but with today's technology it primarily withdraws from the full torso to the sensory extremities: the eyes, the ears, and especially the fingertips.

The exact same remains the case with so many other experiences we do not typically consider being virtual worlds, such as those noted earlier: going to the movies; watching TV; listening over the telephone, to the radio, or live with other people in conversation or storytelling; playing; competing in games; even reading books, where words create meaning. As philosopher Pierre Lévy notes in his *Becoming Virtual: Reality in the Digital Age,* "Since its Mesopotamian origin the text has been a virtual object, abstract, independent of any particular substrate."[40] He applies this not just to fictional stories but to nonfiction as well, for "writing desynchronizes and delocalizes" and "has led to methods of communication in which messages are often separated in time and space from their source."[41] As just one handy example, we wrote the words on this page at a completely different moment and place than you are reading them. (And those reading them on any sort of digital reader have the added virtualness of seeing these same words nicely pixilated from their corresponding bits.)

But when it comes to fiction, to the creations of the imagination, recall what digital media Professor Janet Murray said about how we actively create belief: "When we enter into a fictional world, we do not merely 'suspend' a critical faculty; we also exercise a creative faculty."[42] We do not need digital technology to exercise that creative faculty, but it intensifies our creativity, increases its capabilities, and maximizes its realization to make anything that can be dreamt experienceable, not only in our imagination, but visually, audibly, and increasingly through the other senses as well.

And when it comes to imagination, the possibilities are infinite.

Applying Virtuality

Virtuality is indeed the realm that most takes advantage of imagination, for its essence is again its utter immateriality, unencumbered by the physical world, communicated through a screen but existing only in the mind. Although we provided no principles for the other anchor realm of Reality, for it seemed, well, redundant,, it certainly seems appropriate here to do so for Virtuality. So embrace these principles to bring the power of No-Time, No-Space, and No-Matter to your offerings:

∞ First, *envision how you can make the material immaterial* initially in your imagination, and then through digital technology.

∞ Similarly, *envision how you can make the real virtual* by using digital technology to create places that do not exist in the physical world.

∞ And then of course *envision how you can make the actual autonomous* by playing with time. Review all the ways we discussed for doing so at the end of Chapter 5, "Warped Reality," but recognize too that digital technology makes it so much easier to go into the past or future while enabling whole new ways, such as the timeshifting available with DVRs, or the ability to instantly pause the action and then pick up right where you left off as with most any computer game.

∞ *Embrace the seven foundational attributes of Virtuality* discussed at the beginning of the chapter that characterize nearly all of Virtuality:

–World creation: Create a virtual world, in particular one with "worldness," to use Celia Pearce's term, "a sense of coherence, completeness, and consistency within the world's environment, aesthetics, and rules."[43]

–A sense of place: That world should not be generic, amorphous, or indistinct, but should have the feel of the real about it.

–A feeling of immersion: Make Reality recede as Virtuality advances.

–Narrative: Enact a drama through imaginative storytelling.

–Agency: Give the customer control of his own destiny and thereby let him become the hero, or at least a hero, of the story.

–Individual representation: Provide the means for the customer to represent himself virtually, via some sort of avatar.

–Real experience: Recognize that the experience customers have inside their minds are real—even if the substance the experience is made out of is immaterial, the place in which it happens is virtual, and the events autonomous—and therefore work hard to create belief, providing touch points of Reality for them to grasp.

∞ Go beyond these foundational attributes to *incorporate other aspects characteristic of state-of-the-art Virtuality experiences*:[44]

–Three-dimensional: Although text-based representations no longer cut it, even 2D graphical worlds look positively primitive; Virtuality experiences should as much as possible visually look like real, three-dimensional places.

–Persistence: To go from mere game to fully realized world, the place must live on, even when any particular customer exits the world.

–Embodiment: Avatars come to not just identify people but to represent their identity through an emotional bond.

–Sociality: We are not alone; we are immersed with and interact with (the avatars of) other people. In almost all multiplayer games, it takes multiple players to achieve any goals of significance.

–AI-populated: We also are not alone in that many characters are in fact "bots," powered by artificial intelligence to enhance the play experience.

–Contributory: Individual customers shape the virtual world, adding to (and sometimes subtracting from) it while affecting the experiences of the other people within it.

–Explorable: Even in first-person shooter games players can go where they want at the pace they want.

–Rule-bound: The world abides not just by the rules of physics but by the rules of their creators to enact the social environment they desire; failure to abide by them can result in some cases in death (or even worse, expulsion).

–Market-based: An internal economy—often with exchange rates to the real-world economy—allows people to buy and sell offerings found in-world or created from their own imaginations.

–Reputation: Avatars become known for what they have done, what they can do, what they know, and who they are, often via ranks and levels that immediately identify them to others.

∞ Go even further to *consider attributes not yet there, but coming in the labs and on the horizon*:

–Accessibility: Anywhere, anywhen, anyhow from wherever people happen to be, whenever they want, using whatever device they wish.

–Fully sensory: Virtual worlds remain primarily visual, with the ability to engage the ears via voice only a recent addition; tactile is next up, and then we will see what applications, if any, await the ability to taste and smell.[45]

–Emotive AI: Characters powered by artificial intelligence will eventually be able to respond emotionally, not just logically, to the cues given them.

–Natural: Keyboards and mice will eventually go away as we increasingly interact via gestures, voice, and even thought.

∞ But do not stop there. We are not trying to accumulate a definitive list but to spark your creativity and imagination. So *seek out other attributes*, attributes that no one else has thought of, attributes *that emerge only with time, ingenuity, and the expansion of technological capability.*

∞ With all of these as your toolbox, now think about how to *re-create reality virtually,* creating customer value using such platforms as Google Earth, Google Maps, or Microsoft's Virtual Earth. Or your own.

∞ *Simulate reality* as well, providing the means by which your customers can learn about what is important to them before encountering it in Reality.

∞ Turn your attention from your customers to your workers to *employ games, virtual worlds, and other forms of Virtuality as the means to run your business.*

∞ *Embrace the everyday,* for you do not need to create an entirely new virtual world for your customers or your employees; you can make countless improvements in all the ways we already, as people, incorporate Virtuality into our lives.

∞ Understand that anything you can digitize you can customize; once something is represented in zeroes and ones, those ones can be changed instantaneously back to zeroes, and vice versa. So *seek to customize anything and everything that makes sense* (recognizing that not everything will), from avatars to interactions to the virtual worlds themselves.

∞ *Use your imagination.* Virtuality existed long before digital technology, and today as then it exists solely within the imagination. The possibilities may be endless, but the explorers are many; use your imagination to find the right possibilities for you, for your customers, for your company.

∞ And then *create belief.*

Game designer Harvey Smith says the most immersive experiences depend on good design and the ability to create a coherent and believable game world, not on fancy technology: "Despite all the gadgets that are now available, he says, 'nothing is as immersive as a good book.'"[46] Acknowledging that a good book *is* a gadget of Virtuality, you still have nothing without belief. By getting your customers to actively create belief within your Virtuality offerings, you can create the value they increasingly seek on the digital frontier, becoming their guides in leading them to *cosmos incogniti* never before imagined.

The Realms of the Virtual

A counterweight to Reality in the Multiverse model, Virtuality anchors the Realms of the Virtual, depicted in Figure 6.2. The other three realms to be discussed—Augmented Virtuality, Physical Virtuality, and Mirrored Virtuality—all take this realm as their starting point, as each revolves around the No-Space axis encompassing virtual places. These realms each have their roots in Virtuality, which (as with the Realms of the Real introduced in Chapter 2, "Reality") stretches out to encompass aspects of its opposite anchor, in this case Reality: shifting from No-Matter to Matter yields Augmented Virtuality, swapping No-Time for Time produces Mirrored Virtuality, and substituting *both* variables engenders Physical Virtuality.

It again would be just as accurate to say that Reality reaches out to *pull* a Virtuality-based experience in its direction by flipping appropriate dimensions from Virtuality-based to Reality-based: from bits to atoms for Augmented Virtuality, from autonomous to actual for Mirrored Virtuality, and then flipping both for Physical Virtuality. Creating experiences in these four realms all involve making virtual places, although

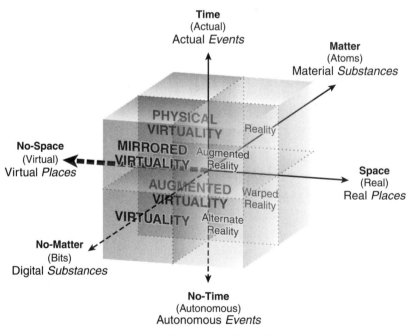

Figure 6.2 The Realms of the Virtual

some enact autonomous and some actual events, and some construct with digital and some with material substances. So even though the next three realms all maintain the texture of the virtual about them, they each take on one or more facets of the real and thereby provide even further opportunities for discovery.

7

Augmented Virtuality

BRINGING THE MATERIAL
INTO THE VIRTUAL

For Valentine's Day 2010, I (Joe) wanted to send cards to my two girls, Becca and Lizzie, who were both away at college. So I went down to the local Hallmark store to pick them out. I found a little section of Disney cards and came across one that highlighted the Disney princesses; I bought two cards to send to each of them.

The caption on the front of the card read, "You're lovely like Aurora, you're brave and kind like Belle, you're Cinderella-sweet . . . you must be magical, as well!" And on the inside, it simply said, "Happy Valentine's Day and Happy Ever After." But here was the kicker: the card offered a surprise: "Watch this card come to life on your computer!" it exclaimed, explaining that all you had to do was to go to www.hallmark.com/extra and follow its instructions.

I had to try it out before sending the cards off. After downloading and running a program particular to the card I purchased, my image came up on the computer screen via the webcam. I picked up the card and placed its front toward the camera—and up popped a three-dimensional animation right on top of the image of the card on the screen! Cinderella herself began singing "Every Girl Can Be a Princess" as a scene from her eponymous movie played. I could still see my own image behind the card, and as I moved it around, the scene changed perspective accordingly, so it could be watched front on or to the side, or even on top. (Turning it over or opening it up caused the program to lose the graphic image of the three princesses on the front, so the animation stopped, only to start over again when I placed the front of the card toward the cam again.) I eventually discovered that if I rotated the card far enough, the *Cinderella* scene was replaced by one starring Belle of *Beauty and the Beast,* and further still brought up Aurora, the star of *Sleeping Beauty.*

I enjoyed seeing all it could do before signing and sending off the identical cards to the two girls.

You can try it out for yourself by going to a Hallmark Store to pick up a free sample, or printing one out at the site, and then following the instructions. When you do, you will notice that the Hallmark page welcomes you by saying, "Watch your cards come to life with Augmented Reality." But it is not Augmented Reality. It is Augmented *Virtuality.*

Bringing the Material into the Virtual

Think about it. Recall our definition of Augmented Reality: using bits to augment our experience of the physical world, overlaying it with digital information. That is not what is going on here. My (and my daughters') primary experience with the Disney princesses did not happen in Reality, but on the computer screen. The webcam-fueled production did not change my real-world experience in any way; rather, it was the *card* that changed my *Virtuality* experience. The physical card—a material piece of matter—altered what I experienced through the cam, on the monitor, in my mind.

That is the exact opposite of Augmented Reality! Rather than the digital enhancing the material, with Augmented Virtuality the material enhances the digital. As seen in Figure 7.1, places are formed in virtual space, events are enacted in autonomous time, and with the augmentation constructed of material substances. The essence of Augmented Virtuality is taking a Virtuality experience and flipping No-Matter to Matter, bits to atoms, by using some material substance to alter, enhance, control, or amend how we experience the virtual world.

You can see this even more clearly with other implementations from the French company Total Immersion, the leader in webcam-based Augmented Virtuality and creator of the Hallmark experience. To promote the movie *Iron Man 2,* it produced a digital marketing campaign in which people can again see themselves through the webcam, but this time with the helmet of Iron Man or another character, War Machine, on their head. As a person's head moves, the helmet moves with it. People can also change the perspective to inside the helmet to view all the information presented to the character (which for that character was Augmented Reality while remaining Augmented Virtuality for the viewer, if you follow!). Each person's head, in other words, becomes the physical trigger that augments the virtual experience.

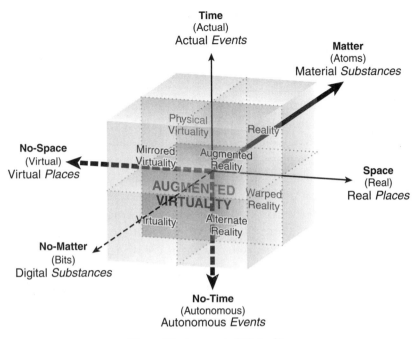

Figure 7.1 Augmented Virtuality

Total Immersion also created the very first implementation we ever heard of, TOPPS baseball cards that audibly introduce each player (complete with cheers, as if at an actual game) and then let the collector manipulate the images to see them hit, pitch, or field on their computer screen. Another developer, James Alliban of London, turned his own business card into an amazing promotional tool at his website, where placing the back of the card, with its graphic marker, in front of a webcam triggers a pixilated 3D image of his own head on top of the card, giving his bio and describing his capabilities. A video of it has been seen hundreds of thousands of times online, but of course it's called "AR Business Card" and not "AV Business Card."[1]

Words have meaning, and it is important to get this right. Much of the strength of the Multiverse lies in understanding the distinctions between realms. To avoid confusion, for example, Layar cofounder Maarten Lens-FitzGerald feels compelled to begin presentations by explaining the difference between proper Augmented Reality as Layar practices it and "webcam-based Augmented Reality" as some mistakenly call it. Discerning the distinctions catalyzes your explorations by giving you conceptual touchpoints to consider in creating customer value.

Bodily Engagement

Other versions of Augmented Virtuality exist besides the webcam kind. In fact, the quintessential example of this realm remains the Wii from Nintendo.

It exploded onto the scene in 2006 (just in time for Christmas) and revolutionized gaming. Its controller, the Wii Remote, senses the direction it is pointed across all three spatial dimensions, along with how fast it is moving, so players can physically manipulate virtual objects. For the first time in any mass-market computer-based game, people could pry their fingertips from their controllers, get their butts off the couch, and put their *body* into the game. You can not only manipulate an avatar to hit a baseball, tennis ball, or golf ball, but physically *be* the one hitting the ball, so to speak; you may physically swing, but it's still a virtual character that hits the virtual ball with a virtual bat. It remains a virtual experience, but the Wii engages both your mind and your body as you physically maneuver the material remote. Nintendo's system became even more realistic when in 2009 it came out with the Wii Motion-Plus, which added a gyroscope to detect the smallest of gyrations of a player's wrist, so now a player can, say, draw a golf shot or put topspin on a table tennis ball.

From the very beginning the Wii engaged not just hardcore teen gamers but the entire family, being particularly popular among women and casual gamers. Even before the Wii, however, there was Activision's *Guitar Hero* (2005), a video game in which players used a guitar replica, developed by Harmonix Music Systems of Cambridge, Massachusetts, to strum to the beat of popular tunes. Harmonix went on to develop more such instrument controllers, creating *Rock Band* with both lead and bass guitars plus drums and a microphone for groups of four to rock out, and the Santa Monica–based Activision responded with *DJ Hero,* where players use facsimile turntables to spin their own music mixes. And even before *Guitar Hero* there was *Dance Dance Revolution* from Japan's Konami, which started as an arcade game in 1998 and later moved in-home to console systems. In *Dance Dance Revolution* players step onto a dance platform or pad and time their dance steps to the music while hitting the spots indicated by patterns on the screen.

Most recently, Sony came out with a similar Augmented Virtuality offering. Its PlayStation enhancement, called the Move, incorporates a Wii Remote–like device that has a sphere on the end that easily can be tracked by a camera called the Eye, enabling much more precision than with Nintendo's Wii in order to control PlayStation games.

Augmenting a virtual experience with a physical object—the Matter of the [No-Time – No-Space – Matter] triumvirate that defines Augmented Virtuality—provides a greater bodily experience than Virtuality alone. The device extends the screen-based experience by drawing it back from the sensory extremities to involve the rest of the body. Further, the experience becomes so much more engaging and robust when the device becomes more sophisticated and intelligent than marked cards and papers placed in front of a webcam. And even though such a device uses digital technology, definitionally that's OK because the experience remains fully one of bits-based Virtuality, with materiality added on top of it, just as Augmented Reality adds digitality atop atoms-based Reality.

Another great benefit ensues: the stimulation of physical activity within a virtual place. You can, in fact, work up quite a sweat playing with the Wii. That's why Nintendo collaborates with the American Heart Association at activeplaynow.com "to promote physically active play as part of a healthy lifestyle."[2] And that's why sports and fitness applications proliferate. In addition to such active games as boxing, Nintendo created the Wii Balance Board, which measures a person's balance and body mass, to enable a number of different physical fitness pursuits through its *Wii Fit* and *Wii Fit Plus* titles, including yoga poses, fitness and aerobic exercises, and a number of balance-based activities.

Others have joined in on using virtual places to promote physical well-being. Respondesign's *Yourself!Fitness* stars Maya, a virtual fitness coach who leads players through exercise routines specific to the abilities and needs of each person. These are done, interestingly, using normal, physical workout objects such as exercise balls, weights, and steps rather than an electronic controller like the Wii Remote, enhancing the virtual experience all the way. And EA Sports, the Electronic Arts unit that is probably the premier producer of sports video games (including *Madden NFL* and *Tiger Woods PGA Tour*), collaborated with manufacturer Toy Island to produce a series of virtual coaching products, including Voice Command Pitching Machine, Voice Command Quarterback, and Sweet Spot Basketball, that "bring classic sports activities to life in a whole new way, utilizing infrared, motion and equilibrium sensors."[3]

As the devices here become less digital and more material, the primary experience may slide from what happens virtually on the screen to what happens physically on the field. This would slip the experience along what we might call an "Augmentation Axis" from Augmented Virtuality to Augmented Reality. The very same technology could then shift commensurately from its primary value being its physicality enhancing the virtual experience to its digitality enhancing the physical experience. In every case, though, *both* aspects remain present, all the time. One can therefore understand the confusion of those who call Augmented Virtuality offerings Augmented Reality, and even vice versa. Still, do keep in mind the distinction as you explore the *cosmos incogniti* of augmentation, seeking value wherever it can best be found.

From the Body to the Mind

While the previous examples of Augmented Virtuality focus on the body, companies can also apply this realm to enhance the mind by increasing what we learn via the base Virtuality experience. Chicago-based VTech Electronics, for example, produces the Wii-like V.Smile Motion Active Learning System, where children bone up on their math, reading, science, and spelling while actively engaging with fun experiences on their TV. And on the webcam-based side of the realm, in London nonprofit Specialist Schools and Academies Trust teamed with James Alliban of Augmatic—he of the amazing business card—to create LearnAR, a set of applications that help teachers and students explore subjects such as math, science, physical education, and languages. In learning about the organs of the body, for example, students can hold a properly marked piece of paper over their own body and via a webcam see all the internal organs displayed on the computer screen in approximately the proper place.

On the intelligent-device side of the spectrum, Amsterdam-based Personal Space Technologies (PST) creates interactive work stations and monitors that let people see virtual objects three-dimensionally. On top of that Virtuality base it then adds plain physical objects that users can move around manually, causing the virtual objects on the screen to move commensurately. (In other contexts we would call them "hockey pucks," although they generally look like big, soft, twelve-sided dice; the reflector dots on each side enable a camera to determine its orientation relative to the virtual object.) The museumgoudA, in Gouda, The Netherlands, for example, digitized its municipal arts collection, and now uses PST offerings to allow visitors to handle, hold, touch, and examine virtual art pieces without risking the slightest damage to the real ones. They simply pick up the physical object that stands in for a virtual artifact (which in turn represents the original work of art!) and freely manipulate it as they look at its image on the screen.

The company started out in health care, where it provides doctors with Personal Space Stations that enable them to view medical images such as X-rays, MRI results, and CAT scans. The doctors can then pick up the same sort of object to manipulate these images, rotating a scan to all sides, zooming in to get a better look, and so forth. The device can even turn its 3D imaging into 4D by displaying a time-elapsed scan as it changes. (Note that if that capability were tied into a real-time scan as it happened, that would fuse Augmented Virtuality with Mirrored Virtuality.) Through it, doctors can effectively hold a beating heart in their hands.

Expanding the Senses

Although all the examples so far result in visual action (with audio accompaniment), other lines of research and application expand the possibilities. The key technology: haptics, where sensors connected to the body can make virtual objects seem real through the application of forces, vibrations, or motion to create tactile sensations. Such "virtual touch" provides a means of information sharing beyond sights and sounds. Long worked on in the laboratory as part of the Virtual Reality thrust, many researchers have created Virtuality environments where subjects interact with their surroundings while wearing body suits with actuators that "push back" to provide people with a sense of touch on various areas of their bodies. Commercialization, however, has come only in highly specialized fields such as avionics and medicine, where doctors use it in training simulations and increasingly for "teleoperations," procedures in which the patient is remote from the doctor, who operates with local instruments (via haptic response) while a robot performs the actual operation on the patient.

There is, of course, one more arena of haptic commercialization: gaming. Dr. Mark Ombrellaro of Bellevue, Washington, founded TN Games as an offshoot of his medical information company, TouchNetworks, to market the 3RD Space Vest. Thanks to air pistons in the vest connected electronically to the game console, players who suit up when they shoot 'em up can actually feel it when they get shot up.[4] Many other virtual touch innovations augment gaming experiences, from something as simple as a joystick controller shaking as your race car rubs against the wall of a virtual racetrack, to something as encompassing as game chairs that move three-dimensionally, in synch with whatever virtual vehicle—motorcycle, car, plane, spaceship—you control, as well as responding tactilely to the virtual environment; for example, you feel the surface of the road over which you are driving.

Fresh Green Light of Rye, New York, uses such driving simulators to teach teens without having to take unprepared drivers on the open road. Cofounder Laura Shuler told us, "Our 'Apple Store meets Driver's Ed' approach is making training cool; one kid recently told me 'these are sick'—the ultimate compliment!" The technology has become so realistic, in fact, that the Sideways Driving Club in Hong Kong counts among its clientele real race car drivers, who train using the Club's gaming simulators. These simulators come complete with "a narrow fiberglass cockpit, realistic steering system and a calibrated brake pedal" that "mimic the feel of a genuine car, while a video screen shows the track and headphones provide realistic sound."[5] Many NASCAR drivers own their own "sim racing" units to prepare for upcoming races. Carl Edwards says he uses it "at tracks where I don't feel real comfortable, specifically the road courses."[6]

Eliminating the Device

Much of Augmented Virtuality involves providing such special-built devices as these driving environments, the *Guitar Hero* guitar, the Wii Remote, the Hallmark card, or Personal Space Technologies' "hockey puck" with its reflector dots. In a different way of thinking about Augmented Virtuality, UK-based Violet produces the Mir:ror, an elegant RFID reader that lets any object drive actions on your personal computer. It comes with a set of RFID (radio-frequency identification) tags that you place on any object, and then you tell your computer what you want to occur whenever that tag is read. So, for example, suppose you have tagged your family's keys; placing your car keys on the Mir:ror looks up the day's weather on the Web, whereas your daughter's house key sends an e-mail to you at work that she arrived at home.

In a similar vein, Personal Space Technologies lets any object—a pen, helmet, tennis racket, even body parts—serve as the virtual manipulation device by placing tracking markers on it, which can then be "seen" by its camera-based Personal Space Tracker. Director Marc Lausberg says, "It's better than the Wii. We can make anything into a 3D interaction device."[7] You can't get more general-purpose than *anything,* an advance owing to moving the technological capabilities from the hand to the camera and its connection to a computer (just as in the webcam-based experiences discussed earlier).

The first commercialized system with such a camera-based interface was of course in games: the EyeToy for Sony's PSP console. Released in

2003, its TV-mounted camera (which evolved into the Eye of the Play-Station Move) recognizes the player's body in order for it to become the physical controller of the virtual experience. It lets your avatar lean, jump, duck, kick, fight, dodge, bat, or perform scores of other actions that mimic your own body movements. In an update to *Dance Dance Revolution,* for example, your hands have to move to the rhythm of the beat, not just your feet.[8]

Microsoft's Kinect technology for its Xbox 360 takes this to a whole new level by adding a microphone for verbal commands, increased resolution, and, most importantly, a second camera, on the infrared spectrum, to see depth. Through it the system can take an image of a player's entire body to place it inside games, so rather than gross motor control of an avatar, Kinect provides rather fine body control over the player's actual image. After its release in November 2010 (just in time for Christmas!), three separate *New York Times* articles (one from a business reporter, another from a business columnist, and the last from a video-game reviewer) all described it breathlessly using the same imagery: It has an "almost magical technology for gesture and voice recognition"; "There's a crazy, magical omigosh rush the first time you try the Kinect. It's an experience you've never had before"; "Most of the time Kinect simply feels like magic."[9]

After playing Xbox 360 Kinect games and experiencing this magic for myself, I (Kim) reflected on my recent Augmented Virtuality experiences—from the Hallmark Card that Joe shared with me, to the Wii, to the Kinect. I noticed a progression of increasing value in the ways these technologies augment Virtuality to create ever more engaging experiences. For example, a Hallmark Webcam Greetings card—simply being a device that launches and, to a limited degree, controls the way the virtual message plays out—has little physical experience nor interactive mental engagement. The card accomplishes its purpose of entertaining you, but that's it.

With *Wii Sports* I play such virtual games as tennis, bowling, boxing, and baseball with the handheld Wii directly controlling my avatar. The level of physical and mental engagement increases as I strive to learn, by trial and error, how to play more effectively. Pursued diligently, the games spur a significant level of physical exercise that initially might go unnoticed but over time produces valuable health benefits. In my ongoing personal transformation quest to find entertaining and engaging physical activity, *Wii Fit Plus* took me to yet a higher level of engagement thanks to the Wii Balance Board. The addition of standing and stepping on this input device provided a greater degree of interaction due to richer real-time feedback on my balance, pace of activity, and overall coordination while performing the *Wii Fit* exercises, treating them in essence as a game.

When the Xbox 360 Kinect came along, my experiences graduated to yet another degree. With this gaming system, no physical device attaches to you or gets stepped on. In this Augmented Virtuality experience, YOU are the matter, constructing the physical control "device." The Kinect cameras profile you, the game learns who you are, and the system then tracks the motion of your whole body and its parts. The comprehensive and tight interactivity between my bodily movements and my virtual avatar boosted my engagement tremendously. Whether shooting down Curvey Creek in *Kinect Adventure: River Rush,* taking dance lessons with *Dance Central,* or exercising to *Your Shape Fitness Evolved,* my every movement comes into play.

Moreover, with the two instructional games my virtual coach commented on my moves, praised me for the correct actions, encouraged me to do right what I had yet to master, gave me very specific critiques to improve my performance (e.g., "Squat lower. Kick higher! Stay in rhythm."), and, in general, matched the workout sessions to challenge me at my current skill level. The instantaneous feedback and continual encouragement from a rather patient and never-tiring coach provides for exceptional learning and workout experiences that move me toward mastery and self-transformation.

Augmented Virtuality technology thus holds the potential for such life-altering activity in many facets of being, such as making work as engaging and intrinsically rewarding as play. We want to play for the experience itself. So why not design other life activities, including work, to be as engaging as play? What if we pursued work for the experience itself, where we surrender ourselves in the flow of its activities to lose our consciousness of actually toiling away? As we shall see further in Chapter 13, "From Design to Deployment," whether we view what we do as work or play comes down to our personal perspective of an activity. As Mark Twain put it, "Work consists of whatever a body is *obliged* to do, [while] Play consists of whatever a body is not obliged to do."[10] Adam Penenberg says in *Fast Company* of the original Augmented Virtuality device, "Nintendo's Wii is so widely used in rehabilitation that some have dubbed it 'Wii-hab.' Patients who have suffered strokes, paralysis, torn rotator cuffs, broken bones, and combat injuries play Wii baseball, boxing, bowling, and tennis. . . . Grueling rehabilitative exercise becomes a game—a competition so engrossing patients can forget they are engaged in occupational therapy."[11]

The capabilities for such nonobligatory play continues to advance rapidly beyond the Wii and even the Kinect. Microsoft sees the latter enabling, in the words of engineer Alex Kipman, "a world where technology more fundamentally understands you, so you don't have to understand it."[12] Virtual Reality pioneer Jaron Lanier, currently Partner Architect at Microsoft Research, wants to take this view even further to encompass us understanding the world. He now works on what he calls "somatic cognition," a "new frontier of human potential" where "the human body is extended by physical objects that map body motion into a theater of thought and strategy."[13] He sees the Kinect camera and its successors as enabling people to map their bodies not just to avatars but to *anything* they wish to study—chemical molecules, mathematical shapes, plants and animals—because people will learn more when they "become the thing" they are studying.[14] His colleagues at Microsoft Research also work on projects advancing the state-of-the-art in Augmented Virtuality beyond the Kinect, such as an armband that directly translates muscle movement into a game controller and, potentially, a controller for all sorts of human-computer interactions.[15] Meanwhile, people across the globe extend the capabilities of the Kinect itself by hacking it to perform ever more varied and amazing feats of augmentation.[16]

Sometimes, though, you do not want a workout via your actions but information to guide your actions. Remember SixthSense, from the MIT Media Lab's Fluid Interfaces Group, and the G-Speak Spatial Operating Environment from Oblong Industries? Described in Chapter 3, "Augmented Reality," for their ability to augment the real world with digital information displayed in front of the user, they seem of a kind with Kinect, at least directionally. And there's that Augmentation Axis again, for although both involve gestures and motion, whether the right realm is Augmented Reality or Augmented Virtuality really depends on *where the primary experience lies,* the Space-based real place of the former or the No-Space-based virtual place of the latter, as well as *its aim,* the Time-centered informational needs of the former or the No-Time-centered gaming aspects of the latter. (Perhaps there are other such axes, planes, or even curves to be discovered within the Multiverse.)

And as with Augmented Reality, over time more and more of Augmented Virtuality will embrace the mobile phone. People can use smartphones not just for their capabilities to bring digital information to any physical location but to bring physical activity to any virtual location.

Already most phone manufacturers are copying the Apple iPhone's accelerometer and motion and proximity sensors, used in applications as trivial as quaffing back a virtual beer to as serious as medical training. And Immersion Corporation of San Jose, California, brings its background in medical and industrial haptics to the mobile phone, licensing "immersive messaging" technology that enables people to *feel* their phones in new ways. Spouses, for example, can send beating hearts as a symbol of their love or simultaneously draw "finger trails" on their individual screens, seen by both parties in a virtual "shared space," with vibration feedback when they touch. The company proclaims, "Digital information remains two-dimensional: something we look at, listen to, and read about. Haptic touch is the missing piece, the sensory element that will transform information into experience."[17]

Through the addition of all these technologies to the mobile phone, over time its use as a physical controller will be integrated into more and more Virtuality environments, augmenting them with the physicality of Matter.

Applying Augmented Virtuality

Using physical substances—whether general-purpose or special-built, whether intelligent devices or body parts—to enhance autonomous events within virtual places is the essence of Augmented Virtuality. Consider how you can apply this realm of the Multiverse to your business through the following principles:

∞ In order to augment Virtuality, you first must *start with a Virtuality experience.* If you already stage one today, consider how you can enhance it through material substances.

∞ If you do not already stage one, you might then *explore the webcam-based version of Augmented Virtuality,* creating a graphic trigger on your physical product. While this often comes off as a gimmick, especially when used just for marketing purposes, integrating it into the offering itself as Hallmark and TOPPS did could yield great value.

∞ Recognize that the physical object always stands in for a virtual artifact. So with Augmented Virtuality you generally must *design two experiences: one virtual and one physical.*

∞ *Engage the body.* In whatever way you implement this realm—with a graphic image, with a Wii-like controller, with a marker-enabled device, or directly with the body itself as a natural interface—the fact that you are using something material will naturally involve the body, so focus on doing so in a way that makes the bodily experience engrossing and absorbing.

∞ Game controllers, musical instruments, sports equipment, vehicles, and medical instruments have all proven amenable to this approach; *seek out new physical controllers/instruments/equipment/ devices as special-purpose controllers.*

∞ And of course, as with much of the Multiverse, *consider shifting from the use of special-built to general-purpose devices.* Always keep up to date with smartphone technology to see how it can be incorporated.

∞ Whether it is the stated goal or not, *ensure greater physical fitness results from the bodily engagement.*

∞ *Focus on intellectual learning* as well.

∞ *Embrace haptic technology and other ways of going beyond sight and sound.* This can make the experience both more engaging as well as more realistic.

∞ Finally, *discern the distinctions between Augmented Virtuality and Augmented Reality to power your explorations.* As we saw throughout this chapter, there seems to be an Augmentation Axis that repeatedly links these two realms. Keeping in mind the exact nature of each, without muddying them together, can double your chances of finding new opportunities.

As evidenced by the relative dearth of viable Augmented Virtuality innovations to date —many are gimmicky and others still in the research labs—companies have spent far more time investigating and applying Augmented Reality than Augmented Virtuality. (So much so that sometimes even when they do the latter they call it the former.) This realm therefore begs for further exploration; look diligently in your business for possibilities to include material substance in otherwise virtual experiences.

8

Physical Virtuality

INSTANTIATING THE VIRTUAL
IN THE MATERIAL

In October 2009 LEGO Systems A/S of Billund, Denmark, updated its website with a new feature: LEGO Design byME. A refreshing of its prior mass customization capabilities, known as LEGOFactory, the new Design byME allows kids (and not a few adults) to design literally *anything* they want—a vehicle, an animal, an architectural wonder, an event, whatever it might be, in facsimile, replica, or newly created, imaginative form—and then after purchase have LEGO package up the exact bricks it takes to make that design and send it to them. Each set comes complete in a box whose image the customer can also design themselves and with a Building Guide that details how to build the design, brick by brick, on the family room floor—or, in our parlance, instantiate the virtual design in real space and actual time.

At the core of the offering is the LEGO Digital Designer, which can be downloaded from the site for free. As the designer, you select from almost 2,000 different elements (not just bricks, but minifigures, wheels, bases, tools, trees, and on and on they go), across over fifty colors (not all elements come in all colors, of course), and then decide exactly where to place each one, in the orientation and configuration you want, with such tools as cloning, hinging, hiding, coloring, and grouping that enable you to get what lies imaginatively in your head out figuratively onto the computer monitor. So you can plan, draft, tinker, and finally perfect your brick-based creation before ever lifting a physical element. Moreover, you can save templates and groupings to refer back to again and again, and even store completed designs to your private gallery on LEGO.com or display them in the Public Gallery. In this way you can show off your designs, which others in the greater LEGO community can find, download, modify, purchase, and build. (Family-friendly LEGO of course examines every design to ensure customers do not infringe trademarks or offend sensibilities.)

Hanne Odegaard, the director overseeing the offering, told us "the most important value we add with Design byME is empowering our consumers to tell their personal stories"—in other words, designing memorabilia for their own LEGO experiences. When we asked what consumers tended to create with the offering, after listing off quite a number of different kinds of models, she concluded, "The possibilities are endless." Absolutely! In fact, if you do not believe there is any such thing as infinite possibility, we dare you to try out LEGO Design byME and find the limit.[1]

Instantiating the Virtual in the Material

This duality of design and build sits at the heart of LEGO Design byME, one readily seen in how the LEGO Group promotes the offering on its website as the combination of two things: "Dreamt byME" and "Built byME." Therein lies the essence of Physical Virtuality: virtual design resulting in physical creation. As seen in Figure 8.1, this realm takes an experience happening in a virtual place and then instantiates, or *realizes*, it in the real world. First you dream it, and then you build it.

This is the specialty of computer-aided-design (CAD) software.[2] A pioneer in the field, Autodesk, based in San Rafael, California, sells AutoCAD and other software tools to designers all over the world for industrial, architecture, engineering and construction, and even media and entertainment applications. To commemorate not only its software but the successes of its customers, the company created the Autodesk Gallery at One Market in San Francisco. Open to the public one day a week while often used as an executive briefing center experience for potential clients, manager Jason Medal-Katz took both of us on a tour of the gallery, noting that the exhibits show how the company's software "helps designers turn ideas into reality" amid "unlimited possibilities."

He further said how once Autodesk announced it would create the gallery, its customers came out of the woodwork to have their designs be the ones on display. (Actually, not their designs, which remain virtual, but the physical manifestations of those designs in the real world of the gallery!) Ford donated a Shelby Cobra GT500, South Africa's ADEPT Airmotive, a high-performance airplane engine; Herman Miller a

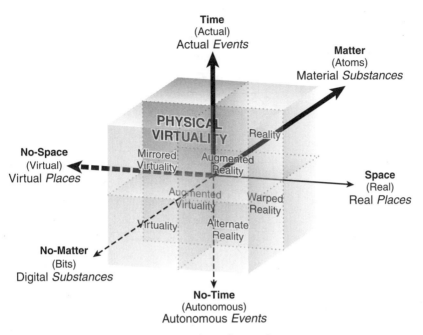

Figure 8.1 Physical Virtuality

Mirra chair; and, interestingly, the LEGO Group a dinosaur, cut out on one side so visitors can see its construction, from one of its LEGOLAND theme parks. The Danish company actually uses Autodesk software to ensure that its own mega models not only can be built but can stand up on their own without support—something its own Digital Designer does on a smaller scale for LEGO Design byME users.

Medal-Katz also pointed out a statement printed on the wall that not only epitomizes Autodesk's capabilities but also exemplifies the very spirit of Physical Virtuality:

> Design has never played a more important role in turning change into opportunity. Everyday, Autodesk customers are recreating the world around us and how we experience it—from new and innovative processes to things never before seen. This gallery showcases some of that daring work and illustrates the ways an idea can become real.

Ideas, conceived in imagination but impossible without digital technology, can, like Velveteen rabbits, become real.

3D Printing

Perhaps the quintessential technology that even further defines Physical Virtuality is 3D printing. Think of inkjet printers, which shoot out multicolored streams of ink onto two-dimensional paper. Slightly simplified, 3D printing adds the third dimension of height, where instead of ink, the printer deposits onto a base plastics or resins with dimensionality to them; the material grows layer by layer and eventually hardens into a physical object. Pioneered by such companies as 3D Systems of Rock Hill, South Carolina, Object Geometries of Rehovot, Israel, Stratasys of Eden Prairie, Minnesota, and Z Corporation, based in Burlington, Massachusetts—the name refers to the third dimension in the standard mathematical notation for spatial axes: *X, Y,* and *Z*—industrial businesses use 3D printing for rapid prototyping, not only imagining but seeing and feeling what a proposed product or part would be like. They can test it, redesign it, and then produce another prototype, much more quickly than with any other method, for as much iteration as it takes to get it exactly right. As David Reis, CEO of Object Geometries, puts it: "Now engineers can think of an idea, print it, hold it in their hand, share it with other people, change it and go back and print another one. Suddenly design becomes much more innovative and creative."[3] Architects use 3D printing not only for design but to demonstrate designs to clients. Other businesses, such as those in jewelry, health care, and art, use it to produce a final product. And combined with 3D scanning, still others use it to replicate existing objects, such as fossils, archaeological artifacts, or bones.

Physical Virtuality, as exemplified by its name, lies at a crossroads between the real and the virtual, because that which in the end people experience in Reality first must be envisioned in Virtuality, with the connecting tissue of being modeled in Physical Virtuality. As Charles Overy, founder of LGM, a building modeler based in Minturn, Colorado, puts it, "We are moving from handcraft to digital craft."[4] Perhaps the first person to put this ideal in motion with 3D printers was Janne Kyttanen, who in 2000 founded Freedom of Creation in Amsterdam to commercialize his own personal designs, freeing him to create art and artifacts he could never produce before.

FigurePrints, based in Vancouver, Washington, does things a bit differently, making real what already exists in Virtuality—specifically, *World of Warcraft* (*WoW*) avatars. It was founded in 2007 by Ed Fries, who as head of Microsoft Games Studio cofounded the Xbox project and is himself one of over 10 million *WoW* players. Players go to the company's website, choose their particular character type from among the scores within the game, and customize its armor, weapons, base, and even the particular pose and expression. Once the player is satisfied, the design goes through pre-processing using Autodesk 3D Studio Max before being printed by a Z Corp printer (with technology licensed from MIT, Z Corp has the only printers in the industry that can deposit in color). The value for *World of Warcraft* players was so high that over 100,000 of them almost immediately signed up for FigurePrints, which had to use a lottery to determine who would get their figures first. Why? Well, as explained by *Desktop Engineering* reporter Susan Smith, "With thousands of hours invested in this game, players seek the items to add to their collections but until now this experience has always been virtual."[5] And with the FigurePrint watching over and inspiring a player's performance, the experience becomes real.

Of course, this general concept of making the virtual real applies to more than what can be printed with resins and plastics. Contour Crafting, invented by Dr. Behrokh Khoshnevis of USC, involves a truck-sized 3D printer to build houses made out of plaster, concrete, and clay. Portland advertising agency Wieden+Kennedy, in concert with StandardRobot and Deeplocal (self-described as "a post-digital shop that helps brands create remarkable experiences that bridge the online and physical worlds"[6]), both of Pittsburgh, built a "Chalkbot" for a Nike campaign. It prints phrases contributed via SMS message on the ground in pixilated chalk for occasions such as at the Tour de France in support of Livestrong. According to Jeff Benjamin, chief creative officer at Crispin Porter + Bogusky in Boulder, Colorado, it's an example that the "digital is breaking out of the computer screen and into the real world."[7]

Scents can now be harvested, analyzed, and deconstructed by perfumers who then build their perfumes molecule by molecule.[8] Meanwhile, the science of molecular gastronomy[9] allows chefs to create food experiences all but unimaginable a few years ago. For example, Homaro Cantu, owner and chef of Moto in Chicago and a pioneer in the field, modified an inkjet printer to shoot out food-based inks onto edible paper, enabling wondrous new multisensory dishes. I (Joe) once took a client to Chicago for an Experience Expedition that included dining at Moto. The evening's courses were listed on a menu that, once we had perused it, we were encouraged to eat. One of the courses was a Cuban sandwich that looked exactly like a Cuban cigar, with the edible "COHIBA, Habana Cuba" label printed using the same technique.

Researchers at Cornell University are working on a 3D food printer for the home,[10] but the most amazing example of Physical Virtuality goes far beyond all this: regenerative medicine company Organovo of San Diego collaborated with the engineering firm Invetech of Melbourne to create a "3D bio-printer" called NovoGen. It can deposit living cells, cultured from bone marrow and fat cells extracted from the individual patient, layer-by-layer with a scaffold to shape the cells properly and let them grow together.[11] Organovo CEO Jack Murphy says, "Scientists and engineers can use the 3D bio-printers to enable placing cells of almost any type into a desired pattern in 3D. Researchers can place liver cells on a preformed scaffold, support kidney cells with a co-printed scaffold, or form adjacent layers of epithelial and stromal soft tissue that grow into a mature tooth. Ultimately the idea would be for surgeons to have . . . the ability to make three-dimensional tissues on demand."[12]

It's also worth mentioning the ability of dentists to make three-dimensional tooth reconstructions on demand, because the method, known as CEREC (for CERamic REContstruction), uses subtractive technology rather than the additive technology of 3D printing. In this process, pioneered by Sirona Dental (a Siemens spinoff based in Bensheim, Germany), dentists capture an image of the actual tooth needing repair and that image is used to create a virtual model of the reconstruction. The digitized rendering is then sent to an in-office milling machine where a porcelain block is cut down, atom by atom, to a crown that perfectly matches the original tooth.

All of these examples illustrate the apex of Physical Virtuality: treating atoms as bits, where matter becomes programmable via virtual design and its physical instantiation.

Mass Customization

This ability to customize an offering on demand for an individual customer and produce it on an efficient, noncraft basis is known as Mass Customization: efficiently serving customers uniquely. This term was coined by Stan Davis once again in his book *Future Perfect*.[13]

When Davis first wrote about it in 1987, Mass Customization was considered an oxymoron. And when I (Joe) wrote my book on the subject in 1993, it was, as the subtitle stated, "The New Frontier in Business Competition."[14] Today it is fast becoming an imperative. Although Lutron Electronics Corporation of Coopersburg, Pennsylvania, has been mass customizing lighting controls for over 40 years, and other businesses, such as LensCrafters and FedEx, could not exist without it, there has been an explosion in the past decade of mass customizers. Many of these are well-known companies who have added this capability to their offerings. These include such big players as Adidas, Nike, and McGraw-Hill. But the capability for mass customization has given rise to many new companies birthed in the capability as well, such as Zazzle, CafePress, Chocri, Spreadshirt, and Blank Label in goods; Peapod, LegalZoom, and Netflix in services; and Pandora in experiences.[15] Carmen Magri, CEO of chocolatier Chocri, calls such businesses "design-your-own companies."[16] MilkOrSugar, a "custom shopping portal" from Amsterdam-based Ilumy, lists 312 customized products (all physical goods) from companies it has vetted across twelve categories.[17]

The core principle they all share to one degree or another is modularity: breaking apart the offering (whether a good, service, experience, or even potentially a transformation[18]) into a set of interchangeable elements that can be reconfigured, dynamically linked together to create different offerings for different people. Mass Customization is not about being everything to everybody—a surefire way to increase costs along with complexity. No, it is about doing only and exactly what each individual customer wants. Modularity (modules + linkage system) enables external combinations to far outpace internal complexity, thereby lowering costs to the point that they are on par with Mass Production (sometimes higher, sometimes about the same, and sometimes even lower, particularly when demand is highly variable, the underlying technology changes quickly, or finished goods inventory costs are high).

When you think of modularity, think once again of LEGO building bricks. What can you build with LEGO elements? Anything! Anything you want, because of the huge number of modules of different sizes, different shapes, and different colors, plus the simple and elegant linkage system for snapping them together.

Of course, the frequent mistake mass customizers make is that they overwhelm people with too much choice, exposing them to all of the possibilities in such a way that their eyes glaze over and they throw up their hands and give up. Always remember that customers do not want choice, they just want exactly what they want. Your job is to present the possibilities to them in a way that they can figure out what they want—even if they do not know what that is or cannot articulate it. This is the task of design tools.

Design Tools

Put simply, design tools match customer needs with company capabilities. More than configurators—common in complex, industrial sales situations—that merely let customers choose among options by description or product code, design tools must be visual, *showing* customers and letting them *experience* the differences between options, the possibilities across modules, the appropriateness and efficacy of the chosen offering.

Consider NedSense enterprises n.v. of Amsterdam. This software provider has served the fashion and textiles industry for over thirty years, providing behind-the-scenes CAD/CAM tools to help designers create their offerings. As it saw more and more of its customers shift toward mass customizing those offerings to distributors, retailers, and consumers, it took the opportunity to lead them in the shift. So it created LOFT, a room and fabric design tool the company calls an "experience engine," to help its customers reach their customers in order to show off, as CEO Pieter Arts told us, "the endless possibilities for people to visualize and share their ideas."

The LOFT experience begins with a digital photograph of a room, either one supplied by the company or one of a consumer's room in her own house. With a few clicks and a lot of processing, the experience engine figures out where the corners of the room are so it can convert the 2D image into a 3D virtual place. The consumer roughly outlines each piece of furniture, which the engine uses to precisely determine their locations within the 3D room. After just a minute or two, the consumer is ready to dream. She can move the furniture around, replace it with other pieces, add a rug, change the curtains, try out new fabrics, all with an easy click. The most amazing part of LOFT's patented technology is its ability to erase an existing fabric on a real piece of furniture (or rug, or curtain, or dress, or anything else that can be made from fabric) and replace it perfectly, so that everything—its curving, its warp and woof, its highlights, its shadows—looks real.

While NedSense initially made LOFT particular to its area of expertise—fabric and textiles—many companies have built general-purpose software that can provide the basis for design tools across any number of industries: design-tool provider cyLEDGE Media GmbH of Vienna maintains a Configurator Database that lists over 600 different Web-based configurators, many of them incorporating full visuals.[19] Many companies use Adobe Flash and more recently Adobe Scene7 to provide visual flair to the online design experience,[20] but to quicken the pace of interaction and enhance the visual experience, Treehouse Logic of Menlo Park places the entire design tool in the browser—including the rules engine, data, and visuals, which integrate with its customers backend e-commerce platforms and Enterprise Resource Planning systems. Consumers can therefore play around with designs very rapidly, without the system having to make the user wait while it goes back to a server for additional information or visuals. Rickshaw Bagworks of San Francisco employs Treehouse Logic for its messenger-bag customizer, proclaiming it enables "Endless possibilities styled by *you.*"[21]

Interestingly, a few companies are creating design tools, often called "virtual mirrors," that encompass the adjacent realm of the Multiverse, Augmented Virtuality. Paris-based FittingBox, for example, enables eyewear manufacturers such as Luxottica, Ray-Ban, and Krys to let consumers see what they would look like in a pair of glasses before they are produced or shipped—with the consumers' own head serving as the physical trigger for the webcam-based virtual try-on experience. Hanulneotech Co., Ltd., of Daegu, South Korea, provides a number of similar tools, including those for virtual hair styling, masks, and, strangely, gold crowns. Its tagline is "Virtual becomes Real,"[22] which is apt even though the Virtual is Augmented by matter. (And, yes, both of these companies mistakenly use the term "Augmented Reality" to describe their offerings.)

Ridemakerz has built its entire business model around a virtual world as design tool. Its *RZ Virtual Experience* lets kids (mostly boys) design, race, and play with virtual cars on racetracks, the open road, in pit crews, and even a wrecking zone. Each kid can then buy the vehicle he designed, which Ridemakerz (formed with significant investment from Build-a-Bear Workshop) mass customizes and ships out for real-world play. As CEO Larry Andreini says, "It's the experience of being able to go online and use an immersive environment and gameplay to try things on or put different wheels on to test performance and play with it and then press the button and turn it into the real toy. We can do that globally without investing to have 300 stores. The viral effect of the virtual world and Internet is the force."[23]

In many situations, such visual design tools are not enough. If it is for an intangible, memorable, or effectual offering—service, experience, transformation—customers may need to experience the possibilities with auditory, tactile, and perhaps other sensory feedback, with the fourth dimension of time (think of 4D as *X, Y, Z,* and *t*) added to pre-experience experiences. Even if the offering is a tangible good, these additional facets can be of great benefit. It would be one thing to merely view a custom-designed vehicle, and another experience entirely to fly around it from any angle, zoom inside it, and smell the leather of the seats as you pass through the window to feel the texture of the steering wheel.

Design tools for inherently personal experiences or intrinsically individual transformations remain few because few companies mass customize such offerings; they are largely craft produced today. One experience example: roller coaster simulators such as at DisneyQuest outside of Walt Disney World and at LEGOLANDs around the world. In 2010 Disney added the Sum of all Thrills ride to the INNOVENTIONS pavilion in Epcot. Sponsored by Raytheon, it lets guests design their own ride on a multitouch table using mathematical rules and engineering tools—it's not a simple Option A or Option B configurator. When they've chosen their particular custom ride among the 1.4 million permutations, they can visually see what the experience will be like on the screen and then go experience it for themselves on the RoboSim 4-D Simulator made by KUKA Robotics Corporation of Augsburg, Germany.

Interestingly, Walt Disney Imagineering produced its own 4D project software for building the complex, story-laden rides for which it is known. First used to create Expedition Everest at Animal Kingdom and since spun out to another company for commercialization, the software takes the concept of a static design tool to embrace changes over time:

> By marrying an architect's 3-D, computer-aided design images with planning software that tracks construction schedules in real time, Disney can create a virtual "movie" of the Expedition Everest project. This 4-D software—the fourth dimension being time—breaks down a 3-D image of a project into millions of pieces of data and then reassembles it step-by-step, in the sequence in which the structure will be built, to visualize how it will all come together.[24]

While mass customizers now customarily use design tools for goods, we need more such tools to envision higher-order offerings. As Stanford Professor Martin Fischer, an expert in 4D visualization who aided in the software development of Disney's tool, said, "The nice thing is that it makes sure that what's inside your head looks the same as what's inside my head."[25]—which then yields an experience inside of the guest's head.

Do It Yourself

Ideally, you want to make the design of the offering, no matter the genre, an experience unto itself, as many people value *designing* and *making* their own offerings almost as much as *having* and *using* them. That's one reason there has been such a push in the past decade or more of a do-it-yourself (DIY) movement in technology. For although we will see additional 4D design tools once more experiences and transformations move out of Craft Production and into Mass Customization, today craft producing one's own technology-infused goods *is* an experience for many people.

Many websites cater to the DIY crowd, including Etsy, a marketplace for handcrafted goods; CustomMade, a clearinghouse for woodworking and furniture artisans; Scrapblog, a community for scrapbookers; Instructables, a sharing site for documenting what people like to do and how to do it; and, at the epicenter of this "maker movement," Makezine, the online manifestation of *Make* magazine from O'Reilly Media of Sebastopol, California. The website, the quarterly magazine, and its annual Maker Faire event all promote hobbyists who use off-the-shelf and personally crafted technology to make real their own imaginings. *Make,* whose slogan is "Technology on your time," is written by makers for makers, although many lack the resources or equipment to realize fully their ideas.

Many companies have stepped up to provide such resources. Ponoko of Wellington, New Zealand, calls itself "the world's easiest making system." From its website: "Ponoko is an online marketplace for everyone to click to make real things. It's where creators, digital fabricators, materials suppliers and buyers meet to make (almost) anything."[26] It works with digital fabrication sources (including not only 3D printers but laser cutters, etc.) around the world in order to produce close to customers, reduce shipping costs, and lessen the environmental impact. Meanwhile, halfway around the world in Eindhoven, the Netherlands, Shapeways was spun out of the Lifestyle Incubator of Royal Philips Electronics to help designers realize their own creations; its website asks, "Have you ever wanted to turn your 3D designs into reality? Enter Shapeways, we create physical models of your digital designs!"[27] Much more than that, it helps connect those designers with consumers who might like the same creations, generally customized to their own specifications, before being 3D printed on the company's Z Corporation ZPrinter 650.

Of course, a 3D printer alone does not a maker make. So enter TechShop, which employs the motto "Build Your Dreams Here." The chain of DIY facilities, with its first workshop lying at the heart of Silicon Valley in Menlo Park, provides members with access to the sorts of tools and equipment that they do not tend to have lying around the house—3D printers, milling machines and lathes, laser and plasma cutters, drill presses and band saws, and just about anything else that *Wired* columnist Clive Thompson categorizes as "atom-hacking tools."[28] Members also can also take workshops and classes from "Dream Coaches" and join with a community of fellow hobbyists to acquire the skills necessary to build what they had only dreamt, whether just for themselves, as a craft hobby to sell to others, or as the precursor to the dream of a big business that just needs to get off the ground.

CEO Mark Hatch told us to think of TechShop as a health club, except it uses tools and workshop equipment instead of exercise gear. "We help people make the things they dream up, but don't have the tools, space, or skills to accomplish on their own. And we make sure that every visit to TechShop is its own unique and engaging experience."

Fab Labs

As digital technology continues to slide down the slope of Moore's Law and becomes more affordable, TechShops could spring up all over the place, putting such technology within the reach of nearly everyone. As Tim O'Reilly, founder of O'Reilly Media, said in a blog post contemplating that day, "How far off is a future in which the creative economy overflows the thin boundary that separates 'information' from 'stuff'?"[29]

That boundary diminishes every day, and even now seems pretty permeable. Where will all this take us? As in so many other arenas, science fiction shows the way: we're heading to the day when in our own homes we have available functionality like that of the replicator from *Star Trek: The Next Generation*. This device physically creates anything a crewmember might ever need—based on virtual specifications lying inside the ship's computer, ready to be called up and customized on command—from a spare part to keep the old spaceship running to, say, a cup of tea, Earl Grey, hot.[30] Amazingly, it is here in the realm of Physical Virtuality where actual realization may be closest to fictional representation, for fabrication laboratories, or *fab labs,* are a here-and-now technology.

The biggest proponent, and foremost researcher, of fab labs is Neil Gershenfeld, the head of MIT's wonderfully named Center for Bits and

Atoms (CBA), who says he is squarely "aiming at making the *Star Trek* replicator."[31] Although originally limited to prototypes of real products, thanks largely to the research and application of Gershenfeld and his colleagues and students, it is now being used to create real products, even electronic devices with their own digital circuitry.

Gershenfeld's describes the CBA, which every year holds the open class "How To Make (Almost) Anything," as "a group of people like me who never understood the boundary between physical science and computer science."[32] Following that to its logical conclusion, he writes in *Fab: The Coming Revolution on Your Desktop—from Personal Computers to Personal Fabrication*:

> The universe is literally as well as metaphorically a computer. Atoms, molecules, bacteria, and billiard balls can all store and transform information. . . . At the intersection of physical science and computer science, programs can process atoms as well as bits, digitizing fabrication in the same way that communications and computation were earlier digitized. Ultimately, this means that a programmable personal fabricator will be able to make anything, including itself, by assembling atoms.[33]

No wonder science fiction writer and technology commentator Bruce Sterling, in *Wired* magazine, calls this capability "The Dream Factory,"[34] an apt epithet for the possibilities that lie within Physical Virtuality!

Gershenfeld's Center for Bits and Atoms is not the only place working on this vision, either. Desktop Factory, a subsidiary of 3D Systems, aims to bring down the cost of 3D printers enough—like laser printers before them, which similarly started as scarce, expensive, shared resources—so every designer who wants one can afford one. eMachineShop—whose founder, Jim Lewis, says he also was inspired by *Star Trek*'s replicator (in yet a second *Wired* piece entitled "The Dream Factory")[35]—lets you access all its tools for cutting, shaping, and bending metal and plastic over the Web. CloudFab, of Pittsburgh, aims to let people access excess digital fabrication resources wherever they reside "in the cloud" that is the Internet. And not to be outdone by the commercial sector, DARPA, the Defense Advanced Research Projects Agency, operates an advanced research project called Programmable Matter whose purpose "is to demonstrate a new functional form of matter" that "can reversibly assemble into complex 3D objects upon external command."[36]

Gershenfeld finds all of this truly revolutionary:

The past few centuries have given us the personalization of expression, consumption, and computation. Now consider what would happen if the physical world outside computers was as malleable as the digital world inside computers. If ordinary people could personalize not just the content of computation but also its physical form. If mass customization lost the "mass" piece and became personal customization, with technology better reflecting the needs and wishes of its users because it's been developed by and for its users. If globalization gets replaced by localization.

The results would be a revolution that contains, rather than replaces, all of the prior revolutions. Industrial production would merge with personal expression, which would merge with digital design, to bring common sense and sensibility to the creation and application of advanced technologies. . . .

That will happen.[37]

How does he know? Because it already has happened, not just at MIT but in sixteen fab labs around the world networked together through the Fab Academy.[38] Fab labs may cost around $50,000 apiece today, but as Gershenfeld predicted in an interview in his office, that will come down soon to $5,000. He foresees the capability of that omni-inspiring *Star Trek* replicator in as little as fifteen or twenty years. And if—excuse us, *when*—that happens, it truly will be beyond Mass Customization as described above. It will indeed be highly personal customization,[39] or as Gershenfeld puts it elsewhere, "It's stuff"—viewing that term in all the physical, material, atomic meaning of the word—"for a market of one."[40] Being able to continually and efficiently innovate offerings of one for markets of one—what could be called Continuous Invention—is the next step in the evolution of business competition, which began with Craft Production, shifted to Mass Production after the Industrial Revolution, then to Continuous Improvement with the rise of Total Quality Management and Lean Production, and then on to Mass Customization in the past few decades.[41]

Applying Physical Virtuality

Continuous Invention. That's where we are headed with Physical Virtuality, whose essence lies in the imaginings of virtual design instantiated in the physical stuff of atoms. Or as Gershenfeld so beautifully sums it up, "Personal fabrication will bring the programmability of the digital worlds we've invented to the physical world we inhabit."[42]

To make that happen in your company, for your individual customers, follow these principles:

∞ *Create a way for your customers to design virtually what they want to create physically.* Help them dream it, and then help them build it.

∞ Think in particular about how you could *use the quintessential technology of 3D printing* to help them realize their dreams.

∞ Go beyond that to *consider all varieties of atom-hacking tools* that might apply in your business.

∞ For new business opportunities, *seek out what already exists only in Virtuality that you could help make physical.* This includes not only things in virtual worlds like *World of Warcraft* but anything from the world of entertainment; companies have already made real such virtual brands as the Bubba Gump Shrimp Co. from *Forrest Gump,* Duff Beer and Kwik-E-Mart from *The Simpsons,* and Stay Puft Marshmallows from *Ghostbusters.*[43]

∞ You can also *use all these tools yourself to make prototypes for engineering purposes or as models for marketing purposes.*

∞ *Invent what has yet to be dreamt.* If the replicator can inspire not only fab labs but also Cantu's rather narrow purpose of edible paper (although he aspires to use it "to deliver food to the masses that are starving"[44]), what could it inspire you to create, in your industry, for your customers? If we can even print human organs in three dimensions, for goodness sake, what other inventions would further humanity and edify us as individuals?

∞ But remember that Physical Reality is a realm, not a technology. Technologies, again, are mere tools we invent to fulfill human purposes. So as with every realm, *always employ technology on behalf of your customers,* in a way that creates value for customers by helping them fulfill their purposes.

∞ *Mass customize your offerings* to give your customers exactly what they want at a price they are willing to pay.

∞ To do that, *modularize your offerings,* breaking them down into constituent elements, or modules, and develop a simple, elegant linkage system for snapping them together.

∞ *Think and work especially hard to mass customize experiences and transformations,* for companies do precious little with these offerings today. And no matter what your industry, you can create value in these higher-order offerings beyond what you can get for mere goods and services.

∞ *Create a design tool to match customer need with company capability*—and thereby avoid the mistake of overwhelming your customers with too much choice.

∞ Although much already is going on in both special- and general-purpose design tools, *conceive of new sorts of design tools* that go beyond today's state of the art. Think especially about applying the other realms of the Multiverse, as some already apply Augmented Virtuality for such tools. For experiences and transformations, do not forget the dimension of time, as the former are revealed over a duration of time and the latter must be sustained through time.

∞ *Make the using of your design tool itself an experience.*

∞ *Embrace the do-it-yourself, or maker, movement.* What can you help customers do themselves? What places, networks, or websites could you create that helps them create?

∞ *Help make the fab-lab future a reality.* What might your company do to realize this vision, whether by embracing Continuous Invention as your own business model or by helping your customers make it their business (or personal) model?

∞ And then when all is said and done, you might even think to *celebrate your customers' virtual designs made real,* à la the Autodesk Gallery at One Market.

Saul Griffith, who got his PhD under Gershenfeld and works on the DARPA project mentioned earlier (and, oh by the way, created the Instructables website), founded Otherlab in San Francisco to bring to market, among other bountiful ideas, offerings based on computational manufacturing and programmable matter. When surveying everything going on in the greater arena of technology invention, he told *Inc.* magazine, "The business landscape looks like infinite possibility."[45]

There is indeed infinite possibility lying within Physical Virtuality (as there is within each and every realm of the Multiverse). Opportunities go well beyond physical goods, to also making real intangible services, memorable experiences, and effectual transformations. Search broadly for possibilities to engage customers in a virtual place you make for them, such as a design tool made to complement and stimulate their imagination, in order that they may construct what moments before existed only in their minds. But if you are a manufacturer of goods that does not yet mass customize its offerings or work with its customers virtually, this is the one realm you can no longer ignore. And for everyone else, it is a realm in which to dream big; for in realizing your dreams, you may just find a way to help your customers realize theirs.

9

Mirrored Virtuality

ABSORBING THE REAL WORLD
INTO THE VIRTUAL

When I (Joe) was a first grader, I moved to Mahwah, New Jersey, just across the Hudson River from New York City and became an avid New York Yankees fan. Throughout several more moves growing up I maintained my love for the team and continued rooting for them no matter where I lived, no matter how they did.

On rare occasions I would go to a game when the Yankees came to whatever town I lived in. I sat glued to the set whenever they were on the TV Game of the Week, but most often I used a powerful shortwave radio tuned to the AM dial to listen to the team play. Late at night, when the sun went down, I could tune in to far-away radio broadcasts, having memorized the station numbers for every team within listening distance so I could follow the Yankees whenever possible. As I listened to the play-by-play, I could at least imagine the game play out in my mind's eye. It was a good experience, but nowhere near as good as seeing the action live.

Today, I don't have to tune the radio and imagine. I can access the Internet and see. I go to MLB.com, the official Major League Baseball website, to pull up its MLB Gameday feature. Starting out as little more than a live box score updating itself as plays are concluded on the field, it has in the past few years become a virtual stadium where I can keep up-to-date on what is happening in the game, in real time. There's a picture and background, with statistics on the current pitcher and batter; a line score with an image of how many runners are on base; a view of the stadium (showing its proper dimensions) with names for each person in the field or on base (hovering the cursor over any player brings up relevant in-game and season statistics); and there is written play-by-play descriptions of every time someone makes an out, gets on base, or anything else happens (like a steal or pitching change).

Most amazingly: next to a generic image of a batter by a virtual home plate and strike zone, MLB Gameday plots every single pitch, showing it from the moment it leaves the pitcher's hand and the route it takes toward the plate. The ball "streaks" green if the pitcher throws it out of the strike zone, red if he makes a strike over the plate, and blue whenever the batter hits it into the field of play. The streak shows precisely where the pitch ends up relative to the plate, with the system informing you how fast it was thrown, with how much break and movement, and what happened if it was hit into play. I can move around the "camera view" in this virtual 3D Gameday world to see the batter from the side, from in front where the pitcher is, or, the default, from behind the batter. And since I pay a membership fee to MLB.com every year to have full access, I can even listen to the local Yankees radio broadcast while watching the virtual game, or toggle over to watch the TV broadcast. It's still not as good as being in the stadium live—a Reality experience rarely available to me—but it's pretty darn close.

Absorbing the Real World into the Virtual

Whether you are a Yankee-lover like me or a Yankee-hater like most other baseball fans (or know nothing about the game), I encourage you to check out MLB Gameday, for there you can see a beautiful example of Mirrored Virtuality. (If golf is your game, you will find similar functionality at PGATour.com with its PGA Tour Shot Tracker, while NASCAR lovers can go to its website for a Live Leaderboard.) This final realm of the Multiverse to be described fully, illustrated in Figure 9.1, involves some representation of the real world being mirrored virtually—formed in a virtual place, constructed from digital substance—but, and this is the key to the realm, enacted in actual time. It is the variable of Time—actual, linear, real time synchronous to what is happening out there, somewhere in the real world—that connects Mirrored Virtuality so tightly to Reality, even though the primary experience is one of Virtuality. Its essence is a virtual expression of Reality that unfolds as it actually happens (or as close to real time as data sensing and movement allows), providing a particular bird's-eye view.

Realize, too, that not only is MLB Gameday an example of this realm, but so is watching a game on TV! For as mentioned in Chapter 6, "Virtuality," TV watching (and radio listening, for that matter) re-

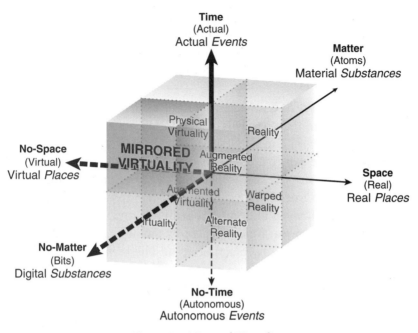

Figure 9.1 Mirrored Virtuality

mains a *virtual* experience; it's not a real-world experience happening to *us* but a vicarious experience we have only through a mediated screen (or speaker). Tie such an experience into real time, as with any sporting event or other live broadcast, and it, too, becomes Mirrored Virtuality. Even a telephone call is, technically if trivially, Mirrored Virtuality for it connects two people into a virtual place (the shared audio space) at the same time, digitally over a wire, through the air, or, increasingly, through the Internet (via VoIP, or Voice over Internet Protocol). So, therefore, is telepresence, pioneered by TeleSuite but today powered by such companies as Cisco and Hewlett-Packard. Here the virtual place encompasses both pristine sound and picture-perfect sight, where the elimination of any lag creates a feeling of real presence and the well-designed surroundings make it feel like the people at both ends are in the same room.

Yale computer science professor David Gelernter presaged and largely described this realm in his 1992 book, *Mirror Worlds*. Mirror Worlds, he explains,

> are software models of some chunk of reality, some piece of the real world going on outside your window. Oceans of information pour endlessly

into the model . . . : so much information that the model can mimic the reality's every move, moment-by-moment. A Mirror World is some huge institution's moving, true-to-life mirror image trapped inside a computer—where you can see and grasp it whole.[1]

Although we're sure he had less prosaic and more consequential chunks of reality in mind than baseball games, Gelernter here perfectly captures the octant of [Time – No-Space – No-Matter], where it is the Time ↔ No-Time axis that differentiates Mirrored Virtuality from Virtuality itself. Inside Virtuality, operating via some sort of avatar, you generally remain free to do whatever you wish to do, whereas inside Mirrored Virtuality you inexorably remain tied into what is happening in the real world, in real time, moment by moment. Because Mirrored Virtuality is so tethered to actual time, it must be a representation of the real world in some way, shape, or form, essentially mirroring reality, and not a complete fantasy or some representation of reality freed from actual time as Virtuality can be.

Today, less than twenty years later, Gelernter's vision has been realized and, in many ways, surpassed. Numerous places within *Second Life* now tie themselves into real-life data feeds, for example. The National Oceanic & Atmospheric Administration operates a real-time weather map of the United States that your avatar can walk through. (Imagine what haptics would bring to this, where you could *feel* thunderstorms rumble or cold fronts pass by.) And the International Spaceflight Museum fashioned virtual models of the International Space Station, the Hubble Space Telescope, and other satellites that, according to Wade Roush, editor of *Xconomy San Francisco*, "your avatar can fly alongside . . . as they orbit a 10-meter-diameter globe in sync with real-world data from the Air Force Space Command."[2]

Note that simply recreating a real place inside of a virtual world is not enough. Virtual world *Twinity*, whose tagline is "Powered by Real Life," contains virtual models of Berlin, Singapore, London, and Miami, with more to come, and describes itself as "a 3D mirror world based on real cities and real people."[3] Intel also uses the term "mirror world" for its *ScienceSim* experimental virtual world, which includes a "Virtual Yellowstone," with topological data of the real Yellowstone National Park in Wyoming, It defines mirror worlds as "that subset of virtual worlds that are based on 'real-world' geographical data (past or present)."[4] But neither is a mirror world as defined by Gelernter, nor Mirrored Virtuality as delineated within the Multiverse, for basing it on real-world geographical data or on real cities or anything else spatially real is not enough. It is tying the activity in such virtual worlds to actual events—absorbing the real world into the virtual—that defines this realm.

Second Earth

Any virtual place that does spatially replicate the real world can become a platform for Mirrored Virtuality if it adds temporal replication as well. But this realm need not be incorporated inside such full-fledged, avatar-based virtual worlds. As discussed in Chapter 6, "Virtuality," the base Virtuality experience can also be built atop maps, satellite photographs, or other such images stitched together, such as those enabled by Google Maps, Google Earth, or Microsoft's Virtual Earth. Flightwise, for example, operates a 3D flight tracker that superimposes small airplane images at their appropriate altitude and positioning within Google Earth (which itself now shows rain or snow in real time). Or consider Ushahidi, a Kenyan nonprofit whose name means "testimony" in Swahili. It began with collecting reports of violence after the disputed 2007 Kenyan elections and pinpointing them on a map, and it now provides "crowdsourcing" tools to track crises in real time, illuminating what exactly is happening from those to whom it is happening. This platform provides a window into such crises as the Haitian and Chilean earthquakes, or more normal but quick-moving events such as monitoring elections in India or even snowplowing in Washington, DC.[5]

Xconomy's Roush sees these visualization tools inevitably merging with virtual worlds like *Second Life* to create what he dubbed "Second Earth":

> The first, relatively simple step toward a Second Earth, many observers predict, will be integrating Second Life's avatars, controls, and modeling tools into the Google Earth environment. Groups of users would then be able to walk, fly, or swim across Google's simulated landscapes and explore intricate 3-D representations of the world's most famous buildings. . . .
>
> A second alternative would be to expand the surface area of Second Life by millions of square kilometers and model the new territory on the real earth, using the same topographical data and surface imagery contained in Google Earth. . . .
>
> But within 10 to 20 years—roughly the same time it took for the Web to become what it is now—something much bigger than either of these alternatives may emerge: a true Metaverse. In Neal Stephenson's 1992

novel *Snow Crash,* a classic of the dystopian "cyberpunk" genre, the Metaverse was a planet-size virtual city that could hold up to 120 million avatars, each representing someone in search of entertainment, trade, or social contact. The Metaverse that's really on the way, some experts believe, will resemble Stephenson's vision, but with many alterations. It will look like the real earth, and it will support even more users than the *Snow Crash* cyberworld, functioning as the agora, laboratory, and gateway for almost every type of information-based pursuit. It will be accessible both in its immersive, virtual-reality form and through peepholes like the screen of your cell phone as you make your way through the real world.[6]

With the simultaneous ability to incorporate real-time data feeds—weather, traffic, population movement, commercial output, stock prices, resource usage, and on and on—such a development would create a platform (or a set of distinct platforms) for the limitless Mirror Worlds envisioned by Gelernter.

Almost two decades ago the Yale professor amazingly and presciently asserted that a Mirror World is more than a mere information service, but rather a *place,* a place where you can stroll around at your leisure and where you can converse with friends and even strangers:[7]

> [It] will be available (like a public park) to however many people are interested, hundreds or thousands or millions at the same time. It will show each visitor exactly what he wants to see—it will sustain a million different views, a million different focuses on the same city simultaneously. Each visitor will zoom in and pan around and roam through the model as he chooses, at whatever pace and level of detail he likes.[8]

And as Roush shows, we are moving closer and closer to such a navigable representation of the earth. Short of that full eventuality, however, much is being done today with the tools we have to create offerings that mirror portions of it.

Predicting the Present

A number of years ago Google discovered that certain search terms could predict accurately whether the searcher (or someone close to the searcher) had the flu and was seeking remedies. So it created Google Flu Trends.[9] There you see a simple map of the world color-coded to the level of flu activity in countries, from minimal to intense. Click on "Animated flu trends for Google Earth" and after a quick add-on download you are inside a similarly color-coded Google Earth that you can move around and zoom into, with longitudinal data for many countries detailed by state or province with a click. In the United States, because data from the Centers for Disease Control and Prevention (CDC) are about two weeks behind, Google Flu Trends provides a real-time warning of spikes in the infectious disease which, should another pandemic ever arrive, could be lifesaving for thousands of people.[10] The CDC itself helped validate the efficacy of the data in the scientific journal *Nature*.[11]

What else might Google searches be mirroring in the real world? You can go to Google Trends and see what is going on with whatever search term in which you find of interest, or take a more detailed look at Google Insights for Search, using various filters.[12] And coming soon: the GPI, or Google Price Index, a real-time version of the government's Consumer Price Index.[13] Hal Varian, Google's chief economist, examined various Google Trends data with a colleague and hypothesized that "this query data may be correlated with the current level of economic activity in given industries and thus may be helpful in predicting the subsequent data releases." He says, "We are not claiming that Google Trends data help predict the future. Rather we are claiming that Google Trends may help in *predicting the present*."[14]

Note that Mirrored Virtuality shares this focus on the present with Augmented Reality; in addition to the Multiverse variable of No-Matter, they have Time in common, both based on actual events happening out there in Reality. So it is natural that one bleeds into the other. Madison-based TrafficCast, for example, provides a Mirrored Virtuality system that analyzes real-time data directly from cars and roads, along with weather conditions, accidents, construction zones, and other information, to accurately predict current travel times and alert authorities to situations in need of attention. And portable navigator provider Tom-Tom, an exemplar of Augmented Reality, not only added real-time traffic updates to some of its devices, but weather and even fuel prices as well. The key to differentiating between these realms is to once again ask: Where does the primary experience occur? The one dimension these two realms differ on is *places,* with one formed from real places in Space and the other from virtual places in No-Space. So, if that primary experience remains in real Space—in Reality, as with the TomTom—then it is Augmented Reality; if the primary experience is one of virtual No-Space—in Virtuality, as with TrafficCast—then it is Mirrored Virtuality, even though in each case the company focuses on the present, on what is actuality happening right now.

Call it the Actuality Axis, to accompany the Augmentation Axis (between Augmented Reality and Augmented Virtuality) discussed in Chapter 7, "Augmented Virtuality." One company whose offerings slide seamlessly along this axis is Ambient Devices, an MIT Media Lab spinoff in Cambridge, Massachusetts. Its first product was the Ambient Orb, "a frosted-glass ball that glows different colors to display real time stock market trends, traffic congestion, pollen forecasts, or any other Ambient information channel: weather, wind speed, pollen, traffic congestion, and more."[15] This clearly belongs in Augmented Reality, providing not a virtual representation of Reality but rather a signal to affect your experience of it, as do more recent products such as the Ambient Umbrella, whose handle glows when rain is in the forecast. Most of the company's product line does, however, provide a virtual representation through a screen, such as its Flurry alarm clock, with the current weather conditions and forecast, and its Baseball ScoreCast, which much like MLB Gameday tracks individual games as they happen. Each of these offerings slide across the Actuality Axis to Mirrored Virtuality.

Real-Time Web

Any real-time data feed could provide the basis for such a focus. Consider the torrents of tweets emanating from all the individual Twitter streams. Trendsmap, from Stateless Systems of Melbourne, analyzes the entire Twitterverse to see what's what, where's where, and who's who. It defines itself as "a real-time mapping of Twitter trends across the world."[16] Pulling it up showcases a map of the world, centered wherever you happen to be, with little, black, translucent boxes highlighting particular words particularly frequent in particular places at this particular time. The bigger, bolder, and brighter the box, the more tweets using the term. You can navigate around the world or zoom in on specific cities or topics, and clicking on a word brings up a box loaded with the Twitter stream referencing that word, constantly updated in real time.[17]

You yourself can informally analyze all the tweets you receive from those you follow to see what is going on in the "where and now" (right now, but all over the place). As one Twitter aficionado, Yuri van Geest, a founder of Mobile Mondays Amsterdam, told us, "It is like standing in a waterfall of information, freely flowing by me. I dip not my body but my mind in that stream to see what is happening, right now, with everyone I know. I could not live without it."

Neither would anyone want to live without the World Wide Web it-self, which increasingly operates in real time.[18] Twitter is just one ele-ment of what's known as the "real-time Web," which Peter Cashmore, CEO of social media news site Mashable, named one of "10 Web trends to watch in 2010." As he put it in a post for CNN.com: "The term repre-sents the growing demand for immediacy in our interactions. Imme-diacy is compelling, engaging, highly addictive . . . it's a sense of living in the now."[19] Reinier Evers, founder of trendwatching.com in Amster-dam, identified this trend toward "Nowism" and defined it this way: "Consumers' ingrained lust for instant gratification is being satisfied by a host of novel, important (offline and online) real-time products, ser-vices and experiences. Consumers are also feverishly contributing to the real-time content avalanche that's building as we speak. As a result, expect your brand and company to have no choice but to finally mirror and join the 'now,' in all its splendid chaos, realness and excitement."[20]

So in addition to Twitter mirroring the real world in real time and thereby joining the now, Facebook, LinkedIn, and other social media sites link people to their connections with real-time updates to what they are doing, who they are seeing, where they are going, how they are doing, maybe even why they care—and all when it happens. Friend-Feed, bought by Facebook in 2009, enables you to share your content (websites, photos, videos, and so on) with your friends, feeding their desire for Nowism. Microsoft's Bing brought the world real-time search. You can, in fact, access just about anything you want in real-time on the Web today—real-time real estate intelligence at Zillow.com, real-time ads via OneRiot, real-time stock information at StockTwits, real-time updates on the location of your package at FedEx.com, real-time density of people in urban areas with SpotRank, real-time news at the wonderfully named TimeSpace: World. And if it is not yet available, just wait; it's coming. As Edo Segal, an early entrepreneur in real-time search with Relegence (since sold to AOL) puts it, "Google organized our memory. Real-time search organizes our consciousness."[21]

The Quantified Self

Mirrored Virtuality also enables us to organize our selves. Mint.com of Mountain View, California, for example, mirrors your finances by ac-cessing, displaying, and analyzing all of your personal banking, credit card, mortgage, loan, and investment transactions. The company, which in 2009 was bought by Intuit, the maker of Quicken, provides a daily updated view of where your money is, where it's going, how close you are to personal goals, and—most importantly for its users—what you could do to improve your financial situation.

If you want to improve your health, you have myriad options. Perhaps the first to mirror your personal fitness was Nike+, where an accelerometer embedded in a shoe tracks the workouts of its wearer, which can then be uploaded to the Web via an Apple iPod. Runners and other athletes log on to nikeplus.com to access information—speed, mileage, elapsed time, calories burned—to see how they are doing, to track their progress against goals, and (naturally) to chat with others in similar situations. Adidas goes one better with its miCoach offering by marrying its tracking components and website to personalized improvement coaching. If you swim competitively instead of run, you can use wireless sensors from Avidasports of Harper Woods, Michigan, to track your precise performance, so your coach can learn of your current stroke tempo, turn time, and so forth, and compare it to your normal races. Fitbit, based in San Francisco, sells a clip-on sensor that measures the number of steps you take each day, your total distance traveled, the calories burned, and even your sleep quality, which you can then track at Fitbit.com. A similar device from Philips, DirectLife, doesn't track your sleep, but it does come with personal fitness and nutrition coaching through its website.

Some people, such as those who suffer from diabetes, need to track more than general fitness. So Bayer came out with the Contour USB, a blood glucose test meter that connects to a computer to upload the meter's readings and display what is happening to the person's body in easily understood ways. The information can be e-mailed to a doctor—and we presume eventually shared directly in a virtual space for effective medical conversations. Many doctors with heart patients now implant defibrillators that not only provide shocks to the heart when needed but can communicate with the patient and the doctor, helping them together manage the situation.[22]

Anything that should be tracked will be tracked. As *Wired* contributing editor Gary Wolf notes, "Almost imperceptibly, numbers are infiltrating the last redoubts of the personal. Sleep, exercise, sex, food, mood, location, alertness, productivity, even spiritual well-being are being tracked and measured, shared and displayed."[23] At the website he, along with fellow *Wired* colleague Kevin Kelly, hosts called "the Quantified Self," Wolf studies this phenomenon, provides tools, and enables "trackers" to discuss their ideas, experiments, and progress.[24] Wolf further notes how digital technology now enables us to quantify ourselves and thereby create Mirror Worlds of our own body and mind:

> Our only method of tracking ourselves was to notice what we were doing and write it down. But even this written record couldn't be analyzed objectively without laborious processing and analysis. . . .
>
> Trackers are exploring an alternate route. Instead of interrogating their inner worlds through talking and writing, they are using numbers. They are constructing a quantified self . . . .
>
> Millions of us track ourselves all the time. We step on a scale and record our weight. We balance a checkbook. We count calories. But when the familiar pen-and-paper methods of self-analysis are enhanced by sensors that monitor our behavior automatically, the process of self-tracking becomes both more alluring and more meaningful. Automated sensors do more than give us facts; they also remind us that our ordinary behavior contains obscure quantitative signals that can be used to inform our behavior, once we learn to read them.[25]

More and more people perform such self-tracking, what some call life-logging or lifestreaming, because we want to do more than *in*form our behavior; we want to *trans*form it. Right now, however, most companies involved in this arena provide sensor goods and/or information and analysis services while enhancing people's life experiences, but few if any use these goods, services, and experiences to actually make possible the transformations we desire.

One person who transformed his life through the capability of digital technology to track not only anything but everything is Gordon Bell, inventor of the VAX minicomputer for Digital Equipment Corporation and now a researcher with Microsoft. The quantified selfers have nothing on him, for since 1998 Bell has digitally recorded everything—his entire life experience, including what he did, who he saw, what he read and wrote, and how he felt. Using his own experience as a guide, Bell says we will soon enter an age of Total Recall, where "your smartphone plus whatever sensors and miscellaneous devices you wear and carry will all be linked together to form a personal digital memory collection-and-management system that will (if you choose) be able to record just about everything you see, hear, and do and keep it all in one big virtual collection in the cloud. The uses of such an archive are limitless."[26]

Topsight & Technology

Bell believes that recording our lives onto digital "e-memory" in real time, all the time, will free our minds:

> With the right software you will be able to mine your digital memory archive for patterns and trends that you could never uncover on your own—graphing, charting, sorting, cross-sectioning, and testing for hidden correlations among all your bits. Imagine if you could bring into a single database all the pictures you take, all the places you visit, all the routes you take, all your notes and annotations, all your e-mails, along with room temperatures, weather conditions, diet, activity, whom you met with, your meeting cancellations, what you read, when you worked, what TV shows you watched, your mood swings, your flashes of inspiration. What would happen if you could take that whole slurry of life-history fragments and run it all through a powerful pattern-detection program? What kinds of patterns might you find?[27]

What you would gain from such a personal Mirror World is what Gelernter recognized as their very raison d'être: *topsight,* which he defines as "an understanding of the big picture." Gelertner explains: "If insight is the illumination to be achieved by penetrating inner depths, topsight is what comes from a far-overhead vantage point, from a bird's eye view that reveals the whole—the big picture; how the parts fit together."[28] Even if you never want to go anywhere near the level that Bell achieves himself and predicts for many of us, it is for reaching exactly such a precious vantage point that we enter the realm of Mirrored Virtuality.

Finding that vantage point requires properly framing the question about that which you seek to uncover truth—although you could take Bell's approach and digitally record absolutely everything as it happens. You must then measure, record, model, track and monitor, analyze, and present the data. Although Mirrored Virtuality is always tied into actual Time, that does not mean you cannot take the virtual representation and replay the past to discover trends or simulate the future to forecast events. For as Bell showed, topsight most of all involves pattern recognition—sifting through the noise to see the meaning in the data. Computers can analyze the raw data to turn it into information, which you can then turn into the knowledge you need to see the patterns that let you determine what actions to take in your own personal or corporate experience, which then can generate the wisdom necessary for true transformation.

Gaining topsight through Mirrored Virtuality requires particular types of technology, elements that together comprise a Mirror World as Gelernter envisioned it and so many of the exemplars achieved. First of all, you need *sensors* to measure and accumulate the raw data. Anything preceded with the term "smart" embeds such sensors in its objects, elements, or infrastructure: smart appliances, smart buildings, smart roads, smart bridges, smart grids. The second requirement is *storage* for all the data you accumulate. This is almost a trivial element to discuss, given the plummeting cost of digital storage and increasingly ability to keep data in the cloud, but keep in mind that it must be absolutely voluminous, and it must be instantaneously accessible for recording, playback, and analysis. Next is some sort of *platform,* a system that connects to all the sensors, provides a mechanism to begin to make sense of the data, and supports some sort of visual or experiential output. Fourth, *tracking and monitoring tools,* which passively watch the data as it comes in and, based on triggers, provide alerts that something requires attention or should be looked at more closely, or even takes action itself automatically. Fifth, *analytics* to more fully understand exactly what is going on, not just in real time as with the tracking and monitoring tools or the whole class of software known as real time analytics, but *through* time in order to analyze historical data, detect patterns, and forecast future trends. And finally, to gain such ongoing topsight regarding any mirror world requires some sort of *dashboard.*

Think of how, at a glance, the dashboard in your car gives you a view of what is happening right now with the vehicle and its surroundings. The new Ford SmartGauge with EcoGuide even turns fuel efficiency into a game by adding the image of a green vine to the dash that grows more branches and buds with efficient driving but withers with leadfoots! The complexities of driving efficiency boil down to a simple display: "You don't have to count the leaves. But if you're in a forest of leaves, you'll know you're doing well."[29] So just like a car dashboard, UK-based Tweetdeck provides you with a visual representation and control panel for your personal Twitterverse. Wowd lets you discover what's going on in real-time on Facebook, and Woopra similarly shows you at a glance what is happening right now with visits to your corporate website. Dashboards can be as specific as Toronto-based Empathica's Mobile Reporting solution for retailers—which "gives them instant access to a mobile dashboard where they can review information on individual location performances"[30]—to as general as the famous Bloomberg Terminal (today really three-terminals-in-one), which provides real-time windows to all the news, information, people, and trades happening right now in the world that could impact decision makers not just in financial services but more broadly in business and government.

What design tools are to Physical Virtuality, dashboards are to Mirrored Virtuality. So, as with design tools, be sure to make the using of the dashboard an experience unto itself!

Applying Mirrored Virtuality

Keep in mind, too, that perhaps your *cosmos incognitus* to be discovered lies not in creating or using your own mirror world as an end offering but in providing one or more of the elements—sensors, storage, platform, tracking and monitoring tools, analytics, and dashboard—that bring Mirrored Virtuality to life.

Whatever the case, from whatever standpoint—offering or tool, user or provider—the essence of this realm is a virtual simulation of Reality that you can watch unfold in real time. Apply these principles to exploit the power of Time to your advantage:

∞ *Help your customers mirror some piece of their Reality*—whether personally or corporately—*in real time.*

∞ To do that, you must first *create a Virtuality experience that represents that Reality* (whether specially or via some available platform).

∞ Then *synchronize Reality and Virtuality together via a real-time data feed* to absorb the real world into the virtual.

∞ Consider what real-world experiences people already experience live on radio, TV, or even rudimentarily on the Web, and then *translate live broadcasts to a virtual world* that relates, accentuates, and extends the action.

∞ *Discern the distinctions between Mirrored Virtuality and Augmented Reality to power your explorations.* Understand the Actuality Axis that links these two realms, and then keep in mind the exact nature of each, without muddying them together, in order to find further opportunities.

∞ *Work to make Second Earth happen,* combining the navigability, exploration tools, and enchantment of virtual worlds with the defined geography, extant situations, and meaningfulness of the one real world.

∞ *Use your creations to predict the present, understand the past, and forecast the future.*

∞ *Take advantage of the real-time Web* to create value for individuals or corporations to see what is going on in the where and now.

∞ *Help people become Quantified Selves,* tracking whatever they want to track. Fitness, health, and finances are already hot topics; what else is out there?

∞ With Mirrored Virtuality in particular, *look beyond experiences to provide transformation offerings that guide customers to change.* Recognize that doing so requires wisdom on both sides.

∞ Consider how you might *help realize Gordon Bell's vision of Total Recall*—while helping your customers determine exactly how much of their life they want to record privately and how little they want to post publicly.

∞ *Always keep in mind how you can provide topsight* via measuring, recording, modeling, tracking and monitoring, analyzing, and presenting.

∞ *Determine your role in creating and/or deploying the key technologies that together yield topsight*: sensors, storage, platforms, tracking and monitoring tools, analytics, and dashboards.

Although it may seem at first blush to be a trivial reflection of reality, on full examination Mirrored Virtuality blossoms into a vast realm of opportunity to manage the previously unmanageable, whether the worldwide spread of diseases or your personal enrichment and transformation. And it all starts simply by digitally (re)constructing Reality in a virtual place and enacting its events in the now—the leading edge of the incessant march of actual time. Infinite opportunities to gain topsight, embrace Total Recall, predict the present, decipher the past, and project the future truly abound within this final realm on the digital frontier.

You are now free to move about the Multiverse. It is yours to exploit.

part IV
GUIDING

10

Multiverse Excursion

REACHING THROUGH THE REALMS

So there it is. The eight realms of the Multiverse in all their glory, de-fined, diagrammed, and copiously explained, with sets of guiding principles that we trust already have you thinking about what it means for your business. The next step is to operationalize what you have learned—to step out into the unknown to explore what possibilities, amid the infinite directions in which you could go, would create the most economic value for your business.

On any journey of exploration into the unknown, it is a given that we cannot know ahead of time what we will discover. But if we can in advance determine at least the nature of what we seek, we can heighten our intuition, tune in our mental receptors, and focus our eyes on the form a discovery may take. When we then move into *cosmos incogniti,* we will be better equipped to see the possibilities that lie before us. The Multiverse should thus provide you with a new lens, a focused way of seeing and making sense of what you discover on your expedition into the unknown.

Exploring the Multiverse

To ensure that your new lens is polished and focused properly, let us here give the very essence of the realms we fully examined in Chapters 2 through 9, respectively:

∞ **Reality:** Staging the richest of experiences, Reality fully engages the five senses, enraptures the whole body, captivates the mind, involves the physical world, and bonds you with your fellow members of humanity.

∞ **Augmented Reality:** Enhancing the world around us, Augmented Reality uses bits to augment our experience of Reality, overlaying it with digital information constructed to enhance, extend, edit, or amend the way we experience the real world.

 ∞ **Alternate Reality:** Creating an alternate view of the real world, Alternate Reality uses Reality as a digital playground via a super-imposed, virtual narrative freed from the bonds of actual time.

 ∞ **Warped Reality:** Playing with time, Warped Reality takes an experience firmly grounded in Reality and shifts it from actual to autonomous time, playing with time in any way possible.

 ∞ **Virtuality:** Crafting the most imaginative of experiences, Virtuality immerses the mind, although generally not the body, in ways that free us from the constraints of Time, Space, and Matter.

 ∞ **Augmented Virtuality:** Bringing the material into the virtual, Augmented Virtuality takes a Virtuality experience and uses some material substance to alter, enhance, control, or amend how we experience the virtual world.

 ∞ **Physical Virtuality:** Instantiating the virtual in the material, Physical Virtuality takes an experience happening in a virtual place and then instantiates, or *real*izes, it in the real world; first you dream it, and then you build it.

∞ **Mirrored Virtuality:** Absorbing the real world into the virtual, Mirrored Virtuality creates a virtual expression of Reality that unfolds as it actually happens, providing a particular bird's-eye view.

So read and reread these—or the version graphically portrayed in Figure 10.1—until you intuitively understand each one. Also refer back to Figure 1.5 in Chapter 1, "Cosmos Incogniti," as necessary until you instinctively know where every realm lies in the framework.

Realize, however, that as you shift now from *understanding* to *ideation,* in the end it's not important how you *classify* any experience you might stage; the only thing that matters is the *efficacy* of the offering. Does it create value for your customers and economic value for your company? So, yes, become good at classifying as an aid to understand-

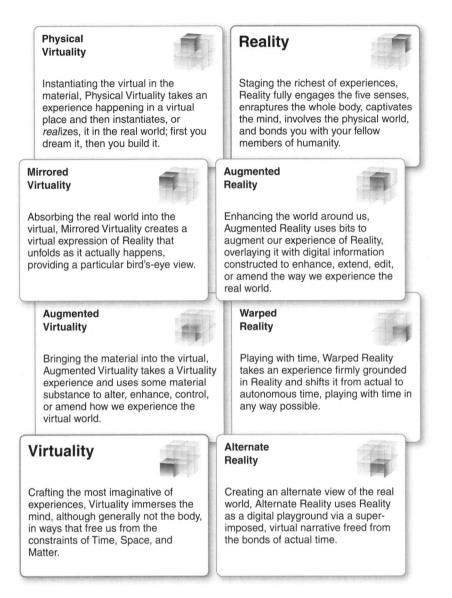

Physical Virtuality

Instantiating the virtual in the material, Physical Virtuality takes an experience happening in a virtual place and then instantiates, or *realizes*, it in the real world; first you dream it, then you build it.

Reality

Staging the richest of experiences, Reality fully engages the five senses, enraptures the whole body, captivates the mind, involves the physical world, and bonds you with your fellow members of humanity.

Mirrored Virtuality

Absorbing the real world into the virtual, Mirrored Virtuality creates a virtual expression of Reality that unfolds as it actually happens, providing a particular bird's-eye view.

Augmented Reality

Enhancing the world around us, Augmented Reality uses bits to augment our experience of Reality, overlaying it with digital information constructed to enhance, extend, edit, or amend the way we experience the real world.

Augmented Virtuality

Bringing the material into the virtual, Augmented Virtuality takes a Virtuality experience and uses some material substance to alter, enhance, control, or amend how we experience the virtual world.

Warped Reality

Playing with time, Warped Reality takes an experience firmly grounded in Reality and shifts it from actual to autonomous time, playing with time in any way possible.

Virtuality

Crafting the most imaginative of experiences, Virtuality immerses the mind, although generally not the body, in ways that free us from the constraints of Time, Space, and Matter.

Alternate Reality

Creating an alternate view of the real world, Alternate Reality uses Reality as a digital playground via a super-imposed, virtual narrative freed from the bonds of actual time.

Figure 10.1 The essences of the Realms

ing, but once you have an idea, shift your thoughts from where it came from to where you can take it in creating a new offering.

In particular here, think not just of new goods and services, but innovative experiences and transformations. These higher-level offerings in the Progression of Economic Value (shown in Figure I.1 back in the

Introduction, "Innovation on the Digital Frontier") create greater value for customers, generally have longer life spans, and make it possible for companies to capture more economic value than the lower-level offerings. So focus your company's innovation on engaging customer experiences and even life-changing transformations in order to create the greatest possible value for each of your individual customers, and therefore the greatest economic value for your company.

Remember, too, that these eight realms of the Multiverse form just one way of looking at our core framework. We referred you back to Figure 1.5 in particular because it shows the framework's full sense-making architecture with its 8-6-3-1 formula: eight realms defined by six variables that comprise three dimensions making up the one Multiverse. Now in Part III, "Guiding," we not only want to cement your understanding of the eight realms (as defined by the three Event, Place, and Substance dimensions) and help you apply them to your business, we also want you to better understand how the one Multiverse incorporates the six variables of actual and autonomous events, real and virtual places, and material and digital substances, and then how to apply *them* to your business independently of the realms.

These realm and variable perspectives, applied with diligence, serve to reveal opportunities hidden from plain sight. Our goal here is to help you make your exploration for and capture of new value *proactive,* to eliminate having to constantly react to your competitors' discoveries, and *effective,* making an otherwise overwhelming task manageable, thorough, and fruitful. But given the vastness of *cosmos incogniti,* with their endless galaxies of opportunity amid infinite possibility, wherever do you begin?

We recommend you conduct two distinct ideation expeditions into the digital frontier. Each of these spur the generation of ideas through a different method, starting from the differing vantage points of first the realms and then the variables, with their own perspectives, approaches, sets of activities, and results. In the remainder of this chapter we will show you how to *Reach through the Realms* with the Multiverse serving as your sense-making guide. This focuses you on methodically exploring each and every one of its eight realms to discover the value creation possibilities they hold in turn. In Chapter 11, "Offering Depiction," we then show you a way of plotting experiences that lets you *Vary the Variables* of the Multiverse. This ignores the realms and instead focuses you on the six variables that define the framework.

These two expeditions yield ideas at the intersection of technology innovation and customer need. You can therefore boost the effectiveness of your Reaching through the Realms and Varying the Variables expeditions by better knowing your customers and the technologies that affect your industry. So we also recommend that you continually look to your customers to observe their behavior and thereby uncover underserved or unmet needs. And remember, as Carver Mead famously said, "Listen to the technology; find out what it is telling you."[1] Through looking at your customer, listening to the technology, and understanding the Multiverse, you are well equipped to begin your first exploration into the digital frontier.

A Structured Walk through the Realms

Columbus, Magellan, Lewis and Clark, Amundsen. Such explorers of *terrae incognitae* in times past all had their maps, however incomplete, to guide them on their journeys. During their expeditions, each imagined the new possibilities their discoveries offered and pursued them vigorously. Sometimes they found what they imagined they would; sometimes they were surprised by what they discovered. With the guiding frameworks of their times, they explored our real world. Now, with the Multiverse as a guide, you can embark on your own exploration of *cosmos incogniti,* not with a map of earthly territories but one of logical territories, more like how mathematicians or physicists use hypotheses to steer their explorations.

Reaching through the Realms systematically explores all eight realms of the Multiverse, incrementally stepping from one to the next, to see what possibilities arise from visiting each and every realm, including looping back to the realm from which you started. Such a comprehensive excursion provides you with new inspirations, ideas, insights, and knowledge gathered along the way.

As you Reach through the Realms you will find yourself in *cosmos* both *cogniti* and *incogniti*. Some will be familiar and perhaps even mundane, whereas other will be bursting with possibility. But also, just as with the incomplete maps for the explorers of old, do not be surprised if at times you fall into a dark void that conveys no illumination to your circumstances, leaving you with no discernible new value creation ideas for your customers. When this happens, just move in another direction and chart a new course. Who knows? Maybe that trajectory will take you back around and position you to explore that same realm from a different vantage point, or simply lead you to richer opportunities elsewhere.

As is also the case with Varying the Variables, the Reaching through the Realm expedition calls for a team of diverse and knowledgeable employees gathered together to jointly explore the possibilities. Select participants who, collectively, cover the full range of business responsibilities in order to discover value creation possibilities and business opportunities from across the full scope of the business. (And be sure to include those charged with looking at the customer as well as those responsible for listening to the technology.) Once the group gathers, kick off the expedition with *immersion*—a learning and understanding session, whether for the first time or as a refresher, to get everyone in Multiverse-thinking mode. Go through the Multiverse, as a whole and realm by realm, with plenty of examples—especially ones they can experience themselves, live!—until everyone has the base knowledge necessary to apply the realms to your business. *Ideation* then begins with the participants dividing into small teams working independently to conduct a structured exploration of the Multiverse realms. After generating ideas at each stage, the teams bring their ideas together for explication, discussion, refinement, and further idea generation. *Selection* then follows with the group choosing those ideas with the greatest value-creating potential to pursue further toward opportunity realization.

We will focus here on the ideation portion of this expedition. To determine where to start ideating, think about a current offering, one you would like to enhance by pushing it out toward the digital frontier. While you might have a very strategic reason for your choice, offerings chosen for other reasons—underperformance, new competition, a sneaking suspicion there's something more of value somewhere, or even at random—can all prompt effective sessions as well. You may also wish to start with just the germ of an idea for a new-to-the-world offering and use the Reaching method to further explore its potential and possibly identify even greater opportunities to create new value. When searching for new ideas beyond your existing offerings, you might even choose another company's offering, possibly a competitor, or even one from another industry that you think might soon impact yours. You never know what ideas generated and insights gained will find their way back into your company's offerings.

Once you choose the experiential offering targeted for innovation, identify its place in the Multiverse, the realm most closely associated with its core value proposition. This realm serves as the offering's *anchor realm*—the starting point for a structured walk through the realms. For example, if a National Football League team charters a Multiverse excursion to innovate its in-stadium offering, Reality anchors the offering. The journey then steps from this realm to proceed through adjacent and then more far-reaching realms to discover what innovations might enhance the in-stadium experience, with a goal of ensuring fans fill the seats at every game. No wonder that in 2009 the Dallas Cowboys brought Virtuality into the field of play when it debuted the world's largest video screen over its field (although not quite "over" enough to avoid being hit by a punt in the first game played there). Guests at the New Meadowlands Stadium in New Jersey (opened in 2010) similarly benefit from Augmented Reality in accessing in-stadium smartphone apps for instant replay, live statistics, and even video feeds from other games, with Virtuality-based fantasy playing against other in-stadium patrons forthcoming.[2]

Suppose you are a medical products company with a live-body-function-imaging offering similar to Luminetx VeinViewer, mentioned in Chapter 3, "Augmented Reality." After centering your offering in this realm, you then start to look right next door in, say, Mirrored Virtuality to reflect remotely in a virtual world what happens to bodies as they function in the real world. If, on the other hand, you offer an interactive virtual world firmly anchored in Virtuality, such as a video game or Web-based retailer, then your Reaching through the Realms expedition heads from there back toward Reality. You may find value in embracing a physical controller to take advantage of Augmented Virtuality, tying the experience into real time with Mirrored Virtuality, or venturing out into the real world via Alternate Reality.

Whatever you wish to explore, the whole offering or some distinctive aspect of it fits in one of the eight realms. That defines the most familiar territory and therefore the logical starting point, or anchor, for your Reaching through the Realms expedition. The structured walk then follows a path from this home base through these four stages, also represented in Figure 10.2:

∞ *Stage One:* Here you explore the three immediately adjacent realms, each one variable different from the anchor, to see what opportunities lie right next door.

∞ *Stage Two:* This takes you further away, examining the three realms that vary from the anchor by not one but two variables,

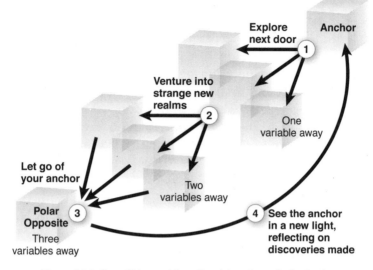

Figure 10.2 Expedition guide to Reaching through the Realms

leaving only one unchanged. This takes the original notion of the offering into strange new territory, making explorations more difficult, but potentially more rewarding.

∞ *Stage Three:* In the next stage you vary all three variables defining the anchor realm at once, essentially letting go of the anchor and starting anew. This realm, the polar opposite from the starting realm, retains the most degrees of freedom from the offering being innovated, allowing for the most far-out ideation.

∞ *Stage Four:* The final stage returns the Multiverse excursion to the beginning, back to the anchor, where you may very well see the offering innovation possibilities in a new light, reflecting the discoveries made throughout the prior stages of the expedition.

In any full exploration through the first three stages of Reaching through the Realms, this fourth and final stage should have you thinking anew about your offerings. For as T. S. Eliot wrote in "Little Gidding,"

> We shall not cease from exploration
> And the end of all our exploring
> Will be to arrive where we started
> And know the place for the first time.[3]

An Electronics Retailer Reaches through the Realms

Now that we have introduced you to the Reaching through the Realms expedition, let's see what one particular company, say, a big electronics retailer, might get out of such an expedition. Although all such retailers have virtual presences at their websites (providing an alternative starting point), we'll focus here on the store itself, anchored as it is in the realm of Reality. Because we don't want to overwhelm you with all the details of just one theoretical example, here we'll provide just enough for you to get a feel for a real-life Reaching ideation expedition.

Stage One: How might we employ Augmented Reality, Warped Reality, and Physical Virtuality, each adjacent to our current store's anchor in Reality?

In this first stage, you and your team go beyond the actual events, material substances, and real places of Reality by reaching into the realms immediately adjacent to it, as shown in Figure 10.3. Augmented Reality, Physical Virtuality, and Warped Realty all differ from Reality by a single variable, each of which you explore one at a time to seek new value-creation possibilities.

The key to Augmented Reality is using digital technology (moving here from Matter to No-Matter) to enhance a customer's experience

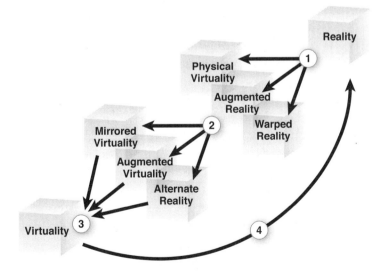

Figure 10.3 Reaching through the Realms—starting from Reality

of the physical store. So let's develop an iPhone app (Good thing we sell them! But we'll port it to other smartphones, too . . .) that becomes the customer's window into our inventory and, more importantly, the guide for his own experience.[4] As the customer walks around, everywhere he points the camera on his app-equipped phone he sees an overlay of information (much of it already on our website) about whatever he's looking at. There are directional arrows to every type of product we have, which he can winnow down to his desired set. Pointing to any one product—whether display merchandise, a box, UPC code, or any other identifier—brings up richer product information and demonstrations, which we'll customize to his needs. He can fully explore everything about that product, compare it to alternatives, experience it in action, find and call over a sales associate, and even buy it, with the item waiting for him at checkout or shipped home . . . .

With Warped Reality, we start back at the vantage point of our store and shift from Time to No-Time. We're still operating in a physical place of Space and Matter, but now we get to explore how to play with our customers' sense of time. What about taking the customer through a time warp surrounding the (still short) history of home electronics? Here's an idea: Let's do an Electronic Age Assessment experience! Let's determine where you, Mr. Customer, lie on the continuum from the 1950s (the Dawn of Time Age, meaning no experience whatsoever with home electronics) through the 1970s (the Stereo Age, where you know your audio equipment backward and forward, including amplifiers, sub-woofers, and the like, but computers remain a new-fangled thing) to the 1990s (the Personal Computer Age, where even they are old hat) to today's world of proliferating devices (call it the Connected Age, with its smartphones, flash drives, netbooks, and tablets, not to mention its Facebooks, Google Earths, and tweets). This could be a standalone experience, or more likely a something a sales associate would do in concert with the customer whenever he determines that someone is looking for a complete overhaul of his electronics environment. The Electronic Age Assessment will then help the associate customize the interactions as he steers the customer to the best, say, home theater system for his situation. And in a further play on time, when they together define that system, we could physically morph our home theater room to represent his own future home, so he sees what it will be like when it's all installed next week . . . .

Now shifting from Space to No-Space, we come to Physical Virtuality, where the goal is to take something that exists solely in the customer's imagination (even if we're the ones who put it there!) and make it real. So let's take our cue here from *The Matrix* and have customers enter our "Electronics Construct"—our virtual store (within the physical one) that starts out completely blank, but morphs to the customer's every whim as we help him select the right home computer, the right home theater, the right gaming station. We're tracking and holding inventory with every selection, so by the time the experience is through, we can physically present that system to the customer. For those that bring in a picture of their home environment, we even digitally morph it to what it will look like once it's all installed and print it out right there and then. What a close!

And let's further realize we have way too much physical inventory that really should be virtual. Just look at all those racks of CDs. They haven't gone away, not just yet, but the need for the inventory sure has. We already let our music aficionados move from Space to No-Space when they put on headphones to listen to any album we have for sale. Let's stop *having* albums for sale until a customer says this is the exact album he is looking for, and then and only then, stamp it out on an actual CD, print out the material for the jewel case, and put it all together complete with personalized (albeit automated) artist signature, if the customer will pay for that extra. Let's then use the same process for DVDs, so that we become the physical counterparts to iTunes and Netflix for as long as customers still buy such physical technologies.

Stage Two: What possibilities await us in the farther reaches of Alternate Reality, Mirrored Virtuality, and Augmented Virtuality?

Let's see: Alternate Reality [No-Time – Space – No-Matter] is about using the real world as a virtual playground, such as for helping customers connect to each other to figure out a mystery. You know, though, there is no reason we couldn't apply this to our sales associates—and thereby make it fun for them and the customers alike. What if we charge each sales associate with determining the customer's "Electronics Identity"? They should see each customer as a puzzle to be solved or mystery to be revealed, with the setting being the store (in fact, every separate store this customer steps foot in). With each associate cast as a persistent, Columbo-like sleuth garnering salient clues through perceptive observations, insightful questions, and telling experiences and collaborating with their colleagues in the other stores. We create a smartphone app (another opportunity to show off our stuff) that leads them through their investigative choices, the completion of each adding one more puzzle piece to our view of this individual customer, until we have a full representation of the identity of each. A prize for solving the mystery sweetens the deal, for knowing each customer increases the opportunity to meet his needs for the next piece of electronics that in turn represents a puzzle piece for his ideal system.

With Mirrored Virtuality [Time – No-Space – No-Matter], we must turn around and create a virtual space as the backdrop for giving customers better understanding of what's going on in the real world with, say, their own sound system, home theater, gaming system, or computer setup. So let's switch roles from store sleuth to playing doctor by offering (for a fee, of course) a system checkup, an ongoing health assessment, and even a "stress test" to customers. First, our customer service personnel could inventory every piece of electronics in the customer's home—healthy ones, aging ones, and those in disrepair. (Hmm . . . this would be a great add-on whenever we're already setting up or fixing a system!) The customer could even do it himself via another smartphone app we provide (point, click, capture!).

That provides the checkup. For the ongoing assessment, we create a virtual representation of the setup, linked via the Internet to each addressable piece of equipment to keep track of everything that happens. (We could even work with the manufacturers to make every reasonable item we sell Internet-addressable.) Customers can go at any time, from anywhere, and view this virtual representation, seeing what has happened over time and what is happening right now. A dashboard lets them know instantly anything that goes wrong (Let's get that in urgent care!), see how components degrade over time (Is it time for replacement?), learn of any anomalies (Is there a patch to fix that?), and track all repairs, changes, and modifications. The stress test looks at possible future scenarios and sees if the system comes through with flying colors or needs some upgrades. Through it all, the customer comes to understand his system, its capabilities, and his own usage, customs, and habits in a way never before possible.

That brings us to Augmented Virtuality [No-Time, No-Space, Matter], where we want to enhance customers' virtual experiences by involving the whole body. We could . . . But wait, we're looking at this from the perspective of our physical store; there's no virtuality to augment! So what if we . . . No, that isn't Augmented Virtuality. How about . . . Hmm, that doesn't work either. Maybe we're in one of those dark voids mentioned earlier where we just can't seem to generate an idea that makes sense. (And if we could, believe us, we would put it in here!)

We'll have to try a different route, come at this realm from a different point of view. Where have we already generated ideas with elements of Virtuality that we could augment? Well, there was that Electronics Construct to guide customers in determining the right system. Then there was the virtual representation of their installed systems we just came up with in thinking about Mirrored Virtuality. Can we now augment them with physicality to get customers bodily involved with the experiences?

Still nothing. Short of outfitting customers with haptic body suits—technology not yet ready for prime commerce time—and the trivial example of having their iPhones shake, rattle, and buzz to warn of something they should pay attention to in their mirrored representation, we still have no good ideas here. Let's not worry about it, and move on.

Stage Three: What ideas can we generate by considering the exact opposite realm—in this case Virtuality?

Pure Virtuality [No-Time – No-Space – No-Matter] always presents many possibilities, with the obvious one being an entirely virtual store. We're not talking about a whipped up website, although that would count as Virtuality, but a truly virtual *place*—one where customers, or rather their avatars, could walk, fly, or teleport around seeking out the best buys in electronics. Yes, that sort of thing was tried in the heyday of *Second Life* (all of four or five years ago), but the problem with those attempts was that they were glorified ghost towns, with no staff, no service, and no sales (and often customers with no shirts). They weren't *experiences.* Our virtual store, on the other hand, will be filled with them, from product demonstrations (watch a live football game on the virtual HDTVs—select any one or take over the video wall!) to special events (dive into a heavy metal concert's virtual mosh pit if that's your thing—avatars don't bruise!) to gaming quests (hunt down and shoot the flying bargain—sure beats the blue light special!). And our virtual store will be filled with our own associates, or rather their avatars, who will guide the experiences of our guests. (No ghost town this!)

Once we get going here, the *cosmos* is the limit. All we have to do is keep in mind that we're designing *experiences,* not a static store; *engaging* customers, not targeting them; getting them to *visit* and *explore,* not selling them merchandise and then booting them out the door. And there's no reason to limit such virtual experiences to customer's own homes. Each one can be accessed from our own physical places, providing yet another opportunity to show off our electronics.

Did you notice something about the virtual product demonstration idea above? It was a *real* football game the avatars were watching, so the tie-in to real time actually places it firmly in the Mirrored Virtuality realm. So what! It doesn't matter what realm an experience ends up residing in; what's important are the ideas sparked by whatever realm we're exploring at the time. The idea's the thing, not slavish devotion to any constraints of the imagination. We're thinking outside the universe here, for goodness sake, so let's not put ourselves in any box. And while we're at it, let's also save judgment on these ideas for a later time when we can refine them, see how we might integrate them, and select the best ones for further investigation and hopefully implementation. (After all, if you don't put them into operation, they're not innovations at all but remain mere ideas.)

Actually, let's do explore a small amount of integration—a little mixing of the ideas through some melding of the realms—here and now. Now that we have associates representing themselves through avatars, why can't they do so in the physical stores? Recall that (Augmented Reality) iPhone app that guides a customer's experience in the store; we'll let them avoid waiting for a live sales associate and call up one immediately—not "call up" in the sense of making a phone call, but in the sense of conjuring a spirit from the great beyond of Virtuality. These virtual associates could be anywhere, support everywhere, and sell everything.

Let's harken back to the (Warped Reality) Electronic Age Assessment too. Although thought of while exploring the real world of Space and Matter (and the unreal world of No-Time), consider how much more engaging this experience could be if it were virtual, where we could instantaneously fly through visual representations of each Age, rather than mere mock-ups. Same goes for morphing our system to match the customers' future system. Such time traveling would be so much more efficient, so much more engaging, so much more effective if experienced virtually rather than physically. And remember the Electronics Identity mystery scenario generated in thinking about Alternate Reality? That, too, would benefit from the influence of Virtuality thinking, especially by having our virtual sales associates join in observing, questioning, and interacting with customers. Finally, let's look back at the big fat zero we came up with in thinking about Augmented Virtuality. Now that we've thought about what a virtual store really should be, we do have some virtual experiences that could benefit from a little physical augmentation. Zapping the flying bargain with a Wii

Remote would be more engaging. Even better, let's create and control the Electronics Construct with Microsoft's Kinect. That would not only make for a great, active, cool experience, but it would help us sell more Xboxes as well!

Stage Four: Go back to the beginning and think anew, with the enlightenment and insights gathered so far, from your anchor realm's point-of-view. How might you pull it all together? And what have you discovered?

Speaking of starts, we began with the vantage point of today's physical store and ventured into a retail cosmos that is now at least a little more *cognitus* than *incognitus.* One aspect of integration that now seems clear is the need to interact with customers wherever, whenever, and however they would like. We're not limited to the confines of the store, to normal retail hours, to physical interactions, nor to Reality itself. All the ideas we've talked about can come together anywhere, anytime, and anyway a customer wants, whenever that individual customer finds himself in the market for a piece of electronics. If we're really good, we can even spark the creation of that market within customers through in-store, at-home, and out-of-this-world experiences that cause them to want to spend time with us, in engaging spaces we have created, around interests that matter to them.

And there's one key discovery we've made, a thread that's been weaving through these ideas: we don't today use our own products enough to sell our own merchandise! How can we expect our offerings to be indispensable in the lives of our customers when they so obviously remain dispensable in our work? Using what we sell to create the greatest engagement for our customers will then yield the greatest economic value for our business.

And so at the end of all our exploration, we have arrived where we started and indeed know the place for the first time.

Moving Your Offering's Anchor

To begin this sample expedition we determined that Reality was the most appropriate anchor realm. But just because your current offering anchors in a particular realm does not mean it must stay there. Anchors hold a ship in place, but you can also raise them from the sea floor in order to move to a new location. During an ideation expedition, consider the possibility that the features of an offering that have anchored it to one realm be discarded and replaced by the features of another realm. You may very well find that you have discovered a way of creating a better value proposition for your customer by arriving at a whole new means of creating and delivering the offering.

USAA serves as an example of this type of realm migration. This financial company recently switched realms in how it deposits a soldier's paycheck. Rather than leaving this offering a Reality-based experience with the physical placement of the check in a teller's hands, USAA discovered greater value for their customers in virtualizing the offering through digitizing the physical check. Now soldiers, many of whom are on long overseas deployments, simply photograph their check with their iPhones and send the photo to USAA for prompt depositing in their bank account.[5]

This immediate digitization of the check changed the essence of the offering from Reality to Virtuality, the polar opposite realm. The physical check was no longer "material" to the experience, nor the soldier's location in space, and actual time essentially became a nonfactor. The paper check, once digitized via the iPhone, frees the offering from the bounds of material substance, real place, and actual events. If USAA were to conduct a Reaching through the Realms ideation expedition for this new check-deposit offering, it could therefore start in Virtuality.

But some offerings are, due to their very definition, unlikely to change realms. For example, an automaker provides a personal auto driving and riding experience, which, by definition, is bound to Reality. But as more and more capabilities come on board that augment the driver's experience (remember that *Wired* piece that increasingly seems to be a work of prediction rather than parody?), we can see the potential for the default experience to be one filled with so much digital technology that Augmented Reality becomes the anchor realm. Similarly, the experience of going to meetings has in many cases shifted from Reality to Mirrored Virtuality with offerings like GoToMeeting, whose only essential tie to Reality is actual time. It doesn't require a special place, just such digital substances as the participants' voices, texting, images, and PowerPoint slides. In the case of a GoToMeeting Reaching expedition, the starting realm would be Mirrored Virtuality, not the Reality of the physical meetings it displaces.

One intriguing possibility for Virtuality-based businesses, especially those with avatar-based virtual worlds: make a complete flip from Virtuality to Reality by conducting a Reaching through the Realms expedition *from the perspective of the avatar.* A virtual world is a virtual *world,* after all, forming all of the *avatar's* Reality. Therefore, the avatar can experience the entire (virtually simulated) Multiverse within the virtual world (once removed, as it were, from the human represented by the avatar).

EVE Online players, for example, already use a dashboard that tells them what's going on in the vast universe their avatars inhabit. For their avatars, that is Mirrored Virtuality. When those avatars use heads-up displays on their spaceships, they are augmenting their reality. So how else might the virtual world enhance the experience of avatars through all eight realms of the Multiverse, and therefore enable the business to enhance the experience of their customers who play through those avatars? Reaching through the Realms is the way to find out.

Reaching Expedition Guidance

The Reaching expedition seeks to generate as many ideas as possible, in the shortest period of time, for creating new customer value on the digital frontier. This approach is no cookbook, but it does provide a method to employ the experience realms of the Multiverse in as fluid a way as possible. With that in mind, here are some guidelines to consider in keeping your ideation expedition on track while at the same time freeing your creativity to perform unlimited ideation:

∞ *Go beyond the visual and aural to engage, or at least evoke, all five senses.* We take experiences in with our senses, so the more senses more effectively engaged or virtually evoked, the richer the experience.

∞ Recognize that you can *engage customers emotionally, physically, intellectually, and/or spiritually.* Almost all experiences must have some level of emotional engagement to be effective; where can you employ the other three kinds?

∞ Since emotional engagement is so important, *consider everywhere emotions can come into play.* What role do the senses play to stir up emotions? How do those emotions bind or attract people to the experience or its intended result? Emotions prompt decisions. What decisions are you looking for your customers to make and what emotions will move them to act? What emotions will people return to experience time and again?

∞ *View your ideas in the context of the bigger picture of the business model.* Does the offering fit with an existing business model or does a new business model need to be created?[6]

∞ *Think of how your ideas expand people's capabilities for sensing, performing, linking, and organizing.* Which capabilities do the technologies you encounter extend or enable? What capabilities are essential to the offering both as it is and as it might be?[7]

∞ Alternatively, for offerings centered on one particular capability, *seek out what possibilities exist across the other three.* If focused on linking, for example, how can you broaden sensing, enhance performing, and provide a means of organizing that currently does not exist? There are always opportunities on the digital frontier to further bolster human capabilities.

∞ *Distinguish multiple types of customers, or personae, served in each realm.* What are the primary characteristics of each persona? Which of them are your customers, but in a different realm? What opportunities do you have for helping currently underserved customers?

∞ Given that, go further to *always examine how your offerings might be tailored to individual customers,* particularly since anything that can be digitized can be customized.

∞ *Distinguish the type of value created by offerings realm by realm.* Look into these offerings, both your own and those of other companies, that create unique value in each realm. What experiences do these other companies stage? How do they create value? What technologies do they employ? Who are their customers? Ideas tend to spring forth from flushing out and diligently examining these en-route discoveries.

∞ *Scrutinize the technologies of the realms.* Which technologies are established in a realm? Which ones are fading, which ones emerging? What human capabilities do they enable? Are new capabilities emerging? How are the technologies employed to create value? What opportunities reveal themselves to apply established technologies? Where might the leading edge of technology cut next? What holes appear where needs cannot be satisfied by existing technologies that point to technology invention opportunities?

∞ Since experiences are the basis for transformations, and transformations provide greater value, *think of what transformations you might build atop your experiences.* What do your customers aspire to become? What core human needs are met by your offerings that could enable a transformation?

Also, as an explorer, be sure to record each possibility discovered throughout this expedition, capturing its essential descriptive elements without reflection during the ideation process. Only afterward should you switch from spontaneity to thoughtfulness in developing enough substance around each idea to more fully understand them. Try in particular to determine the principle or principles behind an idea, as these can then be used for further ideation.

Employing these guidelines, including answering the questions as you go along, makes your innovation process more effective by stimulating idea generation, guiding idea refinement, defining the opportunities, and laying the groundwork for the design of new offerings. By the end of your Reaching through the Realms ideation expedition, your pool of new ideas for creating new value for your customers, and capturing some of it for your company, should be overflowing. But Reaching is not the only idea generation method. The next expedition, Varying the Variables, takes idea generation in a whole new direction.

11

Offering Depiction

VARYING THE VARIABLES

Leonardo da Vinci, Picasso, Frank Lloyd Wright, and, to bring up a current-day business example, IDEO, all discovered new possibilities more as artists and designers than as explorers. Whereas explorers of *terrae incognitae* past used maps to guide their ventures, artists and designers guide their creative process via various forms of expression, including frameworks, methods, rules, and principles. These push them along the path to generating new creative solutions, whether purely artistic, primarily pragmatic, or somewhere in between. Artists often employ the golden ratio. Engineers turn their knowledge of loads, materials, and physics into design theory, guidelines, and rules. Architects follow principles of design to produce both the form and function of their creations. And now designers of experiences have one more valuable tool to add to their repertoire: the Experience Design Canvas, to be employed in conjunction with the Varying the Variables expedition introduced here in this chapter.

The Experience Design Canvas

This new tool focuses squarely on the second number of the 8-6-3-1 architecture at the heart of the Multiverse: the six variables. It is here in this chapter where we take full advantage of these *independent variables of experience design,* as illustrated in Figure 11.1. Through this focus the Experience Design Canvas serves as a platform not only for engendering ideas and discovering opportunities but for designing experiences as well. With the Varying the Variables expedition you do not act as an explorer so much as a designer, depicting experiences (existing or imagined) on the Design Canvas. You select experiential elements from the

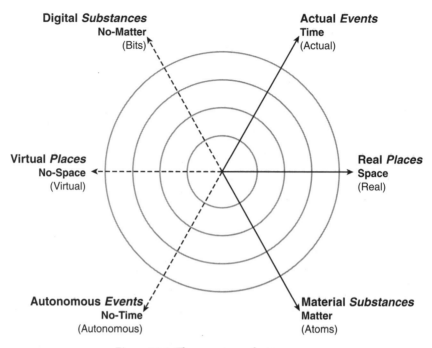

Figure 11.1 The experience design canvas

full palette of variables to depict and design how digital and material substances are constructed, how real and virtual places are formed with those substances, and how autonomous and actual events are enacted in those places.

The Canvas simply takes the six variables of the Multiverse and lays them out in a two-dimensional circle, a process illustrated in Figure 11.2, so you easily can plot the intensity of the six variables within the experiences they together create. Rather than losing fidelity as our view shifts from three to two dimensions, this new perspective deepens understanding and reveals opportunities. In Chapter 1, "Cosmos Incogniti," we described the Multiverse as a sense-making guide for exploring the *cosmos incogniti* that lie beyond the digital frontier. The Experience Design Canvas lets us more fully explore these worlds, shifting them from unknown to a bit more known, by plotting the variables of possibilities to depict them in a way that lets us see the landscape of what's around us.

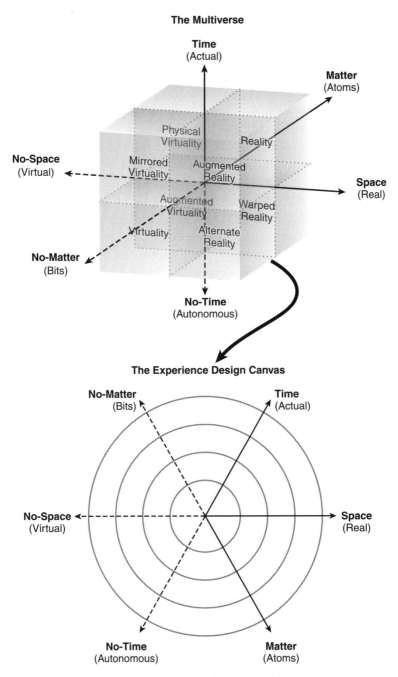

Figure 11.2 From realms to variables

Figure 11.3 then shows each realm of the Multiverse plotted on its respective Canvas, illustrating not only how the 3D to 2D translation works but also revealing the unity of the Multiverse, the Experience Design Canvas, and the 8-6-3-1 architecture. Note the balance and harmony of these realm depictions, with each one positioned across from its polar opposite, forming a progression of patterns between the Realms of the Real on the right side (the same side on which the Space axis resides in the Multiverse framework) and the Realms of the Virtual on the left (where the No-Space axis resides in the Multiverse). The gray areas represent the variables used to create each realm, each one a "pie slice" starting at the middle point, or origin, and extending out to the endmost circle of the Canvas. So Reality, for example, encompasses the three pie slices centered on the lines representing the three variables of Time, Space, and Matter, and Physical Virtuality encompasses the three slices centered on Time, No-Space, and Matter. Of course, the latter realm, along with its opposite, Alternate Reality, looks very different than the others, but this simply results from representing three dimensions onto two; if we were to change the somewhat arbitrary order of the variables—say, Time, Matter, Space instead of Time, Space, Matter—then different realms would have this "split" effect.

Both the Multiverse and its corresponding cousin the Experience Design Canvas serve as ideation tools for discovering new value-creation opportunities. In the case of the eight realms of the Multiverse, the descriptive identifiers such as Alternate Reality or Augmented Virtuality spur idea generation more than if we had identified each of them by their less colorful defining variables (i.e., [No-Time – Space – No-Matter] or [No-Time – No-Space – Matter], respectively). The realm names give aid to understanding, creating eight distinct mental models with easily thought-of exemplars that directionally guide ideation. The Experience Design Canvas foregoes these labels, for once they serve their purpose they only limit thinking to the preexisting mental models, and we don't want to preclude new-to-the-cosmos ideas that do not fit what we currently mean by each label.

This opens us up vast new areas to be explored and exploited. For the conceptual simplifications provided by the realms of the Multiverse limit our thinking to only three variables at a time, those that comprise each realm. Actual experiences can, and more often than not do, extend beyond the strict confines of any one realm, often encompassing elements that have meaning in four, five, or even all six variables. The

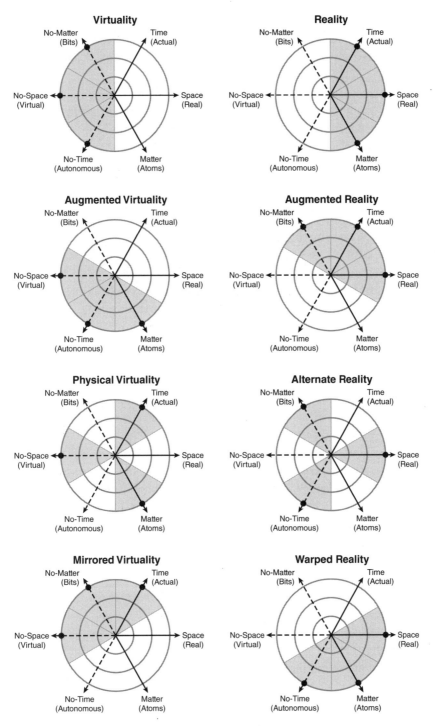

Figure 11.3 The eight Realms of the Multiverse

Experience Design Canvas lets us depict offerings to reflect the involvement of any or all of these variables—enabling us to take a more sophisticated view of value creation beyond the realms themselves by thinking outside the cube.

So here we focus on a different set of labels, with different mental models, by using the more descriptive names for the six variables we introduced in Chapter 1, "Cosmos Incogniti": actual events and autonomous events, real places and virtual places, and material substances and digital substances.

A Variable Design Expedition

Both the Reaching through the Realms expedition, discussed in Chapter 10, "Multiverse Excursion," and Varying the Variables, covered in this chapter, directly harness the power of the Multiverse to guide discovery, but they do so in distinctly different ways. Reaching through the Realms focuses on methodically walking through the Multiverse realm by realm to see what possibilities each one might reveal. Varying the Variables, on the other hand, ignores the realms completely. Instead, it directs your attention to these six variables in order to consider the possibilities of varying their intensities and configurations.

As with the Reaching expedition, we suggest you conduct this as a group exercise with multiple small teams initially working independently before bringing their ideas together for further discussion, refinement, and selection with the overall group. Being more free-form, however, this expedition does not have the same step-by-step approach. Rather, you initiate a Varying the Variables expedition from a variety of ways: by depicting a familiar offering (whether yours or a competitor's), by mapping the variables of an idea generated from your previous ideation exercises, or even by doodling, fiddling, and generally messing around with the variables. You can even start with a blank canvas to try to discover new possibilities.

Once you plot an offering on the canvas, whether an existing one or a new idea, look at the overall pattern of variables. Consider the variables' characteristics, configuration, coherence, complementarity, contrast, and consequence. What characteristics does each variable contribute to the offering? What makes this particular configuration work? Can you see any lack of coherence between the variables involved? Which variables clearly complement one another? Does the contrast between variables enrich or detract from the experience? What consequences result from this particular pattern of variables?

Having now depicted an offering, each team looks for opportunities to create greater value by adjusting the intensity and configuration of variables. If two variables are in conflict, how might the impact of one or the other be reduced? How might one or more variables be doubled or tripled in intensity—perhaps even by an order of magnitude—to yield greater impact overall? How do other competing offerings compare to the one in question? What does this tell you about the value created or, alternatively, how customers sacrifice by not getting exactly what they want?

As you may have gathered, depicting existing offerings or ideas for new offerings encourages unbounded idea generation. Follow a hunch. Scratch an itch. Take a leap into the unknown. Pursue a notion just to see where it leads. Depicting possibilities on the Design Canvas even suits a "blue sky" approach just fine. You never know what ideas will emerge from explorations unencumbered by existing notions of what the offerings should be and what previously has been demonstrated as possible.

Going Beyond the Realms

Now, in order to better understand experience depiction, let us delve deeper into plotting experiences on the Experience Design Canvas. Start by cleansing from your minds—albeit temporarily—what you have so diligently learned about the eight realms. To that end, understand that while plotting the "pure" Multiverse realms (with their three defining variables) on the Design Canvas shows us the Multiverse–Canvas correspondence of idealized realms, depicting the form of *actual* experiences on the Canvas lets us see what's really going on.

Take, for example, an Alternate Reality experience, nominally illustrated on the left side of Figure 11.4 as the distinctive combination of No-Time, Space, and No-Matter. This certainly captures the *essential variables* of any ARG or other experience within this realm, but in such experiences the opposite variables along each of the Event, Place, and Substance dimensions do in fact come in to play, as seen in the *fuller picture* on the right half. Actual time figures prominently, as the players in an ARG cannot ignore the actual events enacted in the real space where the game's events play out. In an urban game, traffic, traffic lights,

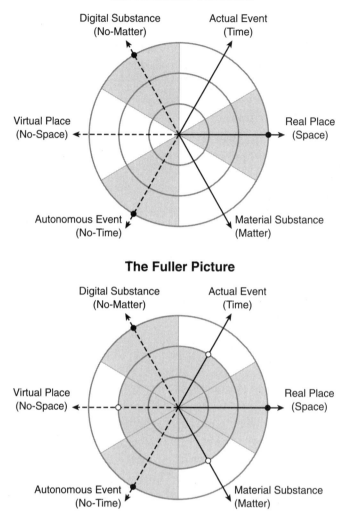

Figure 11.4 Alternate Reality on the Experience Design Canvas

bus schedules, and so forth, all enter into the pace, cadence, rhythm, and timing of the game's events, which the puppet masters manipulate to fit their own schedules. Further, material substances (such as jars of honey and phone booths) and virtual places (such as websites and phone calls) enter into the mix, yielding an experience whose center of gravity still lies in the three prototypical Alternate Reality variables, but actually spreads across all six variables of the Multiverse.

Understanding the fuller picture of Alternate Reality as represented on the Canvas should spur ARG (and other such experience) designers to explicitly define and address the intended configuration of its variables—flushing out ideas regarding variable conflicts, variable intensity, varying configurations, enhancements, manifestations, augmentations, infusions, embedding, and even customer sacrifice elimination. Even further, although the diagram on the bottom half of Figure 11.4 accurately describes ARGs as presently produced, designers and puppet masters could use the ARG format for an even fuller experience, spreading it out even further on the Canvas to encompass the other variables of the Multiverse (actual events, virtual places, and material substances) more fully and simultaneously. Or they could do the opposite: seek to minimize all but the primary Alternate Reality variables (autonomous events, real places, and digital substances) to focus on and intensify the experience, getting it down to its essence.

That is exactly the thrust of the Varying the Variables expedition, to spur on ideation while simultaneously building experience design capability. Though still systematic to a degree, Varying the Variables takes on a more free-form/organic quality than does Reaching through the Realms. It forces us to recognize that any given experience may comprise anywhere from three variables up to and including all six of the possible variables in the Multiverse, so we not only take our capability to faithfully represent the variables of an experience up a notch but also do the same for our understanding, insight, and ideation.

This expedition provides the means to consider enhancing any experience, from adding what might be missing, minimizing what does not add value, combining variables in new ways, or boosting particular variables. It also provides the means for designing experiences from scratch, considering the intensity of each variable one at a time and the interplay between the variables. Beyond focusing on one particular experience, portraying two different experiences on one Canvas provides the means to explicitly compare and contrast them to expose differences in the intensity and configuration of variables. This one-to-one experience comparison serves to deepen understanding, reveal opportunities, identify customer value as well as sacrifice, stimulate ideation, and advance design.

Depicting Experiences

Again, any experience can be characterized by the six variables of the Multiverse to reflect or capture its actuality, autonomy, reality, virtuality, materiality, or digitality. Plotting these variables on the Experience Design Canvas—whether one experience per canvas or two or more for comparison's sake—generates insights and uncovers opportunities that otherwise remain hidden. To understand how, let's see what depicting some easily understood experiences reveals to us.

Think of a real-world experience such as a casual bicycle ride, unenhanced by digital technology, through, say, New York City's Central Park. How would you rate the values of each variable in the Multiverse? Let's take the easy ones first—autonomous events enacted, virtual places formed, and digital substances constructed for this experience are all zero. Nothing digital going on here, folks. That leaves the three variables of Reality–Time with its actual events, Space's real places, and the material substances of Matter. But are the relative intensities of these three variables equal to one another? Or does the significance of Central Park's contribution to the experience mean the magnitude of the real places variable should be greater than the other two? As with any experience, you are the ultimate arbiter, but we think it does. (Of course, we're from Minnesota and do not get to bike in Central Park every day.)

Now consider how you would rate the same variables in an obviously more intense experience in Reality, say, climbing the Matterhorn in Switzerland. Relative to the casual ride in the park, think of how much more expansive is this real place, how much more dependent you are on the material substance of the mountain and your climbing equipment, how much more each and every moment proceeding in this actual event means to your experience as you grapple with the climb. Would each of these variables be ten times as intense? A hundred times? Or perhaps a thousand? Again, we report, you decide.

Now take your analysis of these two experiences and plot them onto the Design Canvas, as we have our opinion in Figure 11.5. You see the six independent yet interrelated variables, three of which are again zero, with the rest dialed up greatly—we're considering it to be a logarithmic scale, so each circle represents an order of magnitude increase in intensity—to reflect the greater impact of the three variables for the mountain-climbing experience. Just by glancing at the area under the curve, as mathematicians say—although in this case it is mul-

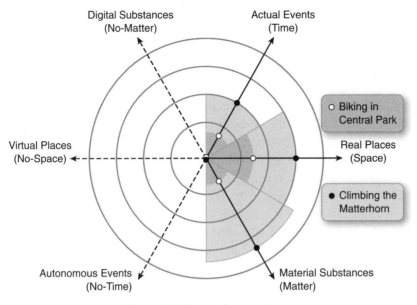

Figure 11.5 Two reality experiences

tiple adjacent curves—you can see how much more intense we believe the mountain-climbing experience is than riding a bike, with the real places and especially material substances contributing a greater portion of that intensity than the flow of actual time.

When using the Canvas, the scale of the variable values can be whatever best serves your purpose. A logarithmic scale serves you well when seeking or designing order of magnitude increases in variable intensity, as we've done here, whereas a linear scale may better serve your need to compare experiences with variables of similar intensity. Once having depicted an experience variable by variable, you can then start thinking about and varying each of them individually and in their collective configuration to discover and depict just the right experience to meet the needs, hopes, and desires of your customers. As just one quick example: turning the climb into a time trial or race would amp up the Time variable commensurate with the other two.

Thinking in Variables

To build up your experience deciphering and depicting skills, think through each of the three dimensions of the Multiverse. Start with the

Event dimension and turn your attention first to events enacted, the *when* of an experience where change and activity—the timing of its events in Time and/or No-Time—play into your customer's perceptions. With actual events, action marches unrelentingly forward to bring a temporal reality to the experience. These events happen in real time with a pace, beat, direction, and rhythm that pushes, prompts, or tugs the experience incessantly forward. Autonomous events, on the other hand, take the experience wherever it wants in time—backward, forward, sideways, jumping around, slowing down, speeding up, and so on—where events becomes malleable with a nonlinear temporality. These events may not move synchronously, nor exist in the now of reality, but yet still may overlap with actual events. Along this variable of autonomous events, look for experiences that take your customers off the endless conveyer belt of stacked events flowing in reality's timeframe to bring them the rewards of autonomous events.

Next, study the Place dimension, the *where* of an experience formed in Space and/or No-Space. Real places bring real-world familiarity to an experience with an emotional appeal that comes from reality's social and cultural familiarity, what futurist Jerry Paffendorf refers to as the "gravity of reality."[1] Virtual places, on the other hand, bring the experience designer free exercise of imagination to invent new places within the limits of the technology employed to bring them into virtual being. (Note how James Cameron scripted *Avatar* more than a decade before he could film the movie as he waited for technology to catch up with his dreams.[2])

Finally, consider the Substance dimension, the *what* of an experience constructed in Matter and/or No-Matter. Material substances—whether natural or man-made objects, devices, materials, plants, or animals—first evoke physical sensations followed by the emotions they trigger. These substances can soothe, support, stimulate, shake, strike, shift, shove, or soar your physical being. In their more forceful renditions, they can bump, burn, blast, and bombard your senses. Digital substances, on the other hand, address the senses in a very different manner, coming to the individual in the form of text, graphics, or imagery enhanced by sounds and occasionally other senses. They evoke a variety of emotions, sans the physical impacts, by tweaking your emotions, tugging at your heart, tickling your funny bone, titillating your fancy, triggering your imagination, transporting you to your peaceful spot, tapping your libido, tempting you to anger, taking you down, terrorizing your very being, or touching you deeply in a multitude of ways and degrees.

Playing on the Experience Design Canvas

With this introduction to the variables of the Multiverse and the Experience Design Canvas, you can now go to work discovering new value for your customers on the digital frontier, specifically by playing with the variables of experience. Start by selecting a current offering and plotting it on the canvas. This should produce a lively discussion right off the bat about the relative value or intensity of each variable and the inevitable comparison of the experience in question with other experiences. You could of course even bring customers into this discussion, or ethnographically observe them using an existing or prototyped offering. Once you have produced the six-variable representation of the experience, start playing with its variables to see what ideas emerge. Look for alternative types of value being created, intensified or reduced emotions, or the achievement of a new level of human capability.

As you play with the variables and their overall configuration, think of what each one lends to an experience and how it affects the customer value of that experience. The Variables of Experience box, with its characterization of each variable, can help get you started. As you practice your own Multiverse-enabled experience design, add to these descriptions as you discover more of what each variable contributes to the types of experiences you develop. As you do this, you should find your ideation capability grows—spurred on with your new insights—to flush out ever-greater possibilities to create new economic value.

For example, play with the variables to see what happens when you intensify the digital substances of a previously reality-centered experience. What changes? What value might be added, what value might be taken away? And how does the overall value of the Substance dimension change? Consider a wide variety of variable intensities and mixes, as well as overall experiential forms. Consider the forms of the experience over time; you could even plot each segment in time with its own unique Canvas. Does this give you any ideas about where the current form can be enhanced to add value? Maybe previous forms of the offering lost one form of value in exchange for another. Maybe technology steered it one way for a time and now new technology stands ready to take it in another direction.

Get a little crazy. Stretch your imagination by considering what happens if you could double the order of magnitude of one variable. What might an offering look like that was one—no, make it *two* orders of magnitude greater? What would the value be to your customers? What

THE VARIABLES OF EXPERIENCE

- *Time's actual events*—the very realness of the now; anticipation of waiting for events that must occur in sequence; the intensity of the course, rhythm, or beat of real time; the satisfying reward of mastering events in actual time.
- *No-Time's autonomous events*—the excitement of experiencing another time; the freedom of escaping the now; the satisfaction of insights gained from other temporal perspectives; flow experiences; escapes; the emotions from memories of past experiences.
- *Space's real places*—the perception of a real sense of place; the promise of realness; the familiarity of the physical world around us.
- *No-Space's virtual places*—the anticipation of fantasy and imagination; the promise of creatively conjured places; places tailored to evoke emotions, offer unique perspectives, hold out new possibilities.
- *Matter's material substances*—the physicality of matter, with all its roughness, smoothness, heat, cold, sharpness, dullness, shapes, and so on; cool devices, tools, toys, structures, and so forth.
- *No-Matter's digital substances*—the accessing of information; connecting; the ability to express the creative imagination; the anticipation of newly expressed ideas, things, and even worlds.

technology exists, or is emerging, that would enable this? Now consider more than one variable at a time. Is it possible to create an experience where every variable is relatively equal? What might it look like? What customer value would it have? What might the experience be if all six variables doubled in intensity at once? Can you stage the exact opposite experience by flipping the intensity of every variable to its opposing intensity? What customer value might that have? What does this reveal about the original experience? If you take the Reality experience of driving a NASCAR race car and flip the variables, you end up with iRacing.com, a Virtuality racing experience safe for novices but also real enough to train professional drivers. Do the same with football and you get the *Madden NFL* video games from EA Sports, where you too can take to the gridiron without a care for conditioning or possible injury—and where NFL players themselves enjoy the experience.

Even when you get a little crazy, ideation works best when you have some purpose in mind to focus the exercise. Although you do not want to focus so hard on a particular customer need that you cannot expand your thinking enough to generate significant new value-creating ideas, you also should not venture so far and wide that you leave your business and company somewhere back over the receding horizon. But when a particular customer focus strikes you as too narrow, look for ideas that leverage your company's current and developing competencies, that employ technologies from other industries within your grasp to master, and that embrace emerging technologies that could soon apply to your business or that one day might help you further your company's pursuit of its chosen purpose. After all, when opportunities exist for a company to leap from iMacs to iPods to iTunes to iPhones to iPads as Apple did, you do not want to constrain your ideation to miss such game-changing opportunities.

Playing with Substance

Consider the possibilities the Varying the Variables expedition presents as we illustrate several different offerings and their changes over time. We'll start with an example that plays out only on the Substance dimension—transitions in music album art, as shown in Figure 11.6. In the days when music was most commonly sold as analog patterns carved in one long spiral on a vinyl disc—for those unfamiliar with such a strange thing, look up "gramophone record" on *Wikipedia*[3]—the cardboard album jackets became an advanced art form thriving on a little over one square foot. With the advent of the jewel case to hold digitized music on a compact disc, album-art real estate decreased to one-sixth its former size, with the front "cover" being a removable booklet of multiple pages.[4] In one sense, this moved album art down the Substance dimension, providing less material to work with, at least as far as what is visible on the real estate of the shrink-wrapped jewel case is concerned. But this was only the beginning of what digitization wrought on album art.

The next step, from CD to MP3, broke the 1:1 relationship between the material media and the music. People now store multiple albums or songs on their digital memory devices, losing the physical medium for the album art and leaving only the miniscule thumbnail icon that may or may not, depending on the setup, display with a song listed on a hard drive or music player. But the virtualization of the album also held the solution to the problem, as digitally interactive album art arose on the Internet to bring a richer experience to the listener than was ever possible with the cardboard-based media of long ago. Users now can access

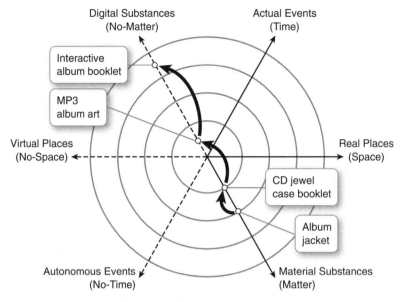

Figure 11.6 Playing with substance

interactive multimedia content, including artist videos, band photos and even "animated lyrics and liner notes," as Apple boasts concerning its iTunes LP offering, which invited you to "experience a beautifully designed, interactive world right in your iTunes library."[5]

In time, as digital tablet devices like the iPad and universal Internet connectivity become commonplace, you will be able to view this album art anytime, anywhere—whether lounging in your favorite chair or seated in an airplane. Digitization brought with it a wave of enhancements to the music experience—indexing, searching, arranging, selecting themed playlists, and so forth, none of which was lost on Apple. What digitization took away from the physical it replaced many times over in the virtual.

Playing with Presence

Next, consider the evolution of groups communicating from disparate locations. The telephone, whether in the form of land lines, cell phones, or VoIP applications such as Skype, offers people the opportunity to meet virtually. Figure 11.7 plots the teleconference experience on the

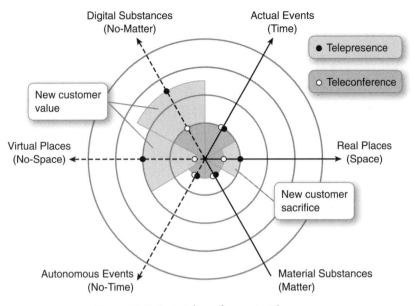

Figure 11.7 From teleconference to telepresence

Experience Design Canvas. Note the dominance of digital substances and actual events. Real space reflects a small commitment to the location of the telecommunications device, though this becomes minimal when using a mobile phone compared to, say, a normal office environment. The phone device shows as a minor material substance factor. The notion that teleconferencing in its own small way eases the grip of time by alleviating the requirement that meeting participants gather together in one physical place gets reflected as a small dose of autonomous events. Finally, there is very little virtual place in the teleconference experience (just the tiny shared space over the wire, through the ether, or across the Internet).

Now compare teleconferencing to telepresence, a much more experiential offering centered in Mirrored Virtuality. In addition to actual events, of course, virtual places and digital substances become the dominant variables, creating new customer value far exceeding that of teleconferencing due to not only the lifelike video presence of the participants but also the functionality of collaboration apps supporting joint participation in activities and the sharing of information.

Notice there is also, almost paradoxically, a greater intensity or role for real places due to the specialized rooms required to conduct a telepresence session. For the most part, this is not an added value to the experience, but rather a new customer sacrifice, because the attendees must gather in specific physical locations. Maybe one day Cisco, HP, or another supplier will replace the telepresence room with virtual reality goggles and ear phones to create an even better experience of "being there" without physically being there, freeing the participants to collaborate regardless of their physical location.[6]

Playing with Emotion

Telepresence illustrates how an increase in a variable may not actually add value to the experience, but rather can cause customers to sacrifice. *Customer sacrifice* is the difference between what a customer settles for and what he wants exactly. In any experience design pay attention to where you might be introducing such sacrifice, whether unintentionally or as a consequence of value added elsewhere, and further how you might eliminate sacrifices that customers encounter in current or competitive offerings.

This notion of value versus sacrifice, or negative value, also comes out in Hallmark Cards' Augmented Virtuality offering highlighted in Chapter 7, "Augmented Virtuality." Hallmark did not have the benefit of the Multiverse when describing its new offering as Augmented Reality, but now that we have it, using the lens of the six variables yields a richer, more nuanced interpretation for both its traditional card-only offering and its new augmented offering.

The traditional card experience fits in a particular spot in the flow of actual events because it commemorates, celebrates, anticipates, or simply accompanies some, uh, actual event. Card givers often intend for the card-receiving experience to happen in a special place: delivered to one's place of work to celebrate a milestone with coworkers, sent to a loved one's home to be relished in an easy chair, dropped off as a blessing at a wedding, or given in person at a social gathering intending to elicit a spontaneous laugh. The material substance of the card itself contains the pictures and words that trigger the recipient's imaginative and emotional response—serving this purpose not just on receipt but often many times over as the recipient views the card again and again.

But the pictures and words (including added personal inscriptions) often also activate an autonomous time and virtual place. The giver uses these elements to invoke particular emotions, typically of comfort, joy, or

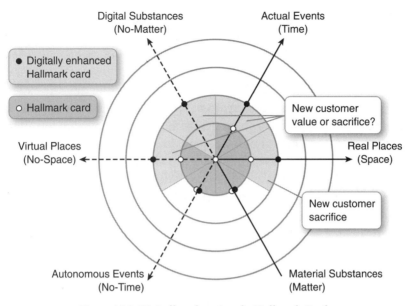

Figure 11.8 Digitally enhancing the Hallmark Card

humor, that transport (we could say "teleport") the receiver to a different time and place—memories of a pleasant past, hope of better times to come, a fantasy environment, or even a shared humorous space connecting sender to receiver over many miles and moments. Place virtualizes as time warps to bring the recipient to the remembered past or expectant future (and, yes, sometimes a thankful present, but one more intensely felt and appreciated). As you can see from the core plot of the Hallmark card in Figure 11.8, the traditional card experience, nominally residing in Reality, actually embraces not just three but *five* of the six variables, illustrating the richness of experience possible with greeting cards and other such social expressions!

Now consider how Hallmark enhanced this experience with its Augmented Virtuality offering, where software downloaded from its website enables recipients to view an entertaining animation when the physical card is placed in front of a webcam. When given such a digitally enhanced card, a recipient actually has pretty much the exact same experience at first, and only afterward goes to his computer for the new, Virtuality-dominated experience. So the total experience actually involves a second, separate event that adds to the first, one of a significantly different nature. Here, the video displayed on the computer screen digitally creates a predesigned virtual place, rather than the virtual place existing solely in the cardholder's imagination. It is a primarily entertainment experience with a linear structure, without the spontaneity of the traditional recipient's autonomous flights of fancy. And if you happen to tilt the card too much and lose the video, on restarting the experience you must start all over again at the beginning. Moreover, this all must happen in front of a computer, with a functioning camera, after a not insignificant amount of time spent downloading the application to make the video work. Depending on the recipient, this add-on experience could have significant value —as it did with Joe's daughters when he sent them ones for Valentine's Day—or not be worth the trouble, for as the digitally enhanced Hallmark card is depicted in Figure 11.8, it clearly entails some new customer sacrifice.

Realize, however, that the current implementation is an interim step for what will certainly be possible in the future—and we applaud Hallmark for experimenting at this early stage in the technology's development. Imagine the day when such virtual experiences become embedded in the physical cards themselves, eliminating the sacrifice of the virtual place and downloaded software on the computer. Card givers could then, for example, add customized digital substances, displaying pictures or videos of the recipient's past or the recollections of friends and loved ones of their past lives together. How much better would the experience be to open the card and see a holographic video playing above the card—just like Hallmark Sound Cards already embed audio clips? Other possibilities abound, such as using an iPad as the social expression delivery mechanism, or expanding the material substance of the card, for very special occasions, to become some sort of glass-like cube containing the card's message in the form of custom pictures, narration, and videos that play on touching the device, eliminating the card altogether while maintaining the social expression that emotionally connects giver and recipient together. Finally, how far away are we from artificial intelligence capabilities that would enable the card recipient to carry on a conversation with the holograph of a loved one, living or passed on? How much better might this expand and intensify the previous plain-old-card experience?

The card is only a medium through which to deliver a virtual experience, the story on the card and the emotions it evokes. The physical card serves, as it always has, as the personal memento that re-triggers the emotional sentiments when glanced at, as well as a public testimony that you have friends who acknowledge your uniqueness.

Playing Guitar

For one last example, consider the *Guitar Hero World Tour* video game introduced in 2008. It physically includes peripheral lead, bass, and rhythm guitars as well as drums and a microphone for vocals. Imagine the experience of five players gathered around a large-screen TV, several of them playing the digital renditions of real instruments while others perform as vocalists, as they lose themselves in the rhythm, mood, collaboration, and focus required to adhere to the pace of the game. This game, too, is nominally Augmented Virtuality, but a closer examination reveals that, like ARGs, it encompasses all six Multiverse variables, none of them producing much customer sacrifice. There is an element of autonomous time for those lost in their performance, the actual time of the music, the virtual place as portrayed on the TV display, the real place of the gathering, the material instruments and microphones, and the most dominant variable of all, the digital substance of music.

As indicated by its depiction in Figure 11.9, this experience has it all—Reality and Virtuality fused together (not to mention authenticity, immersion, emotion, and action), with all variables high in intensity. No wonder the game became such a hit! The interplay of all the variables immerses the players in a virtual place and flow in time by linking their

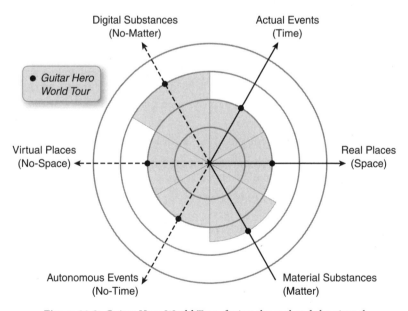

Figure 11.9 *Guitar Hero World Tour:* fusing the real and the virtual

physical bodies and minds in the activity of real-world playing and sing-ing, bathing the virtual world in digital music. The emotional warmth of those gathered to engage in a common purpose shows in the players' intense looks and glowing smiles. The visible feedback of the guitar player's fingering of the frets extends his senses, spurs on his perfor-mance, and links him to the others who are organized in the overall context of the game.

Let *Guitar Hero World Tour* further open your thinking to the di-verse possibilities for designing digital experiences. Some may be "pure and simple," like a singularly Virtuality or Reality experience, some may be augmented while anchored in Virtuality or Reality, and others may break the bonds of both of these realms to create an entirely new kind of experience.

Variable Guidance

However you use these examples and insights to bring your expedition to an end, learn to Vary the Variables the way children approach playing with LEGO building bricks: fiddling with the variables of the Multiverse, changing their magnitude and their configuration to see what discov-eries you make, what insights reveal themselves, and what ideas arise. Consider it serious play.[7]

Varying the Variables takes idea generation for experience design to a whole new level. Keep in mind that although no authoritative formula exists for depicting the variables of experiences on the Design Canvas, it proves a superb catalyst for serious idea generation and even design initiation, if not refinement. With this in mind, here are some guide-lines to enrich your capabilities in these areas:

∞ *Know your experiential variables.* Honing in on the variables of the Multiverse opens the door to a whole new perspective on the makeup of an experience. To employ this perspective, start by thinking of, and becoming very familiar with, the way each vari-able contributes to the whole experience. Become practiced in analyzing your own personal experiences. Become proficient at knowing how each variable acts to enlarge an experience, embel-lish its nature, boost its value, and enrich it to entice engagement.

∞ *Put all the variables to work.* Your company instantiates experi-ences from events enacted, places formed, and substances constructed. Each of these three dimensions consists of two variables to be both scrutinized in existing offerings and imagined in various configurations for possible new offerings. Always consider each variable's inclusion, exclusion, and intensity relative to one another within the experience in question, its absolute intensity in consideration of the intention of the experience, and its relative contribution compared to other experiences.

∞ *More is more.* Look for opportunities to turn up the intensity of one or more variables of an experience. Challenge yourself to dial up one variable at a time in order of magnitude. How does this change the experience? What potential value does this create? And how might it be accomplished?

∞ *Less is more.* Refine the selection and intensity of some variable to create a pure experience. Eschew any variable that takes away from the essence of an experience, like deep-sixing your mobile phone before entering a health club for your workout or massage, or turning the voice off on your GPS navigator to enjoy the conversation with your passenger.

∞ *Eliminate sacrifice.* Minimize or even eliminate any unneeded, unnecessary, and unwanted variable (or aspects thereof). We pointed out in the Hallmark example the sacrifice the customer makes by having computer interactions as part of the digital experience. Target eliminating such sacrifices to clarify the experience.

∞ *Mass customize the offering.* Mass customizing eliminates customer sacrifice, and digitization enables mass customizing. So as we've emphasized before (and will again), seek to design Multiversal experiences to order, tailoring them to create customer-unique offerings that engage targeted senses, extend custom capabilities, and selectively evoke specific emotions.

∞ *Context, context, context.* Keep in mind that all experiences are personal in nature. The guest of an experience is its most essential contextual element. For example, the father of my (Kim's) good friend recently visited the USS *Arizona* Memorial in Hawaii where his brother died in the opening days of WWII in the Pacific. For him, this place evoked an intense emotional response due to his loss over sixty years ago. Other guests come simply to learn more about a historical event that never touched them personally.

Still others may view this place indifferently and be more drawn to watching the fish swimming over the sunken battleship than the memorial to those killed in battle. How can you design for each context? Each guest?

∞ *Harmonize the variables.* Be sensitive to how one variable of an experience affects the others. Have you ever, for instance, been to a promotional event where to give it gravitas the organizers erect some striking structure, such as stunningly massive columns? During the course of the event you go stand next to one of the columns, where a rap of your knuckles produces only a hollow sound from the obviously fake prop. All of the sudden the once authentic-looking column loses its luster, and you begin to notice the speaker and the rest of the event begin to look less authentic as well. Inconsistencies in the visual versus material aspects take away from the whole experience.

∞ *Examine variable capabilities.* Identify how the technologies associated with each variable enable and expand human capabilities in order to be aware of the various technology→human capability→value creation progressions involved. For example, we have seen many examples of value created by virtual substances (No-Matter) that enhance and extend our sensing, linking, performing, and organizing capability. What capabilities are associated with the other variables? How might you extend and enhance people's capabilities?

∞ *Explore the four possibilities for juxtaposing real and virtual variables* to create new value in Multiversal experiences:

- *Enrich the real with the virtual.* Look for opportunities to add some virtual element to enhance the real experience. Augmented Reality has a host of examples, but the same can be done for other realms and configurations of variables. Just pick a real variable and look at its virtual counterpart for possibilities.

- *Manifest the virtual in the real.* Look for opportunities to bring the virtual into the real, like how 3D printing brings material substance to the virtual. What other types of opportunities exist to make the virtual real?

– *Infuse the virtual into the real.* Look for opportunities to instill the virtual into the real, to blend the two together for a more robust experience. ARGs and *Guitar Hero* do this to great extents. Where and how else might this be done?

– *Embed the real in the virtual.* We already do this, lots of it. That's what Mirrored Virtuality is all about. But what other opportunities exist? How would the experience be more engaging by bringing all three Reality variables into Virtuality?

∞ Finally, *iterate your ideation, definition, selection, and design.* Performing multiple iterations yields ever more bountiful results. Though very practical, people rarely practice iterative inquiry, presuming they will be plowing the same ground twice for little or no additional gain. In actuality, iterative inquiry nearly always reveals significant, new, valuable ideas for anywhere from three to five, and sometimes even more, iterations. Intrepid idea explorers who have the patience, persistence, diligence, and courage to iterate through the same process multiple times will discover the most valuable gems.

When you follow these guidelines, your pool of ideas should be overflowing even more than following the Reaching through the Realms expedition.

Turning Possibilities into Opportunities

Note that your explorations build progressively from one to the next. Each one enriches the others as you build knowledge and insights regarding the possibilities and opportunities opening up to your company on the digital frontier. Through diligent pursuit of Multiverse ideation expeditions you grow your capabilities to first gain insights from the perspectives of each realm and then on to envision the power of each variable. These enable you to build foresight emanating from the promise of technology and to create tomorrow's hindsight today through unfettered perceptions of what truly meeting your customer needs looks like.

While Reaching through the Realms *searches and imagines* to discover new possibilities, the Varying the Variables expedition *depicts and designs* to not only generate ideas but define new offerings. In this exploratory progression, the Multiverse expeditions get you beyond mere possibilities to newly formulated opportunities that—accompanied with perceptive analysis, excellent decision making, and flawless execution, of course!—can be designed and deployed to create economic value for your company.

In all your ideation efforts, complement your discovery of value by understanding the five genres of offerings identified in the Progression of Economic Value delineating the flow in customer value from commodities to goods and services and on to experiences and transformations. Then focus your opportunity search on where the greatest value can be created—seek to solve customer problems, identify their latent needs, find alternatives for them to use their time and resources in ways that improve their lives, extend their current capabilities, and enable them to do things they otherwise are not able to do. In a broad sense, these are the things humanity always has done with the technology available to it and invented by it. We now find ourselves on the digital frontier with the opportunities to create new value stretching out to and beyond our very imagination, just waiting to be discovered.

12

Third Spaces

FUSING THE REAL AND THE VIRTUAL

You walk up to a whiteboard and begin drawing a diagram to share ideas with colleagues. They hear everything you say and see everything you draw, but they are not there, at least not really. Rather, you see them only virtually, represented as avatars *through* the clear whiteboard. At their individual locations, they, in turn, see you—strike that; they see *your avatar* through the whiteboard, and you see whatever they draw or write on it as you collaborate together. You gauge each other's reactions not only by what your colleagues say but by seeing where their avatars look, their facial expressions, and their gestures, which all mirror their own bodies.

So that's Mirrored Virtuality, yes, just like telepresence? Well, sure, in both you see the others virtually in real time via digital technology, but with telepresence you see the actual person's picture, not an avatar. And you can't draw on the digital image; here, your real-world activities affect the virtual collaborative space via Augmented Virtuality— but for your colleagues this appears as Augmented Reality, because for them your virtual actions affect their real-world space!

In the end, it doesn't matter what realm it resides in, or what you call it. It's just a great shared experience, enhancing the work of you and your colleagues. It's also not yet an offering, but rather a project at the Georgia Institute of Technology called ClearWorlds, which uses such "virtual whiteboards . . . as a bridge between the physical and virtual world."[1]

Meanwhile, researchers at the University of South Australia work to develop "through-walls collaboration, in which users in an intelligent meeting room can work in real time with field operatives to view and manipulate data."[2] Here again what is real for one person is virtual for another, and vice versa, as now you can collaborate with colleagues out anywhere in the physical world, not cooped up in a souped-up conference room. Going a little farther afield, computer scientists at Stanford University's Media X center seek to scale up a virtual world to planetary size, where "physical sensors in the real world seed their virtual reflections, users can visually browse a sea of information, and virtual avatars convey physical social cues to bring distance interaction to the level of actual presence."[3]

Not to be outdone, the Responsive Environments Group at the MIT Media Lab, led by Joseph Paradiso, created ShadowLab, a *Second Life*-version of the Media Lab's third floor housing the group. Not only does the ShadowLab change based on real-time sensors in the real world, shadowing (i.e., mirroring) it, but things happen in the Media Lab based on what avatars do in the virtual world! The Responsive Environments Group seeks to create a "persistent virtual presence," with "people continuously straddling the boundary between real and virtual" so that "they're never truly offline," allowing avatars in the ShadowLab to "know something about what the user is doing in the real world." "In principle, a touch from an authorized avatar in virtual space can reach out to the corresponding dormant user in the real world . . . , perhaps asking for live interaction or to bring the user more fully into the virtual sphere."[4]

Fusing the Real and the Virtual

Again, don't bother trying to figure out which realm (singular) this is in, as it crosses the boundaries of a number of realms (plural). Paradiso calls them "cross-reality environments,"[5] for they effectively fuse Reality and Virtuality into a *third space,* neither completely one nor the other, but crossing or transversing the environment's events (actually and autonomously), places (really and virtually), and substances (materially and digitally).[6] The Metaverse Roadmap group developed an early and useful model for how Reality and Virtually fuse together, determining that the term Metaverse had grown beyond Neal Stephenson's original fictional conception of complete Virtuality "to include aspects of the physical world objects, actors, interfaces, and networks that construct and interact with virtual environments." The Metaverse, according to the group, represents the convergence of virtually enhanced physical reality and physically persistent virtual space: "It is a fusion of both, while allowing users to experience it as either."[7]

Such virtually enhanced and physically persistent—and we could just as easily say physically enhanced and virtually persistent—third spaces have made their way out of the lab. The YouTube Symphony Orchestra, for example, launched in late 2008, involved real musicians submitting virtual auditions over YouTube to be virtually judged by real symphony experts, with the finalists voted on by the entire virtual YouTube community. The winners, all amateurs, came together for a live concert on April 15, 2009, at Carnegie Hall, led by famed conductor Michael Tilson Thomas, and YouTube featured a virtual mashup of videos of their individual real auditions playing the specially commissioned "Internet Symphony No. 1 'Eroica,'" by composer Tan Dun.[8]

If you prefer the theatre over the symphony, you could head from Manhattan to Brooklyn for the Game Play Festival, which, according to the *New York Times'* videogame reviewer, Seth Schiesel, "is the most ambitious effort I know of to fuse the techniques and live presentation of theater with the themes, structures and technology of interactive electronic entertainment, also known as video games."[9] The July 2010 festival featured such shows as "Theatre of the Arcade," which in Reality provided an alternate *Virtuality* in which classic games such as *Pac-Man, Super Mario,* and *Asteroids* were reimagined, and "Grand Theft Ovid," where the audience watched live students tell timeless stories acted out by their avatars, projected on a screen, in such games as *Grand Theft Auto, World of Warcraft,* and the *Legend of Zelda.*

Turnabout is fair play; in another article Schiesel notes how "as games become more real, the experience of them is bringing them closer to art."[10] He's thinking here in particular of those games like *Power Gig* and *Rock Band 3* that go beyond *Guitar Hero* and the original *Rock Band* to incorporate real musical instruments, as well as the Kinect system that incorporates the full body. "Throughout," he concludes, "from the personal to the physical, the line between the real and the virtual is beginning to fade."[11]

Students in a number of North Carolina high schools involved with Project K-nect (no relation), thought up by Shawn Gross of Digital Millennial Consulting of Arlington, Virginia, and funded by San Diego-based Qualcomm, were given smartphones to enhance their classroom learning of math.[12] They could access additional instruction and information asynchronously in off-hours, ask teachers and classmates questions at any time from school or home and then await the answers to come at some later time, and use their phones' video cameras to film their group projects or explanations of how to solve particular types of problems—seventy-five videos in one week, in fact, on solving linear equations. Meanwhile, Katie Salen at Parsons The New School for Design founded Quest to Learn, a new school in New York City that brings custom video games into the live classroom, formally labeled a "hybrid physical-digital space" but which Salen more informally calls a "possibility space"; she and the teachers manage the space, and the classes, like a yearlong video game itself.[13]

Different elements of any one experience can also encompass multiple realms, creating experiences that transverse the Multiverse (for both guests and employees). Visiting Walt Disney World in Orlando, for example, clearly makes for one of the happiest experiences in Reality, but recall how the company makes use of Alternate Reality with its Kim Possible experience at Epcot. It embraces Warped Reality, with Main Street USA harkening back to a bygone era, and also in how it manages queues to change guests' perception of time. In today's "cultural shift toward impatience" even that's not enough, as Disney increasingly turns to technology to warp its waiting time reality "to get you to the fun faster."[14] It now operates a wait-time command center below Cinderella's Castle to monitor wait times throughout Walt Disney World (Mirrored Virtuality). When necessary, the center calls for additional ride capacity and/or a mini-parade to route guests to underutilized areas of the park (both in the theme park's base Reality). Disney added videogames to the waiting areas of particularly long-lined rides (Virtuality), while its smartphone app Mobile Magic lets guests see where characters are out in the park (Augmented Reality). Finally, the company is experimenting with wristbands that identify guests connected to in-character technology, so that the cast members playing characters will know whom they've already met and where, guest names, and so forth (Augmented Reality for the cast members to enhance Reality for the guests).

You create a third space whenever you transverse even one boundary between two realms within any given experience. Recall how Layar could not only enhance your current surroundings through its Augmented Reality technology but also, with some apps, could give you a "time slider" that lets you see those surroundings into the past or future, shifting over into the No-Time realm of Alternate Reality as part of one experience. Other apps turn the phone into a gun to shoot down virtual objects, sliding over into Augmented Virtuality. Or consider SensAble Technologies of Woburn, Massachusetts, which provides 3D design and modeling tools clearly within the borders of Physical Virtuality, but its

FreeForm and ClayTools applications enable users to use a haptic device it developed, called PHANTOM, that provides force feedback operating on 3D models. It lets you, for example, model with virtual clay just as if it were real clay. The addition of haptics causes the experience to reside simultaneously in Physical and Augmented Virtualities.

Further, properly understood, *even those experiences residing within one solitary realm*—outside of the anchors themselves—create a third space that is neither fully of Reality nor entirely of Virtuality. Each of the other Realms of the Real—Augmented Reality, Alternate Reality, and Warped Reality—has at least one un-real (i.e., virtual) variable, whether it be digital substances, autonomous events, or both. Likewise, each of the other Realms of the Virtual—Augmented Virtuality, Physical Virtuality, and Mirrored Virtuality—has at least one un-virtual (i.e., real) variable, whether it be material substances, actual events, or both.

Defining Third Spaces

A third space, therefore, is *any experience not purely Reality or Virtuality*. Third spaces include those experiences within any one of the six other realms of the Multiverse as well as those transversal experiences that cross any boundary between realms, thereby encompassing not just three but four, five, or all six variables.[15]

Realize, too, that *most* experiences—if not nearly all of them outside those you can clearly place within the pure anchors—resist clear classification into any one, single, solitary realm defined by three hard and fast variables. Recall our discussion in the previous chapter (Chapter 11, "Offering Depiction"), on how even something as simple as a purely physical Hallmark card embraced not just three but *five* of the six variables. While the traditional card experience fits easily into Reality— with the material card being read in a particular place in the flow of actual time as it commemorates, celebrates, anticipates, or simply accompanies some event—it also often activates an autonomous time and virtual place, transporting the receiver to a different time and place in the remembered past or expectant future. So while its center of gravity within the Multiverse, if you will, lies in its core material substance, it reaches out to encompass all variables except the opposite one on the Substance dimension. Then, when Hallmark adds digital substances to the experience through its nominally Augmented Virtuality (but, remember, mislabeled Augmented Reality) cards, the center of gravity shifts over to digital substances as now all six realms factor into the experience (as Figure 11.8 in Chapter 11, "Offering Depiction," shows).

So think of the realms as having soft boundaries that blur at the edges, more often than not blending aspects of multiple realms fused into one unified experience. The three core variables of any particular realm provide the center of gravity or *essence* of the experience, whereas any one, two, or three of the noncore variables extend, enhance, enlarge, embellish, boost, or intensify the experience, increasing the value created within each individual customer.

That certainly is the case with all of Alternate Reality, also discussed in Chapter 11. As revealed in its plot on the Experience Design Canvas, experiences within this realm encompass not just the essential variables of autonomous events, real places, and digital substances but the more peripheral—yet still crucial—variables of actual events, virtual places, and material substances. The same holds true for most experiences centered in the other realms. All variables remain at play to one degree or another. By realizing this, you can more explicitly and intentionally take advantage of these variables to provide a fuller, more robust experience—an overtly *transversal* experience—with greater engagement and value.

Now, we intentionally waited until this point to reveal all this in order to ease your understanding and use of the Multiverse model. It's a complicated enough beast without right off the bat being forced to think about multiple realms at a time. Thinking solely in terms of single realms bestows, we believe, great value in discovering the *cosmos incogniti* lying beyond the digital frontier. We do want you to start your ideation process by Reaching through the Realms, realm by realm, and only then go on to Varying the Variables, where you can more explicitly design transversal experiences by thinking of each variable first independently of the others, and then in fuller and more robust combinations.

When, as a result, you create third spaces that fuse the real and the virtual, you necessarily draw from Reality and from Virtuality, *both* of which lie at the core of what it means to be human.

It's Really All Real

According to some social scientists, there is no such thing as objective truth, that in fact reality is socially constructed.[16] On the other hand, we (along with most readers, surely) recognize the reality of Reality. No matter where an experience resides in or across the Multiverse, it still requires a real, live, living, breathing person to do the experiencing. Escape into your mind's eye with a good book, and still you lay on a couch in your family room, breathing the air. Explore the beauty of a virtual world or simply surf the web to your heart's content, and still you sit in front of a screen, controlling the action with your hands on a keyboard, mouse, or other device. Play a Kinect game or model virtual clay, and still your physical hands and arms move, shaping the on-screen activity. Visit a living history museum for the day or participate, whenever you can afford a few minutes or hours, in an ARG, and still you move inexorably along with the universe's arrow of time, growing older moment by moment as your work piles up at the office or home.

There's no escaping the reality: *it's really all real.*

So design for the real place in which your customers reside, no matter how virtual the place you wish to take them. Every experience is a transversal experience in this regard, always incorporating the real place also being experienced by the real person, in the actual time available to him and with the material substances before him.

Further recognize that *Reality is the source of all experience,* whether through the direct engagement of the senses in Reality itself or by triggering emotions evoked by those senses via virtual means. And as we have emphasized multiple times, Reality still provides the richest of sensorial experiences. For example, we may be able to bring the elements of the rainforest to our offerings—say, through a tropical plant conservatory, a Web-surfing excursion seeking information about tropical forests, or even a virtual jungle tour—but we can never replicate the experience of being there: squishing the mud, feeling the springy humus, stubbing your toes on roots, smelling the verdant flora, hearing the birds' calls and the monkeys' hollers, and feeling the stifling hot humid air as rays of sunlight pierce the canopy high above.[17]

Reality also supplies the referent for all representations; even the most fantastical require some relationship to people's experience for them to comprehend.[18] The principles closing each of the chapters on the other realms all refer directly to the relationship between each realm and Reality, as summarized here:

∞ Warped Reality takes a Reality experience and plays with its sense of time without straying from material substances or real places.

∞ Augmented Reality uses Reality as the background—or better yet, as the foreground—for the experience.

∞ Alternate Reality uses Reality as a playground, superimposing the virtual onto the real to create an alternate view.

∞ Physical Virtuality takes things the other way by instantiating in Reality what you imagine in Virtuality.

∞ Augmented Virtuality takes a Virtuality experience and incorporates elements of material Reality to engage your mind and (real) body.

∞ Mirrored Virtuality reflects Reality, creating a simulation of the real world tied into actual time, moment by moment.

∞ Virtuality, even with its utter immateriality unencumbered by the real world, still hearkens back to Reality to give our imagination touchpoints to grasp.

So although we may define Virtuality as the polar opposite of Reality in order to present a handy conceptual framework that provides us with insights to stimulate our ideation, we never truly leave Reality behind. It's really all real.

It's Virtually All Virtual

According to some cosmological scientists, underlying the physical matter of the Universe—below the levels of molecules, atoms, and even subatomic particles such as quarks, muons, and bosons that collectively make up all of Reality—lies one more level, *the* fundamental level. And it is comprised of bits, of zeros and ones.[19] While we find that view fascinating, if unproven (and probably unprovable), you need not believe it, or even comprehend it, to understand how Virtuality underlies all our experiences of Reality.[20] So yes, no matter where an experience resides in or across the Multiverse, it still requires a real, live, living, breathing person to do the experiencing. But where does that experience truly happen? The experience does not reside in either material or digital substances; they merely create the props. The experience does not occur in either real or virtual places; they merely fashion the stage. The experience does not transpire in either actual or autonomous events; they merely shape the drama. *The experience happens inside each person.* As we noted earlier in Chapter 6, "Virtuality," the actual experience is your internal reaction to the external stimuli staged in front of you, whether those stimuli are generated via Reality, Virtuality, or a third space anywhere in between. All experiences truly exist only in the mind.

There's no escaping the verity: *it's virtually all virtual.*

So design for the mind no matter what you want to do with the body. Every experience is a Virtuality experience in this regard as well, always happening in the mind, the autonomous and immaterial virtual place inside of the real person.

Further realize that *Virtuality serves as the font of extraordinary experience,* for all experiences must engage the mind no matter whether the stimuli come through the direct engagement of the senses in Reality or indirectly in Virtuality. As much as experiences reside in Reality, the generation of new value today comes primarily from Virtuality. It can take you places Reality alone would never let you go. Its ability to create what mankind wishes is unprecedented, extraordinary, and limitless.

Virtuality also furnishes the inspiration for all imaginings; even the most grounded of new experiences require thoughtful innovativeness to engage people today.[21] The principles closing the chapters on the other realms all refer, even if indirectly, to the relationship between each realm and Virtuality, as summarized here:

∞ Mirrored Virtuality creates a Virtuality experience tied into actual time, moment by moment reflecting Reality.

∞ Augmented Virtuality engages your real body via material substances to enhance a Virtuality experience.

∞ Physical Virtuality takes what you imagine in Virtuality and instantiates it in Reality.

∞ Alternate Reality takes an otherwise Virtuality experience and superimposes it on the real world, using the latter as a playground for the former.

∞ Augmented Reality takes a real-world experience and enhances it with elements of Virtuality, extending them not only visually but also along audio, tactile, and kinesthetic dimensions.

∞ Warped Reality takes Virtuality's autonomous events into an otherwise real-world experience, opening the door to playing with time without straying from material substances or real places.

∞ Reality, the epitome of the physical world, harkens back to the Virtuality of the imagination that creates and defines its experiences.

So although we may define Reality as the polar opposite of Virtuality in order to present a handy conceptual framework that provides us with insights to stimulate our ideation, we never truly leave Virtuality behind.[22] It's virtually all virtual.

From Ideation to Design

Now you have it all—everything we know about the Multiverse (and probably then some). We trust this fuller understanding of Multiversal experiences serves as an enriching catalyst for refining and putting meat on the bones of your new value creation ideas. The more thoroughly you comprehend and explicitly consider all the factors at play, the more clearly you will see how to innovate new offerings that fulfill the promise inherent within digital technology.

Your knowledge of each of the eight realms (with the plethora of examples given throughout the book) should help you generate initial ideas for consideration. Your knowledge of the six variables should further broaden the scope of ideas, and knowing how each of them can always be brought to bear in any offering should deepen those ideas. Your knowledge of how every experience needs to be depicted in terms of Events, Places, and Substances, the three dimensions of the single Multiverse, should help you more clearly define exactly how each idea turns into an offering. And now your fuller understanding of the true nature of the Multiverse—how it portrays third spaces that are really all real and virtually all virtual—should help you see how each offering would truly affect each customer.

13

From Design to Deployment

ACT INTO THE FUTURE

Infinite possibility holds the danger that the *cosmos* of our imagination become so vast that, like David Livingstone in Africa, you become lost and succumb to despair at ever finding a way out. If, however, you keep your focus clearly on creating customer value and persevere in your ideation expeditions, you should have a rich pool of ideas for third places that fuse the real and the virtual. From these you can then select those that would create the most experiential value for your customers, and the most economic value for your company. You next must take these selected ideas down the path from design to deployment.

In taking the next step, design, understand that whereas the Multiverse provides a new sense-making guide to discovering never-before-realized value, viewing any Multiversal offering through the format (and lens) of the Experience Design Canvas—versus just the eight-realm Multiverse itself—will prove fruitful. So *encompass a full complement of variables* by mapping your offering onto the Design Canvas and then examine it variable by variable, seeking to make it more *robust* by dialing up or down the right variables to create the right experience.

Experience Design

Of course there is still more to do beyond that exercise. The path of experience design remains well-worn with many ideas, tools, and frameworks to help you do it effectively and profitably. Although experience design, particularly of the digital kind, is still in its infancy, we especially recommend the following books to assist you in your endeavors: Nathan Shedroff's *Experience Design 1* (with *Experience Design 2* published in 2011), Mark Stephen Meadow's *Pause & Effect,* Jesse Schell's

The Art of Game Design, Dan Saffer's *Designing for Interaction,* and David Lee King's *Designing the Digital Experience.*[1]

And two more books (Joe writes humbly): *The Experience Economy* and *Authenticity.* For designing Multiversal experiences fits the overall worldview contained in these books (with an updated edition of the former published in 2011 shortly before this book). They therefore offer great help in designing experiences encompassing not just Reality but the entire array of the Multiverse, experiences that are not just robust but cohesive, rich, individual, authentic, and compelling. We encourage you to read these books in full, paying particular attention to these design principles, each with their own framework:

∞ *THEME the experience*: In order to make it *cohesive,* establish the organizing principle that binds the experience together, enabling you to determine what is in and what is out of the experience.[2]

∞ *Hit the sweet spot*: Every *rich* experience must appeal to all four aspects: entertainment, education, escapism, and esthetics—the 4Es—to engage customers in a multiplicity of ways, draw them in more fully, and get them to spend more time.[3]

∞ *Eliminate customer sacrifice*: For an experience to engage each and every *individual,* understand the difference between what a customer settles for and what he wants exactly—his customer sacrifice, as mentioned in Chapter 11, "Offering Depiction"—and then mass customize your Multiversal experience in order to efficiently serve customers uniquely, meeting each individual, living, breathing customer's wants and needs.[4]

∞ *Render authenticity*: For customers to perceive your experience as *authentic*—and here we are contrasting the real and the fake, not fusing the real and the virtual—requires recognizing how you meet (or not) the two key standards of authenticity: Is the offering true to itself? Is it what it says it is?[5]

∞ Finally, *embrace dramatic structure*: To make your experience *compelling,* understand that for today's Experience Economy, work *is* theatre, and therefore in order to grab people's attention and hold it, experiences must have a dramatic structure that draws them into the experience, engages them, provides a payoff, and concludes.[6]

Even a totally virtual experience with no live workers must understand and embrace theatre in order to truly engage and connect with guests. That's why literary scholar Marie-Laure Ryan relates narrative to the three dimensions of the Multiverse when she notes in *Narrative as Virtual Reality* that virtual worlds "are mentally constructed by the reader as environments that stretch in space, exist in time, and serve as habitat for a population of animate agents. These three dimensions correspond to what have long been recognized as the three basic components of narrative grammar: setting, plot, and characters."[7]

If you follow these principles, you cannot help but excel at creating customer value on the digital frontier through innovative experiences that effectively fuse the real and the virtual.

Game Design in Learning, Work, and Life

Of course, as you have probably gathered from our realm discussions, the greatest impetus for ongoing innovation throughout the Multiverse is games (and not, as is so often said of new technology, the pornography industry). Gaming infuses every realm. Game design, therefore, has become a major subset of experience design. It not only *can* inform greatly the design of all sorts of experiences, it already *is* doing so. Often going by the awkward term "gamification," companies today apply game design to many facets of learning, work, and even life.[8]

We have also seen this throughout the book, as businesses take what they have discovered in gaming and expand it to encompass other environs. Think of Quest to Learn, the school in New York City mentioned in Chapter 12, "Third Spaces," that treats the classroom as a yearlong video game.[9] Consider Jane McGonigal's appeal in the *Harvard Business Review* to apply Alternate Reality to training, strategy, innovation, and other business pursuits to effect "the New Business Reality"; Byron Reeves and Leighton Read's plea to use multiplayer Virtuality games in redesigning work itself; and our own thoughts on how Augmented Virtuality could make work as engaging and intrinsically rewarding as play. Recall also how Augmented Reality can be used not just to inform our travels but transform our lives through sensory prosthetics. And contemplate how Mirrored Virtuality gives us topsight to enhance our learning, enables us to track everything going on in our business, and allows us to quantify the activity of our bodies and our minds to improve both. Remember, for example, the new Ford

SmartGauge with EcoGuide mentioned in Chapter 9, "Mirrored Virtuality," which adds a virtual green vine to the dash that flourishes with efficient driving but shrivels with speed demons? It's a perfect, albeit simple, example of applying game mechanics—every driver desires to see his leaves grow and sprout rather than wither and die—to transform our behavior and thereby enhance the world.

Although many companies now incorporate into their offerings such game mechanics as points, rewards, badges, levels, and so forth, Amy Jo Kim, an expert in online social architecture and cofounder of game designer Shufflebrain, was quick to point out to us how short-sighted that is: "It's like putting the right ingredients in the refrigerator and thinking that's all it takes to make a great meal."[10] No, there are many other elements and tasks to create a great experience based on gaming, foremost among them, Kim said, was "the unfolding power of story."

Jesse Schell, professor at Carnegie Mellon's Entertainment Technology Center (ETC) and CEO of Schell Games, echoes this in his aforementioned book *The Art of Game Design* through what he calls the "Lens of the Elemental Tetrad" (the seventh of one hundred lenses for designing games). In it he identifies the four elements of a game: *mechanics* and *story* comprise the first two, and *aesthetics*[11] ("how your game looks, sounds, smells, tastes, and feels") and *technology* ("the medium in which the aesthetics take place, in which the mechanics will occur, and through which the story will be told") complete the Tetrad.[12]

One more element seems crucial, however. In a conversation with Schell he talked about how whenever you apply game design to broader environs than gaming, you must be very careful about tackling incentives and motivations, and he put us onto Alfie Kohn's book *Punished by Rewards*. Kohn rails against traditional carrot-and-stick methods of parenting children, teaching students, and managing workers, and among his prescriptions one item stands out: *purpose*. As he puts it:

> What is a good job? Let us start by aiming high: at its best, it offers a chance to engage in *meaningful* work. The sense of doing something that matters is not the same as a feeling of intrinsic motivation. It isn't just that the process of working provides enjoyment, but that the product being made (or the service provided [or experience staged, or transformation guided]) seems worthwhile and even important, perhaps because it makes a contribution to a larger community. Mihaly Csikszentmihalyi, who has spent much of his career describing the pure pleasure of "flow" experiences, points out that beyond such enjoyment

"one must still ask, 'What are the consequences of this particular activity?'" The question is not just "Are we having fun yet?" but "Are we making a difference?"[13]

So in addition to mechanics and story, to aesthetics and technology, in whatever experience you design be sure to embrace purpose, to understand the meaningful ends to which your experience is but the engaging means.

In doing so, you will find yourself going beyond experiences to transformation offerings. *All* applications of game design to learning, work, and life—all "gamification"—occur only when the customer seeks change or when such change is sought by someone else (not just businesses but teachers, managers, parents and spouses, doctors, and all others responsible for or concerned with the well-being or productivity of others). You (whether corporately or personally) must take special care in this latter case, morally speaking, that (1) your desire for change in others edifies (builds up, not tears down) and (2) the means (the experiences by which all transformations occur) are justified in full.

Game design, appropriately done with a proper sense of purpose, can certainly inform the means of experiences. Back in 2002, I (Joe) gave a talk on the Experience Economy at PopTech, a popular culture-meets-technology conference held every year in Camden, Maine. I was paired with General Paul Gorman, retired, under whose command the United States Army created its rather effective recruiting game *America's Army*. During the Q&A portion of our time, an audience member stood up and asked when someone was going to make a game that would help make the world a peaceful place, rather than one that encouraged them to be soldiers. The place erupted in spontaneous applause.

The moderator was about to go on to another question when I stopped her, pointing out to everyone that there had been only two times during the entire conference when the audience clapped spontaneously to a remark. This moment, and the day before when an earlier speaker railed against "those Republicans" in Congress who had the temerity to contend that violent games affected people. When that speaker in essence called out "Hogwash!" nearly everyone clapped. So now I asked, "Which is it? You applaud when someone says games can't possibly change people, and then you applaud when someone suggests we should have a game that changes people!"

Although many do not like to admit it, the truth of course lies in the latter.[14] Games can and do change people, as we are all the products of our experiences. That is exactly why game design has escaped the bounds of mere play to affect, and effect change in, all facets of life. It is also why you should embrace its tenets—mechanics, story, aesthetics, and technology—in designing your experiences, but only when you couple them to a core purpose, not only for how your customers themselves benefit from your offerings, but for your company itself. Are you making a difference?

Exploring as a Way of Life

Even though unlimited opportunities to make a difference await companies who go in search of them, the future's uncertainty, unpredictability, and mystery make for an intriguing, if not baffling, management puzzle to solve. The way forward is to *act into the future*.[15] Only through action do you turn speculation into knowledge, discover otherwise indeterminable consequences, and encounter the serendipitous opportunities that inevitably emerge. *Pushing* your way into the future with comprehensive plans to be achieved at all costs only serves to frustrate. As no one knows what the future holds, extensive plans based on conjecture, strictly adhered to, blind your company to the opportunities and issues revealed while you proceed according to plan.

Instead, *pull* your way into the future by learning to act, and acting to learn. You then evolve your company as well as its offerings with every step forward. Do not view this approach to discovering and creating the future, this exploration and exploitation, as a once-and-done exercise, of course. Innovation must be an ongoing activity of all thriving businesses, lest you get in the position of not having the next big thing designed as your last big thing starts its inexorable decline, or even worse, find yourself failing to exploit what you have already discovered.

Exploring *cosmos incogniti* in order to look into the possibilities they hold only serves your company's purpose well when pursued as a way of life. When done as an occasional project or as a response to immediate crises, inevitably the pace of your company's evolution lags behind that of its ecosystem as planned, directed, periodic explorations prove less dynamic than that of your collective competition (especially startups).

Only by engaging your people in ongoing exploration and exploitation orchestrated to continually rejuvenate your company's offerings can you hope to perpetuate your company, and seek to pursue its purpose, indefinitely.[16] Only a virtuous cycle of perpetual exploration and exploitation produces a persistent competitive advantage.

Being Good

As you go about this, you also cannot help but run into a number of issues and implications that rise to the fore when shifting offerings from Reality to the third spaces that fuse it with Virtuality. Every new technology of note raises the ire of someone, for inevitably something valuable gets lost and many someones get left behind as the ground shifts underneath them, causing inevitable longing and heartache. This is especially true of digital technology, for as we have seen throughout it may very well be the most sweeping, significant, and revolutionary set of technologies ever invented. And it's not all anti-technologists; you don't have to be a Luddite to be concerned about what escaping the stability of Reality for the vicissitudes of Virtuality is doing to mankind. Even the most diehard of geeks, hackers, gamers, and all manner of technological enthusiasts may have legitimate qualms about the implications of infusing every aspect of our lives so thoroughly with digital technology that we cannot escape it, even for a moment.

So you would be wise, as you advance from experience design to offering deployment, to not only be aware of the potentially deleterious effects but to take them into account in your offerings, in your business purpose, and also in your life. We cannot of course deal here with everything negative that anyone has ever said about digital technology and its effects on our lives; others have, you can be sure, and we trust will continue to. But let us address the eight key issues that we think most affect experiences of the Multiverse, with our thoughts on how you should approach them. Some of these are valid issues that can be ameliorated. Some are false ideas, or generally so, but they reflect a real concern that must be handled. And some are implications of the Multiverse both true and false, depending on the circumstances, or problems where we remain unsure of the final outcome but still can and should be taken into account. We do encourage you to think on these things.

We are in a constant state of information overload, always on and never off. This so often is the case. Do we really need even more bits in our lives? Surfing the Web, reading blogs, answering your e-mail, updating your Facebook page, having the Twitterverse wash over you—each and every one in and of themselves can be a good thing. You learn, you inform, you connect. Recognize, though, that even on the negative side hype often exceeds actuality. University of Texas professors Craig Watkins and Erin Lee found that "Facebook is not supplanting face-to-face interactions between friends, family and colleagues." Rather, they believe that "there is sufficient evidence that social media afford opportunities for new expressions of friendship, intimacy, and community."[17]

But we only have twenty-four hours a day, seven days a week, 365 days a year. The key here, then, is one of balance, a viewpoint eloquently encouraged by William Powers in *Hamlet's BlackBerry: A Practical Philosophy for Building a Good Life in the Digital Age* and, earlier, by Thomas Hylland Eriksen in *The Tyranny of the Moment: Fast and Slow Time in the Information Age*.[18] When, where, how, and how often we access third spaces is a matter of personal choice—something for you to consider both with your offerings and in your personal life. As with any good and engaging activity, some will go overboard, even become addicted. Unless you actually design your offerings to *be* addictive—not a far-fetched idea when it comes to gaming, and something that alone would flip the switch, in most people's minds, from good to evil— recognize that you must compete with all the other ways people may spend their time, and you must compete well in order to create value. Recognize, too, the value to be had in intentionally making offerings less addictive, freeing up actual time to be spent elsewhere in the Multiverse on more enriching and edifying experiences.

Digital technology encourages us to provide information that should remain private. This, too, is oh so true, and many young people in particular will come to dread how much information about themselves and their activities they have put online, seemingly forever.

But recognize that they do so because it has value for them today. Not a day goes by without warnings about this issue or stories of someone who has been bit by it, so it most likely will be like a pendulum, which once it swings too far in one direction naturally falls back toward the center. In your business, never ask anything of your customers, nor collect any piece of data of their activities, that you do not intend to use *on behalf* of that *same* customer. Always protect that data you do collect, no matter what. Do not allow customer data to seep out of your hands into others, regardless of how profitable it may be to you, without explicit customer approval. Teach your customers to be smart about it. And on customer request, provide the means for their own data to be erased—permanently, thoroughly, and utterly. In short, *be good.*

Digital technology, with videogames and the Internet itself at the top of the list, is bad for us, turning our brains to mush. This is more than every generation's complaint that the next generation is going to pot (a cycle of life going back at least as far as Plato), for again digital technology is different than all previous technologies—more enticing, more customized, more immersive, less expensive, more ubiquitous. IT curmudgeon Nicholas Carr complains in his latest book, *The Shallows: What the Internet Is Doing to Our Brains,* that, well, the Internet is doing not good stuff to our brains.[19] Journalist Maggie Jackson asserts in *Distracted* that our ability to focus is being so degraded we risk a new "dark age."[20] Emory University professor Mark Bauerlein even goes so far as to call young people growing up amid all of today's digital technology the "Dumbest Generation."[21] Of course, for every book bemoaning the effects of digital technology there seems to be ten extolling its virtues, notably including Steven Johnson's *Everything Bad Is Good for You: How Today's Popular Culture Is Actually Making Us Smarter,* David Shaffer's *How Computer Games Help Children Learn,* and James Paul Gee's *What Video Games Have to Teach Us about Learning and Literacy.*[22]

Where does the truth lie? Probably in both camps, with harmful effects predominating for some people, beneficial effects for others, and with most people somewhere in between. For society overall, we firmly believe the genuine benefits far outweigh the valid detriments, and in any case, at this point there's no turning back. The question is what we *do* with digital technology in general and the Multiverse in particular that matters. Forget about which camp you are in, or the desire to be proven right; which camp is made more likely by your offerings, and if the first, *what will you do about it?*

We are amusing ourselves to death with all these experiences. From the title of Neil Postman's 1985 book, *Amusing Ourselves to Death,* where the late cultural critic joined many others in bemoaning how electronic media—most notably television, but the point certainly applies to all of the Multiverse—was reshaping our culture, turning everything, "politics, religion, news, athletics, education and commerce," into "congenial adjuncts of show business"[23] with few, if any, redeeming qualities relative to the written word and internal reflection.

There certainly is a lot of truth to this, although one man's mere amusement is another man's engaging experience, and as book authors we certainly believe people should spend more time with the written word and reflecting on what they have learned. *Selah.* Later, in 1992's

Technopoly, Postman encourages us to consciously choose or deny technologies, recognizing that "every technology is both a burden and a blessing"; when, therefore, "we admit a new technology to the culture, we must do so with our eyes wide open."[24]

Although he was talking more culturally than individually, it again comes down to informed choice. As individuals, we should choose carefully what technologies we use, what offerings we consume, in what experiences we partake—and just as importantly as what, we must choose when and for how long. As a society, we should open our eyes to the natural effects of new experiences, new offerings, and new technologies—which are not neutral but bias action and thinking in particular directions, not always foreseeable—to counter the deleterious and promote the edifying. As a business, you should understand those effects in your own commercial output and strive to go beyond mere amusement to *making a positive impact* on your customers, and on the world.

Digital technology, and social media in particular, fragments, regurgitates, and impersonalizes not only text and ideas but people as well. In *You Are Not a Gadget,* a far-ranging diatribe to which the sentence above does not do justice, Jaron Lanier rails against "the worship of the illusions of bits" that has resulted in "this widespread practice of fragmentary, impersonal communications [that] has demeaned interpersonal interaction."[25] He echoes others in this regard, but as the foremost popularizer of Virtual Reality, his words have a weight others do not.

All of this can be true, and too often is the case, but it need not be—else Lanier would not have bothered to write his manifesto. So *always examine the consequences of your offerings,* the directions in which it encourages humanity to go. All commerce, not just digital offerings, involves moral choice.[26] What choices are you making? And what choices are you encouraging your customers to make?

Virtuality goes so far as to fragment personal identity. Online, you can be whoever you want to be. In Facebook or LinkedIn, your profile represents who you are—but perhaps very differently on each. In virtual worlds, you create your avatar's appearance and build up from scratch its characteristics and behaviors—your Virtuality personality. Are these all merely representations, with greater or lesser relationship to who you really are? Are these multiple personae manifesting themselves in different arenas? Or are these presentations of a "protean self," in the phrase of psychologist Robert Lifton, that "is multiple but integrated . . . a sense of self without being one self"?[27] And what does it all mean for the authenticity not of economic offerings, but of us as human beings?

Although we are unwilling to give up on the concept of a unitary self, we understand that, after Erving Goffman,[28] all of us present ourselves differently in front of different people; these distinct presentations may or may not be authentic to who we really are. It is clear that the Multiverse multiplies the opportunities for individual multiplicity, and as individuals we should embrace the view that Sherry Turkle, founder of the MIT Initiative on Technology and Self, expresses in *Life on the Screen*: "Without a deep understanding of the many selves that we express in the virtual we cannot use our experiences there to enrich the real. If we cultivate our awareness of what stands behind our screen personae, we are more likely to succeed in using virtual experience for personal transformation."[29] As corporations, you should seek to use your offerings to *help* individuals enrich the real and *guide* them to transform.

Technology causes alienation, interceding in and replacing human relationships. This has been an issue at least since Karl Marx used it as the pretext for his theories (with capitalism as the alienating technology *du jour*), but again there is no doubt that digital technology exacerbates the problem. As noted above, we can be always on and never off, which so often means *not with* the people with whom we share this space in Reality, here and now. When sharing space in Virtuality, we effortlessly can represent ourselves falsely, should we so choose. We so easily slip into different online personae that some may feel their identities pulling apart into multiple selves, as Turkle found. And so thoroughly, immersively, and constantly can we be engaged by third spaces that many can become alienated from that first space, from real life itself, and the human companionship that makes it, well, humane. It's not without reason that many decry the increasing use of humanlike robots in classrooms and soft, cuddly, animal-like robots in nursing homes or, increasingly in Japan, the personal homes of the elderly.[30]

But particularly in the case of the elderly, these robots are not replacing a human connection; they are filling a human void. As long as such voids exist, people should seek to fill them *in person,* but businesses can and should ameliorate the rest—including helping people form real relationships and connect on a personal level.[31] As we wrote in Chapter 2, "Reality," if technology is not used to *make a human connection*—a positive and enduring one—with and especially between your current and prospective customers, what is the point?

People desire to keep in Reality that which they hold most dear. Whereas the previous issue, as with many others, stems from an age-old problem intensified by technology, the final issue we address here is wholly new, emerging from the propensity of Virtuality in general, and simulations of Reality in particular, "to make some things seem more real," in the words of MIT Professor Turkle.[32] In her fascinating study of how faculty members across a variety of disciplines embrace (or not) simulations within their domains of expertise, *Simulation and Its Discontents,* Turkle found that people tended to want to hold back what they held most dear, to make some "sacred space" a "simulation-free zone" that was "off-limits for the computer."[33] For architects it was drawing; for civil engineers it was structural analysis; for chemists, the lecture hall; for physicists, experiments.

As we ponder the Multiverse itself, this is the question we ask you to consider and reflect on: When it comes to the domain of humanity itself, of what it means to be human, what do we hold most dear? *Selah.*

Into the Future

As Lanier tells us, "the most important thing about a technology is how it changes people."[34] Digital technology changes people, individually and collectively. We are not sure how it will wash out, as all these issues—and more that could have been covered—weave together, extend, and amplify each other in unforeseen ways. The primary thing to do as you act into the future, designing and deploying experience offerings inspired by the Multiverse, is *be aware.* Don't just let all these changes wash over you, unthinkingly. Examine not only your self but your business, and our society. Then and only then can you be prepared for what the future holds, and perhaps be one who makes it happen.

Now, we are not futurists. We do not tell you what is *going* to happen; we tell you what *is* happening, right now, that perhaps you do not yet see. The Multiverse is such a sense-making tool for perceiving the present in a new way. As with any tool, it can be used wisely or unwisely, in edifying or deleterious ways, for good or for evil. Be wise. Choose good. And then imagine what could be.

It's oft been said that the mechanization that came with the Industrial Economy caused us to view ourselves in terms of machine metaphors—the brain as a determinant mechanism, for example. With the rise of the Service Economy and its dependence on information technology, computer metaphors abounded, with the brain as information processor. With the emergence of the Experience Economy and the Multiverse, we hope to see the concomitant rise of metaphors of imagination—the mind as limitless imagineer. We are not mechanisms or processors; we are ones who use the tremendous resources of digital technology to create what we imagine. We now truly are limited only by our imaginations, which stretch out to embrace infinite possibility.

Afterword

TO INFINITY AND BEYOND

Some of you may wonder if talking about "infinite" possibility is gross overstatement, just so much hyperbole. Well, yes; yes it is—but not by much in any practical sense. To see our point, consider again the LEGO brick, a simple thing of material substance that illustrates that possibility may not be infinite—but it is genuinely immeasurable, and truly limitless.

To Infinity . . .

Take, for example, the relatively simple case of six 2×4 bricks (those with eight studs on top)—and we'll even ignore color. In 1999 LEGO published the number of possibilities that could be built with just these six bricks: an astounding 102,981,500.[1] This turned out to be a considerable underestimate, however, as it only counted designs where each brick was on top of another in some way—so each of the almost 103 million designs reach precisely six bricks high. But you can also put bricks side by side, yielding five-brick-high combinations as well as four-, three-, and two-brick-high combinations. Søren Eilers and Bergfinnur Durhuus of the University of Copenhagen, plus high school student Mikkel Abrahamsen, who instigated the quest for the right answer, showed that the true number for six 2×4 bricks is 915,103,765![2]

Now imagine (or pull out of your kids' treasure trove) twenty-five LEGO bricks, still 2×4s, and still all the same color. And then consider this number: 130,881,177,000,000,000,000,000,000,000,000,000,000. That is not the number of different designs you can make with them. No, that is the *number of years* they estimate it would take to figure out that precise number![3] In case you were wondering, that is nigh on 131 duodecillion. Years.

The good Danish mathematicians cannot, unfortunately, calculate the number of combinations for any arbitrary number N of 2×4 bricks of identical color, but they estimate it to be around 100^N (that's the number 100 followed by N zeros).[4] Now think about this: according to LEGO, there are 3,900 distinct types of elements (again, not just bricks but minifigures, wheels, trees, etc.) with fifty-eight different colors, yielding a total of over 7,500 "active combinations" (relatively few elements come in more than one color). Realize, too, that LEGO produces about 21 billion elements a year these days. (Two years worth, each element atop the other, would reach almost to the moon.) And, finally, consider that 485 billion total elements have been produced since it began in 1949 (with about 1,000 more elements manufactured every second).[5]

So how many possible designs could be built with all those LEGO elements? Innumerable. Incalculable. But infinite? No, not infinite, but vastly beyond human comprehension, yes.[6]

And all those elements comprise just one tiny, tiny category of material substances. Just as all the virtual elements you can manipulate in LEGO's Physical Virtuality offering, Design byME, comprise just one tiny, tiny category of digital substances you could employ in your offerings. And all the material substances in the known universe comprise a tiny, tiny fraction of all the digital substances you could bring to bear in the *cosmos incogniti* of the Multiverse. And these two variables come together to form only one of the three dimensions of the model, whose arrows on either end extend out, further and further, reaching toward infinity. And with them go the eight realms, expanding ever outward, encompassing ever more possibility, creating deeper and more intense experiences through the innovations resulting from our imaginings.

And of that there truly is no end.

. . . and Beyond

But that also is not all there is. Beyond the real and the virtual, beyond the universe of Time, Space, and Matter, and the Multiverse incorporating No-Time, No-Space, and No-Matter, lays another realm: the eternal. In eternity there exists the truly Infinite. The word "eternal" does not mean simply everlasting, perpetual, or unceasing. It denotes, according to the *Oxford English Dictionary,* that which "always has existed and always will exist," that which is "not subject to time relations."[7] In other words, eternity lies *outside* of time. It moreover lies outside of space (always existing and not subject to distance relations) and outside of matter (always existing and not subject to physical relations). It lies beyond both universe and Multiverse, both Reality and Virtuality, both actuality and possibility, both experience and imaginings. Before any of these were, it is.

In eternity exists the truly Infinite, that which is self-existent. And that existence speaks to the ultimate purpose for everything we do with the possibility that is set before us. To what eternal end are your business, your acts, and your self the means? Your answer may or may not help you create economic value, but it will help you reach beyond, to find the Infinite.

notes

All website references were valid as of January 3, 2011, unless otherwise indicated.

Foreword

1. Sean Leahy, "Stadium vs. Home: Can the NFL make being there match what's on TV?" *USA Today*, September 1, 2010.

2. Stan Davis, in the Foreword to B. Joseph Pine II, *Mass Customization: The New Frontier in Business Competition* (Boston: Harvard Business School Press, 1993), x–xi.

3. B. Joseph Pine II and James H. Gilmore, *The Experience Economy*, Updated Edition (Boston: Harvard Business Review Press, 2011), 76.

4. Ken Auletta's book, *Googled: The End of the World as We Know It* (New York: Penguin Press, 2009), masterfully chronicles the triumph of the mathematical algorithm over "old media." Its subtitle points to the belief system in place at not only Google (and Amazon) but most of the digital innovators of our age. Note that even the old guard that was slow to respond to the digital revolution (can you say, newspapers?) missed the shift precisely because their own behavior demonstrated a view of the digital as completely alien to their businesses.

5. Daniel Lyons, "The Customer Is Always Right," *Newsweek*, December 21, 2009. Bezos' complete answer to the first question: "I do. I don't know how long it will take. You know, we love stories and we love narrative; we love to get lost in an author's world. That's not going to go away; that's going to thrive. But the physical book really has had a 500-year run. It's probably the most successful technology ever. It's hard to come up with things that have had a longer run. If Gutenberg were alive today, he would recognize the physical book and know how to operate it immediately. Given how much change there has been everywhere else, what's remarkable is how stable the book has been for so long. But no technology, not even one as elegant as the book, lasts forever."

6. For an introduction to the role physical libraries have in promoting an appreciation for human knowledge, see David Brooks, "The Medium Is the Medium," *New York Times*, July 8, 2010. For a peek at a future without physical books, watch an episode or two of MTV's *Cribs*, which takes viewers on tours of the houses of well-known athletes, musicians, and other "celebrity" role models; there's nary a book to be found in these narcissist containers.

7. Jaron Lanier, *You Are Not a Gadget: A Manifesto* (New York: Alfred a Knopf, 2010), 27.

8. Dalton Conley, *Elsewhere U.S.A.: How We Got from the Company Man, Family Dinners, and the Affluent Society to the Home Office, Blackberry Moms, and Economic Anxiety* (New York: Pantheon Books, 2009), 7.

9. David F. Nobel, *The Religion of Technology: The Divinity of Man and the Spirit of Invention* (New York: Penguin Books, 1999), 206–207.

10. I am indebted to Bill Brokaw for this valediction. See www.brokaw.com.

Introduction

1. For a more complete description of this fundamental shift in the fabric of all developed economies, see B. Joseph Pine II and James H. Gilmore, *The Experience Economy: Work Is Theatre & Every Business a Stage* (Boston: Harvard Business School Press, 1999), now in an updated edition, *The Experience Economy* (Boston: Harvard Business Review Press, 2011), to which all future citations will refer.

2. True commodities, being fungible, cannot be innovated, although of course new commodities may be discovered and old ones refined or processed in new ways.

3. We have had many people tell us about the iPhone unboxing experience, and have seen it for ourselves, but in the writing here we read the normally irascible Lucy Kellaway's poetic ode to the App Store guidelines in her "Business Life" column in the *Financial Times*: "I have found the words to describe Apple's glory." Lucy Kellaway, September 20, 2010.

4. Alan Kay, "Computer Software," *Scientific American,* vol. 251, no. 3, September 1984, 52–59, cited in Brenda Laurel, *Computers as Theatre* (Reading, Massachusetts: Addison-Wesley Publishing Company,1993), 32.

5. Jaron Lanier, *You Are Not a Gadget: A Manifesto* (New York: Alfred A. Knopf, 2010), 103.

6. Laurel, *Computers as Theatre,* 32–33.

7. "F-8 Digital Fly-By-Wire Aircraft," *NASA Dryden Fact Sheet,* www.nasa.gov/centers/dryden/news/FactSheets/FS-024-DFRC.html.

8. An illustration from W. Brian Arthur, *The Nature of Technology: What It Is and How It Evolves* (New York: Free Press, 2009), 72–73.

9. The impediments to reaching literally everyone in the world are primarily political (retarding wealth creation in undeveloped countries) and cultural (with many groups of people resisting new digital technology, not necessarily without cause, even—such as the Amish—in the United States). Even many poor people today have digital phones; witness the rise of mobile phone usage in both India and Africa.

10. Andrew S. Grove, "Intel Keynote Transcript, Comdex Fall '96," *Intel,* November 18, 1996, available at www.intel.com/pressroom/archive/speeches/ag111896.htm.

1. Cosmos Incogniti

1. Stan Davis, *Future Perfect* (Reading, Massachusetts: Addison-Wesley, 1987), 5.

2. Ibid., 7.

3. Ibid., 92. Another path-breaking notion from this book, in the chapter "Mass Customizing" (138–190), inspired B. Joseph Pine II, *Mass Customization: The*

New Frontier in Business Competition (Boston: Harvard Business School Press, 1993).

4. In ibid., 102, Davis provides the equation.

VALUE OF A DELIVERABLE = INFORMATION / MASS,

citing Paul Hawken's statement in *The Next Economy* (New York: Holt, Rinehart & Winston, 1983), 11: "The single most important trend to understand is the changing ratio between mass and information in goods and services." See also Diane Coyle, *The Weightless World: Strategies for Managing the Digital Economy* (Cambridge, Massachusetts: The MIT Press, 1998).

5. Nicholas Negroponte, *Being Digital* (New York: Alfred A. Knopf, 1995), 11–20 in particular.

6. Anne Friedberg relates screens to the three dimensions of the Multiverse on the first page of *The Virtual Window: From Alberti to Microsoft* (Cambridge, Massachusetts: MIT Press, 2006), 1 (italics removed): "The screen is a component piece of architecture, rendering a wall permeable to ventilation in new ways: a 'virtual window' that changes the materiality of built space, adding new apertures that dramatically alter our conception of space and (even more radically) of time."

7. In cosmology, this term refers to the unproved (and unprovable) hypothesis that our known universe is one of many, each with its own set of distinct physical laws. Related more directly to using digital technology to create customer value, a company based in Mountain View, California, called Multiverse says its mission is to build a platform for companies to create particular virtual worlds, and eventually to have them interact with each other; see www.multiverse.net and www.mv-places.com.

8. We discuss this relationship between the real and the virtual at length in Chapter 12, "Third Spaces."

9. Jane McGonigal, "Alternate Reality Gaming: 'Life Imitates ARG,'" PowerPoint presentation created for the MacArthur Foundation Board of Directors, November 2004, available at *Jane McGonigal,* www.avantgame.com/writings.htm#PRESENTA-TION%20MEDIA.

10. In the end analysis, it doesn't matter whether you call such experiences Reality or Warped Reality, and people will differ on their perceptions of particular experiences (even the same experience at different times). What matters is using the labels and the realms to innovate new offerings.

11. David Gelernter, *Mirror Worlds: or the Day Software Puts the Universe in a Shoebox . . . How It Will Happen and What It Will Mean* (New York: Oxford University Press, 1992), 3.

12. We discuss creating experiences that take advantage of both variables on either side of a dimension, and provide a model for thinking about it—the Experience Design Canvas—in Chapter 11, "Offering Depiction."

2. Reality

1. We are not commenting here on authenticity as the new consumer sensibility, which the lead author did elsewhere—in James H. Gilmore and B. Joseph Pine II,

Authenticity: What Consumers Really *Want* (Boston: Harvard Business Press, 2007), with particular focus on technology and economic offerings in Chapter 5, 81–94. Rather, our point here is simply that technology does not lessen the Reality-based nature of real life.

2. W. Brian Arthur, *The Nature of Technology: What It Is and How It Evolves* (New York: Free Press, 2009), 28.

3. Ibid., 70 and 145.

3. Augmented Reality

1. "In the Driver's Seat," *Time,* www.time.com/time/specials/packages/article/0, 28804,1939342_1939430_1939727,00.html. Note that FanVision has since been reduced to a 6'×4' palmprint with an even larger screen size than before.

2. Laurie Mallis, "Birth of the DIAD," *Upside: The UPS Blog,* December 7, 2009, blog.ups.com/2009/12/07/birth-of-the-diad/.

3. Christine Perey, "Shopping with AR," *O'Reilly Radar,* radar.oreilly.com/2009/10/ shopping-with-ar.html. Although an interactive catalog that we can choose to browse or not browse whenever we want sounds intriguing, we do hope the world does not turn into a cluttered landscape of virtual billboards, instigating a battle among advertisers for the "virtual estate" that potentially lies in front of us, always.

4. David Pogue, "The Pogies: Best Ideas of the Year," *New York Times,* December 30, 2010.

5. Sam Altman, "The Life Graph: You Are Your Location," *Wall Street Journal,* March 11, 2010, voices.allthingsd.com/20100311/the-life-graph-you-are-your-location/.

6. Gary Hayes, former director of Australia's Laboratory for Advanced Media Production and founder of MUVEDesign in Sydney, Australia, provides a model for "16 Top Augmented Reality Business Models" on his blog, *Personalizemedia,* September 14, 2009, www.personalizemedia.com/16-top-augmented-reality-business-models.

7. "About Medtronic Surgical Navigation Systems," *Medtronic,* www.medtronic .com/for-healthcare-professionals/products-therapies/spinal-orthopedics/surgical -navigation-imaging/surgical-navigation-systems/index.htm.

8. See T. C. Browne and Mike Donfrancesco, "Using Motion Control to Guide Augmented Reality Manufacturing Systems," *Motion Control Technology,* nasatech .com/motion/features/feat_1007.html.

9. Chris Baker, "Found: Artifacts from the Future," *Wired,* 16.01, January 2008, 168.

10. Kristina Grifantini, "GM Develops Augmented Reality Windshield," *Technology Review Blog,* March 17, 2010, www.technologyreview.com/blog/editors/24936/ ?nlid=2828&a=f.

11. Columnist David Pogue, in "Apps We Wish We Had," *New York Times,* July 15, 2010, asked his Twitter followers what, you might have guessed, apps they wished they had, and "one hugely popular category was 'Shazam for other things,'" like movies and TV.

12. "RJDJ," *iTunes Preview,* itunes.apple.com/us/app/rjdj/id290626964?mt=8.

13. See Takayuki Hoshi, Masafumi Takahashiy, Kei Nakatsumaz, and Hiroyuki Shinoda, "Touchable Holography," www.alab.t.u-tokyo.ac.jp/~siggraph/09/Touch ableHolography/SIGGRAPH09TouchableHolography.pdf.

14. Kristina Grifantini, "Augmented-Reality Floor Tiling," *Technology Review Blogs*, April 28, 2010, www.technologyreview.com/blog/editors/25114/?a=f.

15. Morgan Stanfield, "Hugh Herr: Beyond the Merely Human," *The O&P Edge*, March 2010, www.oandp.com/articles/2010-03_08.asp.

16. Herr works hard on how his prosthetics look, not just how they function, for he fully believes that people will want to "augment their appearance, not just their performance"; quoted in Paul Hochman, "Bionic Legs, i-Limbs, and Other Super Human Prostheses You'll Envy," *Fast Company*, February 2010, 87.

17. This replaces an elbow ligament, such as on the throwing arm of Tommy John, the first professional athlete to undergo the operation successfully, with a tendon from elsewhere in the body.

18. See, for example, William Saletan, "The Beam in Your Eye: If steroids are cheating, why isn't LASIK?" *Slate*, April 18, 2005, www.slate.com/id/2116858/.

19. In Stanfield, "Hugh Herr: Beyond the Merely Human," Herr contends: "If the Paralympic committees do not ban advancements in technology, 100 years from now the jumping heights and running times and whatnot for the Paralympics will all be superior to that of the Olympics. It will make the Paralympics the preferred spectator sport—it will just be more exciting."

20. See "Pattie Maes and Pranav Mistry demo SixthSense," *TED*, www.ted.com/index.php/talks/pattie_maes_demos_the_sixth_sense.html, and "About," *sixthsense*, www.pranavmistry.com/projects/sixthsense/.

21. See, for example, ibid., plus Norman Chan, "TED 2009: The Sixth Sense Is Actually a Minority Report-like Internet Interface," *MaximumPC*, www.maximumpc.com/article/news/ted_2009_the_sixth_sense_actually_a_minorityreport_internet_interface.

22. "John Underkoffler points to the future of UI," *TED*, www.ted.com/talks/john_underkoffler_drive_3d_data_with_a_gesture.html.

23. Keith Kelsen, *Unleashing the Power of Digital Signage: Content Strategies for the 5th Screen* (Amsterdam: Elsevier, 2010), 219.

24. And not all of these technologies, whether software or hardware, necessarily work well enough to be useful, as is often the case with new technologies in their first release or two. As Mark Schatzker noted in a review of travel apps for *Condé Nast Traveler*, January 2011, 44, after actually using a number of them on a trip to Rome, "The problem is that we are in the early, heady days of travel apps and AR. It's three seconds after the big bang, metaphorically speaking, and the universe is still jumbled and chaotic."

25. If movies were the first screen, TV the second, personal computers the third, mobile phones and PDAs the fourth, and digital signage the fifth—see Kelsen, *Unleashing the Power of Digital Signage* —then consider the retina as the zeroth screen.

26. Few have also followed in the footsteps of Steve Mann, a professor at the University of Toronto who helped found the Wearable Computers group at the MIT Media Lab, who has worn a computer that mediates his vision since the early 1980s. See Steve Mann with Hal Niedzviecki, *Cyborg: Digital Destiny and Human Possibility in the Age of the Wearable Computer* (Toronto: Doubleday Canada, 2001). Mann believes his "Mediated Reality" differs from Augmented Reality, as least as it was thought of at the time, but it readily fits within the parameters of this realm.

27. Quoted in Liz Karagianis, "Climbing Higher," *SPECTRVM*, Fall 2010, 5.

4. Alternate Reality

1. Jane McGonigal, "The Puppet Master Problem: Design for Real-World, Mission-Based Gaming," in Pat Harrigan and Noah Wardrip-Fruin, editors, *Second Person: Role-Playing and Story in Games and Playable Media* (Cambridge, Massachusetts: MIT Press, 2007), 251–2. The name *I Love Bees* derived from the point of first contact: a jar of honey a few prominent people received in the mail containing letters that spelled the title phrase, which sent people to the supposed beekeeping site www.ilovebees.com, at which something was obviously not right (an effect that still remains active long after the game was completed, at least as of our last access).

2. See "Alternate Reality Games," *Sean Stewart,* www.seanstewart.org/interactive/args/. A great resource on ARGs can be found in Adam Martin, Brooke Thompson, and Tom Chatfield, editors, "2006 Alternate Reality Games White Paper," *The IGDA Alternate Reality Games SIG,* archives.igda.org/arg/resources/IGDA-AlternateReality Games-Whitepaper-2006.pdf.

3. Henry Jenkins, "Game Design as Narrative Architecture," in Noah Wardrop-Fruin and Pat Harrigan, editors, *First Person: New Media as Story, Performance, and Game* (Cambridge, Massachusetts: MIT Press, 2004), 128.

4. See McGonigal, "The Puppet Master Problem," and "A Real Little Game: The Performance of Belief in Pervasive Play," *Digital Games Research Association (DiGRA) "Level Up" Conference Proceedings,* November 2003, www.avantgame.com/MCGO NIGAL%20A%20Real%20Little%20Game%20DiGRA%202003.pdf.

5. "Games Now Playing," *ARGNet: Alternate Reality Gaming Network,* www.argn.com/now_playing/.

6. Note that such elements add a degree of material substance, or Matter, to the experience. As mentioned in Chapter 1, "Cosmos Incogniti," experiences often bleed into other realms, adding elements of other variables than the defining ones for that realm. This will be fully explored in Chapter 11, "Offering Depiction," with Alternate Reality as a particular example, as experiences within it seem to permeate boundaries more readily than those of most other realms.

7. "Beyond the Fourth Wall," *Sean Stewart,* www.seanstewart.org.

8. "Disney's Kim Possible World Showcase Adventure," *Walt Disney World Resort,* disneyworld.disney.go.com/parks/epcot/attractions/kim-possible/.

9. Markus Montola, "Games and Pervasive Games," 12, in Markus Montola, Jaakko Stenros, and Annika Waern, *Pervasive Games: Theory and Design: Experiences on the Boundary Between Life and Play* (Amsterdam: Morgan Kaufmann Publishers, 2009).

10. Ibid., 12 (capitalization deleted), 14, and 13, respectively. Note that he and his fellow editors treat ARGs as a subset of pervasive games, not the other way around as we do. This view arises from thinking of pervasive gaming arising more from the live action role-playing games (LARPs) of Warped Reality, discussed in Chapter 5, "Warped Reality," than from the computer games of Virtuality as discussed in this chapter. ARG designer Sean Stewart wrote the foreword, and on xiii he incorporates both approaches by defining pervasive games as "entertainments that leap off the board, console or screen and into your real life."

11. *SCVNGR,* www.scvngr.com.

12. Quoted in David Segal, "Just Manic Enough: Seeking the Perfect Entrepreneur," *New York Times,* September 19, 2010.

13. "LocoMatrix—GPS gaming for everyone," *LocoMatrix,* www.locomatrix.com.

14. Ibid. See also the "active urban games" of *Encounter,* which asks if you are "ready to jump into the world of real adventures?" at en.cx.

15. "Welcome to Geocaching," *Geocaching—The Official Global GPS Cache Hunt Site,* www.geocaching.com.

16. "Team Building Events," *geoteaming,* geoteaming.com.

17. "What's a GoCar?" *GoCar Tours,* www.gocartours.com/pages/what-is-a-gocar.html.

18. "DigiWall—Takes fun to new heights!" *DigiWall,* www.digiwall.se/experience/.

19. Tom Chatfield, *Fun Inc.: Why Gaming Will Dominate the Twenty-First Century* (New York: Pegasus Books, 2010), 52. He goes on to add, "This is true of all art and media to some extent."

20. Gary Hayes, "Future of Location Based Augmented Reality Story Games," *Personalizemedia,* October 25, 2010, www.personalizemedia.com/future-of-location-based-augmented-reality-story-games.

21. "timescope (2005)," *ART+COM,* www.artcom.net/index.php?option=com_acprojects&page=6&id=38&Itemid=115&details=0&lang=en.

22. Peter Wayner, "When All the World's a Staged Game," *New York Times,* November 11, 2009.

23. "Jane McGonigal: Gaming Can Make a Better World," *TED,* www.ted.com/talks/jane_mcgonigal_gaming_can_make_a_better_world.html.

24. See *World Without Oil* at www.worldwithoutoil.com.

25. "Superstruct FAQ," *Institute for the Future,* www.iftf.org/node/2096.

26. Jane McGonigal, "Making Alternate Reality the New Business Reality," *Harvard Business Review,* February 2008, 29. Note that despite the reference here (and others elsewhere) to ARGs as a genre of "entertainment," they are not true entertainment experiences marked by passive-absorption, but more escapist experiences in which the individual is actively immersed. The best of them, for most players, surely hit the "sweet spot" between the four aspects of experiences discussed briefly in Chapter 13, "From Design to Deployment," and in detail in B. Joseph Pine II and James H. Gilmore, *The Experience Economy,* updated edition (Boston: Harvard Business Review Press, 2011), Chapter 2, 41–64.

27. McGonigal, ibid. See her full-length treatment of this topic, *Reality Is Broken: Why Games Make Us Better and How They Can Change the World* (New York: The Penguin Press HC, 2011).

28. This point is further made by David Edery and Ethan Mollick, *Changing the Game: How Video Games Are Transforming the Future of Business* (Upper Saddle River, New Jersey: Pearson Education, 2009), 127: "ARGs possess qualities that make them uniquely powerful for increasing the ability of employees and companies to deal with unusual events. First, ARGs are interwoven with reality—players interact with the ARG using the same tools that they use every day. . . . ARGs also unfold over long periods, allowing players to experience a scenario from the first day through final resolution. Committing a little time each day to an ongoing ARG allows employees to effectively train while they work. And, most important, a good ARG is both fun and deeply immersive, creating a believable world in which individuals want to solve problems and resolve mysteries. A good ARG can lead entire teams to voluntarily train themselves and push their co-workers to improve."

29. Construction equipment also provides a great (and play-full) consumer experience at Dig This in Steamboat Springs, Colorado, "the *first ever* heavy equipment play arena in the United States"; see *Dig This,* www.digthis.info/#Home.

30. For a discussion of how many organizations of learning use ARGs, see "ARGs in institutions: museums, libraries, schools, and beyond," *Jeff Watson,* remotedevice. net/blog/args-in-institutions.

5. Warped Reality

1. Mihaly Csikszentmihalyi, *Flow: The Psychology of Optimal Experience* (New York: HarperPerennial, 1990), 66.

2. Ibid., 67.

3. "List of historical reenactment groups," *Wikipedia,* en.wikipedia.org/wiki/ List_of_historical_reenactment_groups.

4. For a great discussion of LARPs and other such imaginary realms, including some virtual, see Ethan Gilsdorf, *Fantasy Freaks and Gaming Geeks: An Epic Quest for Reality Among Role Players, Online Gamers, and Other Dwellers of Imaginary Realms* (Guilford, Connecticut: The Lyons Press, 2009).

5. Unfortunately for this golfer (Joe), the course's website at www.oakhurstlinks .com indicates it is no longer open to the public since 2007. We still love it as an example.

6. Peter Laundy, "That's it! Rocketing new business ideas into implementation," *Doblin,* unpublished essay.

7. See "Historical Preenactment Society," *Facebook,* www.facebook.com/group .php?gid=18669064520.

8. "What Is Vintage Base Ball," *Vintage Base Ball Association,* www.vbba.org/ Main/What%20Is%20Vintage%20Base%20Ball.htm.

9. Doris Kearns Goodwin, cited in Louis D. Rubin, Jr., editor, *The Quotable Baseball Fanatic* (New York: The Lyons Press, 2000), 137.

10. Christopher Caldwell, "Games prey on your mind," *Financial Times,* March 12, 2010. The quotes are from problem gamblers cited by Natasha Dow Schüll in "Digital Gambling: The Coincidence of Desire and Design," *The Annals of the American Academy of Political and Social Science,* vol. 597, 2005, 65–81.

11. Sally Harrison-Pepper, *Drawing a Circle in the Square: Street Performing in New York's Washington Square Park* (Jackson: University of Mississippi Press, 1990), 71.

12. Csikszentmihalyi, *Flow,* quoted in Michel Benamou and Charles Caramello, *Performance in Postmodern Culture* (Madison: Coda Press, 1977), 33.

13. Thomas Hylland Eriksen, *The Tyranny of the Moment: Fast and Slow Time in the Information Age* (London: Pluto Press, 2001), 2–3.

14. Ibid., 6.

15. Aaron M. Sackett, Leif D. Nelson, Tom Meyvis, Benjamin A. Converse, and Anna L. Sackett, "You're Having Fun When Time Flies: The Hedonic Consequences of Subjective Time Progression," *Psychological Science,* November 30, 2009, pss.sagepub. com/content/early/2009/11/25/0956797609354832.full.pdf+html.

16. "Time flew by . . . I must have been enjoying myself," *BPS Research Digest,* January 27, 2010, bps-research-digest.blogspot.com/2010/01/time-flew-by-i-must-have-been-enjoying.html.

17. In the story of *Somewhere in Time* (1980), based on the novel *Bid Time Return* by Richard Matheson (New York: Ballantine Books, 1976), playwright Richard Collier (played by the late Christopher Reeve) goes back in time to meet, and then falls in love with, the beautiful actress Elise McKenna (played by the beautiful actress Jane Seymour). The time travel is accomplished more or less by sheer force of will within surroundings that completely recreate the past timeframe. The climax of the movie occurs when Richard pulls out of his pocket a single, solitary penny from the present day, which destroys the illusion and brings him back to the present day. Experience designers should similarly look after every single, solitary detail in staging their experiences lest belief be destroyed.

6. Virtuality

1. "Colossal Cave Adventure," *Wikipedia,* en.wikipedia.org/wiki/Colossal_Cave_Adventure. This reproduces the exact spacing (within lines, such as the extra space after "BUILDING," and across lines, such as the extra line after the computer game's response). The only user input here are the three commands, ".RUN ADV11," "YES," and "GO IN."

2. The level of agency in the *Colossal Cave Adventure* is still pretty primitive, limited as it is to simple choices that branch off in different directions. In "Response," in Noah Wardrop-Fruin and Pat Harrigan, editors, *First Person: New Media as Story, Performance, and Game* (Cambridge, Massachusetts: MIT Press, 2004), 314, Brenda Laurel says of interactive fiction in general, "There is something deeply unsatisfying about the lack of significance in one's actions as a player; that is, the player knows that he/she is merely selecting one of many preordained 'pathways' and its therefore exercising no more agency than a rat running a maze. To the discerning player, branching architectures lack vitality in the same way as hypertexts."

3. It seems to us that not all Virtuality-based experiences are interactive; movies and books, for example, and at least some virtual art are esthetic or entertainment experiences, and hence passive in nature, which also lessens their agency.

4. Byron Reeves and Clifford Nass, *The Media Equation: How People Treat Computers, Television, and NewMedia Like Real People and Places* (Cambridge, England: Cambridge University Press, 1996), 5.

5. Plato, *The Republic,* translated by Benjamin Jowett (Mineola, New York: Dover Publications, Inc., 2000), Book VII, 177–202.

6. Henry Jenkins makes this point in "Game Design as Narrative Architecture," in *First Person,* 118–130, as does Nicole Lazzaro, in "Why We Play Games: Four Keys to More Emotion Without Story," *XEODesign,* www.xeodesign.com/xeodesign_why weplaygames.pdf, 4, who notes that immersion is often created with less than full fidelity, as "ambiguity, incompleteness, and detail combine to create a living world."

7. Visual representation is a two-edged sword, of course. Sometimes, as with reading, we are better left to our own imagination than to have images made explicit, which can impair or stunt that imagination. On the other hand, sometimes images can fulfill our imagination, letting it bloom and take flight.

8. Samuel Taylor Coleridge, *Biographia Literaria,* from *The Major Works* (New York: Oxford University Press, 2000; originally published in 1817), 314.

9. Janet H. Murray, *Hamlet on the Holodeck: The Future of Narrative in Cyberspace* (New York: The Free Press, 1997), 110.

10. Astute readers will note the high degree of similarity between this discussion and the section "Create Belief" in James H. Gilmore and B. Joseph Pine II, *Authenticity: What Consumers Really Want* (Boston: Harvard Business Press, 2007), 108–110, from which it is borrowed and edited. This shows the tight connection between Virtuality and what we call there Fake-real offerings, offerings that create a *fake reality*—a Virtuality—by creating belief.

11. J. R. R. Tolkien, "On Fairy-Stories," in "Tree and Leaf" in *The Tolkien Reader* (New York: Ballantine Books, 1966), 73 and 60, respectively. Note that Tolkien calls such story-makers "sub-creators" because they create in the image (and imagination) of the Lord of Creation, creating worlds secondary to the world of Reality.

12. Although many businesses have given up on *Second Life* in particular, as a consumer experience it continues to chug along nicely, thank you. According to Erik Sass, "Second Life Chugs Along," *The Social Graf*, July 29, 2010, available at www.mediapost .com/publications/?fa=Articles.showArticle&art_aid=132912&nid=117095, active users "increased from about 25,000 in 2005 to roughly 700,000 in 2009–2010" but more importantly they are spending even more time and money on the site.

13. For understanding the nature of virtual worlds in general, and *Second Life* in particular, and why so very many people spend so very many hours there, we highly recommend Tom Boellstorff, *Coming of Age in Second Life: An Anthropologist Explores the Virtually Human* (Princeton: Princeton University Press, 2008).

14. Edward Castronova, *Exodus to the Virtual World: How Online Fun Is Changing Reality* (New York: Palgrave Macmillan, 2007), 7. For more on time and attention as the currency of experiences, see Gilmore and Pine, *Authenticity*, 172–177, and David W. Norton and B. Joseph Pine II, "Unique experiences: disruptive innovations offer customers more 'time well spent,'" *Strategy & Leadership*, vol. 37, no. 6, 2009, pp. 4–9.

15. Elizabeth Olson, "For FarmVille Players, a Crop from a Real Organic Farm," *New York Times*, July 15, 2010.

16. One key to staying in flow, well understood in gaming but not so much in other aspects of Virtuality, is sub-second response time. Anything but very rapid response time takes us out of what we're doing, destroys our concentration, and gets us thinking (either about the lack of response or other things on our mind). See the IBM white paper, "The Economic Value of Rapid Response Time," by Walter J. Doherty and Ahrvind J. Thadani, GE20-0752-0, November 1982, also available at www.vm.ibm.com/ devpages/jelliott/evrrt.html.

17. Boellstorff, *Coming of Age in Second Life*, 129.

18. "Globe Genie," *Joe McMichael*, web.mit.edu/~jmcmicha/www/.

19. See "Projects," *CyArk*, archive.cyark.org/project-world.

20. Michael Kimmelman, "Scots Aim Lasers at Landmarks," *New York Times*, November 4, 2009.

21. Although virtual, it is a real embassy, inaugurated simultaneously in both SL and RL on May 22, 2007; see "Virtual Embassy—Maldives," *Diplomacy Island*, www .diplomacy.edu/DiplomacyIsland/Embassies/display.asp?Topic=Maldives.

22. In *Upsizing the Individual in the Downsized Organization: Managing in the Wake of Reengineering, Globalization, and Overwhelming Technological Change* (Reading, Massachusetts: Addison-Wesley, 1994), 103–8, Bob Johansen points out the need to design work spaces for Same time/Different time and Same place/Different place. It seems

Same matter/Different matter should also be considered, which we could equate to Real person/Avatar.

23. See "CityOne," *IBM INNOV8,* www-01.ibm.com/software/solutions/soa/innov8/cityone/index.html. Note that Smarter Planet is a Mirrored Virtuality initiative enabling companies to use sensors to track their activities and the effect of those activities on the world.

24. Quoted in Steve Silberman, "The War Room," *Wired,* September 2004, 155.

25. See "Post-Traumatic Stress Disorder Assessment and Treatment (PTSD)," *Institute for Creative Technologies,* ict.usc.edu/projects/ptsd/C45, and Benedict Carey, "Virtual Healing for the Real World," *New York Times,* November 23, 2010.

26. Silberman, "The War Room," 154.

27. "Institute for Creative Technologies," USC Institute for Creative Technologies, ict.usc.edu.

28. "America's Army Medic Training Helps Save a Life," *America's Army,* forum.americasarmy.com/viewtopic.php?t=271086.

29. James Glanz and Alan Schwarz, "From the 'Avatar' Playbook, Pro Teams Adopt 3-D Imaging," *New York Times,* October 3, 2010.

30. Byron Reeves, Thomas W. Malone, and Tony O'Driscoll, "Leadership's Online Labs," *Harvard Business Review,* May 2008, 66.

31. Karl M. Kapp and Tony O'Driscoll, *Learning in 3D: Adding a New Dimension to Enterprise Learning and Collaboration* (San Francisco: Pfeiffer, 2010), 19.

32. Byron Reeves and J. Leighton Read, *Total Engagement: Using Games and Virtual Worlds to Change the Way People Work and Businesses Compete* (Boston: Harvard Business Press, 2009), vii.

33. Ibid, 5.

34. Jaap Bloem, Menno van Doorn, and Sander Duivestein bring this conversational and connecting aspect of the Web together as "the glorious age for Me-Media," in *Me the Media: Rise of the Conversation Society: Past, Present and Future of the Third Media Revolution* (Bariet, The Netherlands: VINT Research Institute of Sogeti, 2009), 12, also available at www.methemedia.com/download/.

35. Frances Cairncross, *The Death of Distance: How the Communications Revolution Is Changing Our Lives* (Boston: Harvard Business School Press, 2001, with the first edition published in 1997), 23–24. She was actually citing awed Victorians who believed that the telegraph meant "the annihilation of space and time." Ah, the good old days.

36. David Weinberger, *Small Pieces Loosely Joined: A Unified Theory of the Web* (Cambridge, Massachusetts: Perseus Publishing, 2002), 24–5.

37. Ibid., 164, Weinberger notes that "words have always built worlds, just as they build the Web," and encourages his readers on 164–5 to dive into *Huckleberry Finn*: "Now you're in the world of a fourteen-year-old boy floating down the Mississippi on a raft. The sky, the clouds, the sound of the river, the way a campfire carves out a warm spot in a moonless night, all of this becomes more present to you than the world your body is occupying as you read. The clang of the phone feels like it's calling you back from another world. Words are *Matrix*-like in their ability to create a world. And because the world that words build is constructed entirely out of meanings, not atoms, the meanings can't slide off that world."

38. Anne Friedberg makes the same point in *The Virtual Window: From Alberti to Microsoft* (Cambridge, Massachusetts: MIT Press, 2006), 7–12, noting that the term

long predates the rise of digital technology. Friedberg, 10, quotes Brian Massumi, in "Line Parable for the Virtual (On the Superiority of the Analog)," in John Beckmann, editor, *The Virtual Dimension* (Princeton: Princeton Architectural Press, 1998), 309: "Nothing is more destructive for the thinking of the virtual than equating it with the digital. All arts and technologies envelop the virtual, in one way or another." Massumi, 306, asserts that "imagination is the mode of thought most precisely suited to this vagueness of the virtual," and Friedberg herself, 11, adds that "once the term 'virtual' is free from its enforced association with the 'digital,' it can more accurately operate as a marker of an ontological, not a media-specific, property"; that is, as its own independent dimension of experience.

39. In "Another Time, Another Space: Virtual Worlds, Myths and Imagination," *Journal of Virtual Worlds Research*, vol. 1, no. 1, July 2008, 2, Maria Beatrice Bittarello also asserts (citing others before her) that "virtual worlds have always existed in literature, religion, and art."

40. Pierre Lévy, translated by Robert Bononno, *Becoming Virtual: Reality in the Digital Age* (New York: Plenum Trade, 1998), 47.

41. Ibid., 51.

42. Murray, *Hamlet on the Holodeck*, 110.

43. Celia Pearce and Artemesia (her avatar), *Communities at Play: Emergent Cultures in Multiplayer Games and Virtual Worlds* (Cambridge, MA: The MIT Press, 2009), 20.

44. In addition to our own research and experiences, these two lists of attributes draw from ones given in Pearce, ibid, 18–20; Castronova, *Exodus to the Virtual World*, 45–62; Reeves and Read, *Total Engagement*, 27–29 and 61–90; and Murray, *Hamlet on the Holodeck*, 71–90 and 126–129.

45. The possibilities here are discussed in Chapter 7, "Augmented Virtuality."

46. "The ultimate game gear," *The Economist Technology Quarterly*, September 8, 2007, 13.

7. Augmented Virtuality

1. See—and we do mean go to the Web and see it—"AR Business Card," *Augmatic*, augmatic.co.uk/vid2.html.

2. American Heart Association and Nintendo, activeplaynow.com.

3. "Toy Island Partners with EA to Develop Innovative Sporting Goods," *Toy Island*, www.toyisland.com/press_release_ea.cfm.

4. Reena Jana, "The (Game) Doctor Is In," *BusinessWeek*, March 3, 2008, 70.

5. "Boy racers," *The Economist*, January 7, 2006, 56.

6. Quoted in Viv Bernstein, "Simulated Racing Gives a Real Advantage to Drivers," *New York Times*, March 4, 2007.

7. Quoted in video, "Virtual Reality made easy," *Product*, www.ps-tech.com/product.

8. Dom Nguyen, "EyeToy Takes Off," *Wired*, August 2004, 60.

9. Respectively, all from the *New York Times*: Ashlee Vance, "With Kinect, Microsoft Aims for a Game Changer," October 23, 2010; David Pogue, "Invitation to Play, and Sweat," November 4, 2010; and Seth Schiesel, "A Home System Leaves Hand Controls in the Dust," November 4, 2010.

10. Mark Twain, *The Adventures of Tom Sawyer* (New York: Barnes & Noble Classics, 2003; originally published in 1876), 19–20.

11. Adam L. Penenberg, "Everyone's a Player," *Fast Company,* December 2010–January 2011, 140.

12. Quoted in Steve Lohr, "Computers That See You, Read You and Even Tell You to Wash," *New York Times,* January 2, 2011.

13. Jaron Lanier, "On the Threshold of the Avatar Era," *Wall Street Journal,* October 23–24, 2010.

14. Ibid.

15. Claire Cain Miller, "Technology Designers Focus on the Fingertips," *The International Herald Tribune,* September 2, 2010, and Tom Simonite, "T. Scott Saponas, 29: Detecting Complex Gestures with an Armband Interface," *Technology Review,* September/October 2010, 49, respectively.

16. See "Gallery," *OpenKinect,* openkinect.org/wiki/Gallery.

17. White paper, "Harnessing Human Touch," *Immersion,* 1, www.immersion.com /docs/harnessing-human-touch.pdf.

8. Physical Virtuality

1. Give up? We discuss the unlimited nature of LEGO building bricks in the Afterword, "To Infinity and Beyond."

2. For a resource on extending CAD with Computer-Aided Manufacturing (CAM) and on to an entire digital factory, see Yves Coze, Nicolas Kawski, Torsten Kulka, Pascal Sire, Philippe Sottocasa, and Jaap Bloem (editors), *Virtual Concept > Real Profit with Digital Manufacturing and Simulation* (Bariet, The Netherlands: Dassault Systèmes and Sogeti, 2009).

3. Quoted in "A factory on your desk," *The Economist Technology Quarterly,* September 5, 2009, 27.

4. Quoted in Ashlee Vance, "A Technology Sets Inventors Free to Dream," *New York Times,* September 14, 2010.

5. Susan Smith, "3D Printing Lets FigurePrints Play Outside the Game," *Desktop Engineering,* March 13, 2008, available at www.zcorp.com/documents/216_2008-0313 -Desktop%20Eng-3DP%20Lets%20Figureprints%20Play%20Outside.pdf.

6. *Deeplocal,* www.deeplocal.com.

7. Cited, if not necessarily quoted, in "Cyber Grand Prix: Wieden + Kennedy for Nike's 'Chalkbot,' DDB Sweden for VW's 'Fun Theory' . . . ," *mikidevic's posterous blog,* June 24, 2010, mikidevic.posterous.com/cyber-grand-prix-wieden-kennedy-for-nikes-cha.

8. Spencer Morgan, "Scent Branding Sweeps the Fragrance Industry, " *Bloomberg BusinessWeek,* June 16, 2010, www.businessweek.com/magazine/content/10_26/ b4184085987358_page_2.htm.

9. The field was created by physical chemist Hervé This; see "How Molecular Gastronomy Works," *HowStuffWorks,* www.howstuffworks.com/molecular-gastronomy .htm/printable.

10. See Daniel L. Cohen, Jeffrey I. Lipton, Meredith Cutler, Deborah Coulter, Anthony Vesco, and Hod Lipson, "Hydrocolloid Printing: A Novel Platform for Customized Food Production," Solid Freeform Fabrication Symposium (SFF'09), August 3–5

2009, available at ccsl.mae.cornell.edu/sites/default/files/SFF09_Cohen1_0.pdf. A summary of the research paper with pictures of sample output can be found at "Printing Food," *Cornell Computational Synthesis Laboratory,* ccsl.mae.cornell.edu/node/194.

11. "Making a bit of me," *The Economist,* February 20, 2010, 77–8.

12. Quoted in "Organovo Develops First Commercial 3D Bio-Printer for Manufacturing Human Tissue and Organs," *News,* www.organovo.com/news/press/17.

13. Stan Davis, *Future Perfect* (Reading, Massachusetts: Addison-Wesley, 1987), 138–190. Davis did so in the chapter immediately after the one entitled "No-Matter" that inspired me (Joe) to conceive of the Multiverse. Long before that, however, Davis inspired my own book on this subject of Mass Customization, and the two concepts converge here in Physical Virtuality. (If I ever run out of ideas, Davis had three other chapters plus an Aftermath and Beforemath in that seminal book.)

14. B. Joseph Pine II, *Mass Customization: The New Frontier in Business Competition* (Boston: Harvard Business School Press, 1993).

15. The decreasing number of exemplars in each category is roughly indicative of the decreasing number of total companies mass customizing up the Progression of Economic Value, including none in transformations that we know of.

16. Quoted in Mikal Belicove, "Mass Customizers Hope for 8 Million Facebook Impressions," *Entrepreneur Daily Dose,* August 5, 2010, blog.entrepreneur.com/2010/08/mass-customizers-hope-for-8-million-facebook-impressions.php.

17. "All Milk or Sugar Products," *MilkOrSugar Custom Shopping,* www.milkorsugar.com/custom_made_products.

18. Commodities, being fungible, cannot be materially changed (merely refined or processed) and thus cannot be customized. If it is tangible and you can customize it, it qualifies as a good.

19. *Configurator Database,* www.configurator-database.com.

20. See "Visual Configurator: The Killer App for Mass Customization," *Scene7,* available at www1.scene7.com/registration/s7visconfigwp.asp?src=Scene7VC_WP_blog.

21. "Rickshaw Bag Customizer," *RickshawBagworks,* www.rickshawbags.com/customize/custom-bag.

22. *Hanulneotech,* www.arhunt.com.

23. Quoted in Joey Seiler, "Ridemakerz, Now in Open Beta, Making the Virtual Real," *EngageDigital,* April 2, 2009, www.engagedigital.com/2009/04/02/ridemakerz-now-in-open-beta-making-the-virtual-real.

24. Joann Muller, "How to Build A Mountain," *Forbes,* October 27, 2003, 87.

25. Quoted in ibid.

26. "About Us," *Ponoko,* www.ponoko.com/about/the-big-idea.

27. "Sign up," *Shapeways,* www.shapeways.com/register.

28. Clive Thompson, "A One-of-a-Kind Revolution," *Wired,* March 2009, 34.

29. Tim O'Reilly, "The Significance of Threadless.com," *O'Reilly Radar,* radar.oreilly.com/archives/2006/11/the-significanc.html.

30. Homaro Cantu calls his inkjet printer modified to print edible paper a "'food replicator' in homage to *Star Trek,*" according to Laura Goodall and Sandrine Ceurstemont, "Futuristic Food," *FirstScience,* www.firstscience.com/home/articles/technology/futuristic-food_1734.html.

31. Quoted in Kevin Maney, "Physics genius plans to make 'Star Trek' replicator a reality," *USA Today,* June 14, 2005.

32. "Neil Gershenfeld on Fab Labs," *TED,* www.ted.com/talks/neil_gershenfeld_on_fab_labs.html.

33. Neil Gershenfeld, *Fab: The Coming Revolution on Your Desktop—from Personal Computers to Personal Fabrication* (New York: Basic Books, 2007), 4. We return to the notion that the universe literally might be a computer in Chapter 12, "Third Spaces."

34. Bruce Sterling, "The Dream Factory," *Wired,* December 2004, 88.

35. Quoted in Clive Thompson, "The Dream Factory," *Wired,* September 2005, 129. As you can tell, *Wired* magazine positively loves Physical Virtuality. In a piece *not* entitled "The Dream Factory," editor in chief Chris Anderson writes ("Atoms Are the New Bits," *Wired,* February 2010, 64): "All these digital trends have begun to play out in the world of atoms, too. The Web was just the proof of concept. Now the revolution hits the real world. In short, atoms are the new bits."

36. "Programmable Matter," *Defense Sciences Office,* www.darpa.mil/dso/thrusts/physci/newphys/program_matter/index.htm.

37. Gershenfeld, *Fab,* 42.

38. "Fab Academy Sites," *Fab Academy,* fabacademy.org/index.php/fab-academy-sites.

39. Highly personal, not "personalized." Personalization, properly understood, is a subset of customization. Think of monogrammed towels or cuffs, custom-printed T-shirts, and the like; all take a standard, off-the-shelf product and then *personalize* it to the individual. It is *cosmetic customization,* one of four different types, where the function of the offering remains standard while the outward *representation* of it is customized; see James H. Gilmore and B. Joseph Pine II, "The Four Faces of Mass Customization," *Harvard Business Review,* vol. 75, no. 1, January/February 1997, 91–101.

40. Quoted in Thompson, "The Dream Factory."

41. This model of the four stages in the evolution of business competition—with Continuous Invention a fifth stage mapped back onto Invention at a higher level—can be found most fully in B. Joseph Pine II, "You're Only As Agile As Your Customers Think," *Agility & Global Competition,* vol. 2, no. 2, Spring 1998, 24–35. It was originally developed by Bart Victor and Andrew C. Boynton; see their *Invented Here: Maximizing Your Organization's Internal Growth and Profitability* (Boston: Harvard Business School Press, 1998) as well as B. Joseph Pine II, Bart Victor, and Andrew C. Boynton, "Making Mass Customization Work," *Harvard Business Review,* vol. 71, no. 5, September–October 1993, 108–119.

42. Gershenfeld, *Fab,* 17.

43. Some of these examples are from Rhymer Rigby, "Fancy a Duff Beer? The real market for fake brands," *Financial Times,* August 23, 2010.

44. Quoted in Jennifer Reingold, "Weird Science," *Fast Company,* May 2006, 49.

45. Josh Dean, "Saul Griffith's House of Cool Ideas," *Inc.,* February 2010, 75.

9. Mirrored Virtuality

1. David Gelernter, *Mirror Worlds: or the Day Software Puts the Universe in a Shoebox . . . How It Will Happen and What It Will Mean* (New York: Oxford University Press, 1992), 3.

2. Wade Roush, "Second Earth," *Technology Review,* July/August 2007, 40. An expanded version of the article is available at www.technologyreview.com/communi cations/18911/page1/.

3. *Twinity,* www.twinity.com/en.

4. Sean Koehl, "From the labs: Virtual Yellowstone in ScienceSim," *Intel Software Network,* January 25, 2010, software.intel.com/en-us/blogs/2010/01/25/from-the-labs -virtual-yellowstone-in-sciencesim/.

5. Anand Giridharadas, "Africa's Gift to Silicon Valley: How to Track a Crisis," *New York Times,* March 14, 2010.

6. Roush, "Second Earth," 41.

7. See Gelertner, *Mirror Worlds,* 6 and 22 in particular.

8. Gelernter, *Mirror Worlds,* 5.

9. *Google Flu Trends,* www.google.org/flutrends/.

10. "How does this work?" *Google Flu Trends,* www.google.org/flutrends/about/ how.html.

11. Jeremy Ginsberg, Matthew H. Mohebbi, Rajan S. Patel, Lynnette Brammer, Mark S. Smolinski, and Larry Brilliant, "Detecting Influenza Epidemics Using Search Engine Query Data," *Nature,* 457, 1012–1014, available at www.nature.com/nature/ journal/v457/n7232/full/nature07634.html.

12. www.google.com/trends and www.google.com/insights/search/#, respectively.

13. Christopher Caldwell, "Government by search engine," *Financial Times,* October 16–17, 2010.

14. Hyunyoung Choi and Hal Varian, "Predicting the Present with Google Trends," *ii,* static.googleusercontent.com/external_content/untrusted_dlcp/www.google.com/ en/us/googleblogs/pdfs/google_predicting_the_present.pdf.

15. "Products," *Ambient Devices,* www.ambientdevices.com/cat/products.html.

16. *Trendsmap,* trendsmap.com.

17. At the exact time of the first draft of this chapter—11: 36AM on Friday morning, July 23, 2010—the particularly hot term in Minnesota is #smbmsp, the Twitter tag for Social Media Breakfast—Minneapolis/Saint Paul, which this morning conducted a session on the topic of "Small Business Gets Social" at Deluxe Corporate Headquarters in Shoreview. Ibid. and *Social Media Breakfast—Minneapolis/Saint Paul,* smbmsp .ning.com (both accessed, naturally, at 11:36AM on July 23, 2010).

18. In an extra sidebar to Roush's article online, available at www.technologyre view.com/communications/18911/page7/, Gelernter says that when he wrote the book, "the response was, 'Let's get serious. We know you're an imaginative guy, and it's an interesting book because it's about effective programming tools, but the general framework was crazy.'" But that was before the rise of the World Wide Web. Gelernter says now he was being too conservative: "Not that the web was anything like mirror worlds in detail. But there was one very important thing—that institutions in the real world would be mirrored in the cybersphere, that I would be able to visit a software version of the DMV or the hospital or the university—and the web really did do that."

19. Peter Cashmore, "10 Web trends to watch in 2010," *CNN.com,* www.cnn.com/ 2009/TECH/12/03/cashmore.web.trends.2010/index.html.

20. "'Nowism': Why currency is the new currency," *trendwatching.com's November 2009 Trend Briefing,* trendwatching.com/trends/nowism/.

21. Quoted in Clive Thompson, "Live in the Moment," *Wired,* October 2009, 46. Elsewhere, in "Beyond Realtime Search: The Dawning of Ambient Streams," *EdoSegal.com,* www.edosegal.com/?p=15, Segal says that real-time search is a misnomer and argues for what he calls "ambient streams": "These are streams of information bubbling up in realtime, which seek us out, surround us, and inform us. They are like a fireplace bathing us in ambient infoheat. I believe that users will not go to a page and type in a search in a search box. Rather the information will appear to them in an ambient way on a range of devices and through different experiences."

22. Gina Kolata, "New Tools for Helping Heart Patients," *New York Times,* June 22, 2010.

23. Gary Wolf, "The Data-Driven Life," *New York Times Sunday Magazine,* May 2, 2010.

24. See *The Quantified Self,* www.quantifiedself.com.

25. Wolf, "The Data-Driven Life." Note that in the article the middle paragraph here actually came before the first paragraph.

26. Gordon Bell and Jim Gemmell, *Total Recall: How the E-Memory Revolution Will Change Everything* (New York: Dutton, 2009), 13.

27. Ibid., 23. Many argue that with all of us leaving a trail of bits online, we also need a way of digitally *forgetting* the past. See in particular Viktor Mayer-Schönberger, *Delete: The Virtue of Forgetting in the Digital Age* (Princeton: Princeton University Press, 2009); Jeffrey Rosen, "The End of Forgetting," *New York Times Sunday Magazine,* July 25, 2010; and Stefan Sonvilla-Weiss, *(In)Visible: Learning to Act in the Metaverse* (New York: SpringerWeinNewYork, 2008), which refers to this possibility as a "kind of universal prosthetic memory." Bell himself, 20, states his digital record is for his personal use, recognizing the need for sharing personal information "cautiously, considering the trustworthiness of the individual recipients." "Public publishing," he continues, "is only for what I am glad to have the world associate with me—forever."

28. Gelernter, *Mirror Worlds,* 52. Interestingly, on pp 185 and 190–193 Gelernter writes of "Chronicle Streams," which his student Eric Freeman extended into the concept of "lifestreams"; see *Lifestreams Project Home Page,* cs-www.cs.yale.edu/homes/freeman/lifestreams.html.

29. Nancy Gioia, Ford's director of hybrid-vehicle programs, as quoted in Matthew Dolan, "Ford Device Stretches Gallons," *Wall Street Journal,* October 29, 2008. In *Fun Inc.: Why Gaming Will Dominate the Twenty-First Century* (New York: Pegasus Books, 2010), 161, Tom Chatfield points out the efficacy of gaming to the design of dashboards: "Because everything can be visualized and managed in real time, it allows people the kind of control over—and understanding of—complicated real environments that they have previously extended to virtual ones. If there's one thing that games have demonstrated over the last thirty years, it's that people have an extraordinary aptitude for managing the use of resources within real-time systems, so long as they have suitably clear data, visuals and interfaces—something the games industry has an unrivalled expertise in providing."

30. "Empathica Launches Mobile Reporting Solution for Multi-Unit Retailers," *Retail Customer Experience,* www.retailcustomerexperience.com/article/177886/Empathica-launches-mobile-reporting-solution-for-multi-unit-retailers.

10. Multiverse Excursion

1. Famously but elusively. We cannot find the original source of the quote, although it is all over the Web and you can find it without an original citation in "Carver Mead," *Wikipedia,* en.wikipedia.org/wiki/Carver_Mead. Our first exposure to it, also without citation, was atop the preface to George Gilder, *Microcosm: The Quantum Revolution in Economics and Technology* (New York: Simon and Schuster, 1989), 11. Not coincidentally, Gilder's book is a wonderful explication of the capabilities of digital technology past, present, and future. Well, "future" from the perspective of 1989 in the hands of a master prognosticator.

2. Michael S. Schmidt, "To Pack a Stadium, Provide Video Better Than TV," *New York Times,* July 28, 2010.

3. T. S. Eliot, "Little Gidding," quoted in *The Four Quartets, Wikiquote,* en.wikiquote.org/wiki/The_Four_Quartets.

4. We note that one electronics retailer, Best Buy, partnered with Shopkick on its app that identifies consumers as they walk in, and then offers them discounts; see Jefferson Graham, "Shopkick app can lead you to discounts and sales," *USA Today,* August 11, 2010, www.usatoday.com/tech/products/2010-08-12-shopkick12_ST_N.htm. We did not include such functionality, because here we want to generate ideas that provide greater customer value, not commoditize ourselves through discounts.

5. Jena McGregor, "USAA's Battle Plan," *Bloomberg BusinessWeek,* March 1, 2010, 40.

6. Apple's iPod would be nothing without iTunes and Apple's business agreements with the owners holding the rights to the music, for example. Getting the business model right plays no small role in Apple's rise to become the largest provider of music to consumers. For more on business models, see Alexander Osterwalder and Yves Pigneur, *Business Model Generation: A Handbook for Visionaries, Game Changers, and Challengers* (Hoboken, New Jersey: John Wiley & Sons, 2010), a book to which Kim contributed.

7. For example, focusing your attention on a specific human capability, such as sensing, or even more specific yet to seeing, tunes your thinking into a narrower set of specific possibilities likely to conjure up more robust ideas across multiple rounds. And on the flipside, once you have generated that great idea to improve seeing, consider the possibilities to capitalize on this new sensing capability to improve performing, linking, and organizing capabilities as well.

11. Offering Depiction

1. Quoted in Daniel Terdiman, "How 'Avatar' may predict the future of virtual worlds," *CNET,* January 28, 2010, news.cnet.com/8301-13772_3-10443265-52.html. Paffendorf, one of the organizers of the Metaverse Roadmap mentioned in Chapter 12, "Third Spaces," adds, "It seems like even in pure virtual worlds, you always get pulled back to real world references" and concludes, "The real world wins, so all the augmented reality things are going to be especially compelling, because they're reality, but plus-plus."

2. "*Avatar* (2009 film)," *Wikipedia,* en.wikipedia.org/wiki/Avatar_(2009_film).

3. See "Gramophone Record," *Wikipedia,* en.wikipedia.org/wiki/Gramophone_record.

4. A record album sleeve or jacket is $12^3/_8 \times 12^3/_8$ inches, making it 153 square inches. A CD jewel case cover is just under twenty-five square inches.

5. "What's New in iTunes?" *Apple,* www.apple.com/itunes/whats-new/ (accessed May 21, 2010; it has changed since—as you might expect with something called "What's New"—with some of these same words on various other iTunes pages).

6. In the meantime, seeking to reduce the dependence on a specialized place, Cisco intends to make it possible for anyone with HDTV to participate in its TelePresence setup; see Peter Burrows, "Innovator: Martin De Beer," *Bloomberg BusinessWeek,* May 17–23, 2010, 38.

7. LEGO SERIOUS PLAY is in fact a small B2B practice, originally initiated by Professor Bart Victor of Vanderbilt University, where people examine their organizations, business models, and offerings by playing, seriously, with LEGO bricks. See "LEGO SERIOUS PLAY—Build Your Way to Better Business," *LEGO SERIOUS PLAY,* www.seriousplay.com.

12. Third Spaces

1. Alex Hill, Matt Bonner, Jacob Schiefer, and Blair MacIntyre, "ClearWorlds: Mixed-Reality Presence through Virtual Clearboards," *IEEE Pervasive Computing,* vol. 8, no. 3, July–September 2009, 56.

2. Bruce H. Thomas and Wayne Pickarski, "Through-Walls Collaboration" in ibid., 42.

3. Daniel Horn, Ewen Cheslack-Postava, Tahir Azim, Michael J. Freedman, and Philip Levis, "Scaling Virtual Worlds with a Physical Metaphor" in ibid., 50.

4. Joshua Lifton, Mathew Laibowitz, Drew Harry, Nan-Wei Gong, Manas Mittal, and Joseph A. Paradiso, "Metaphor and Manifestation—Cross-Reality with Ubiquitous Sensor/Actuator Networks" in ibid., 28.

5. Joseph A. Paradiso and James A. Landay, "Cross-Reality Environments" in ibid., 14–15.

6. We are of course inspired here by sociologist Ray Oldenburg's coining of the term "third place," a physical place set apart from home and work—such as pubs, taverns, cafes, and the like—where a person can interact with others he has come to know as members of the same community, in *The Great Good Place: Cafés, Coffee Shops, Community Centers, Beauty Parlors, General Stores, Bars, Hangouts and How They Get You through the Day* (New York: Marlowe & Company, 1997).

7. John Smart, Jamais Cascio, and Jerry Paffendorf, "Metaverse Roadmap: Pathways to the 3D Web," *Acceleration Studies Foundation,* 2007, www.metaverseroadmap.org/MetaverseRoadmapOverview.pdf, 4. Intriguingly, the 2×2 at the heart of the Metaverse Roadmap includes Augmented Reality, Mirror Worlds, and Virtual Worlds in the exact same relationship to each other as in the Multiverse (with the No-Matter arrow turned directly toward you to form a 2×2 on its digital substance side), with the only difference being Lifelogging instead of our Alternate Reality. As briefly mentioned in Chapter 9, "Mirrored Virtuality," we consider lifelogging to be a form of Mirrored Virtuality related to the "Quantified Self" and Gordon Bell's concept of "Total Recall."

8. See "YouTube Symphony Orchestra," *Wikipedia,* en.wikipedia.org/wiki/You Tube_Symphony_Orchestra. For the Carnegie Hall concert, see "Act One: YouTube Symphony Orchestra @ Carnegie Hall," *YouTube,* www.youtube.com/watch?v=ue JcRmfweSM and "Act Two: YouTube Symphony Orchestra @ Carnegie Hall," *YouTube,* www.youtube.com/watch?v=6cS653udPCM; for the mashup see "'The Internet Symphony Global Mash Up," *YouTube,* www.youtube.com/watch?v=oC4FAyg64OI.

9. Seth Schiesel, "Tragedy and Comedy, Starring Pac-Man," *New York Times,* July 16, 2010.

10. Seth Schiesel, "Motion, Sensitive," *New York Times,* November 28, 2010.

11. Ibid.

12. Elizabeth Svoboda, "Cellphonometry," *Fast Company,* November 2009, 60–62.

13. Sara Corbett, "Games Theory," *New York Times Magazine,* September 19, 2010, 54–61, 66–70; see also "Games lessons," *The Economist,* September 5, 2009, 86–87.

14. Brooks Barnes, "Disney Technology Tackles a Theme-Park Headache: Lines," *New York Times,* December 28, 2010

15. This relates to Henry Jenkins' concept of "transmedia storytelling." In *Convergence Culture: Where Old and New Media Collide* (New York: New York University Press, 2006), 95, he describes how a "transmedia story unfolds across multiple media platforms, with each new text making a distinctive and valuable contribution to the whole." Jesse Schell also provides a good discussion of transmedia storytelling, with at the end a set of principles for what encompasses them, in "Transmedia Worlds," *Slideshare,* www.slideshare.net/jesseschell/transmedia-worlds-3656102, with the video here: transmythology.com/2010/11/14/jesse-schell-dust-or-magic-conference/. See also *The Art of Game Design,* 300–307.

16. See, for example, Walter Truett Anderson, *Reality Isn't What It Used to Be: Theatrical Politics, Ready-to-Wear Religion, Global Myths, Primitive Chic, and Other Wonders of the Postmodern World* (New York: HarperCollins Publishers, 1990). There is of course a fatal flaw with socially constructed realities (SCRs) and all such "there is no objective truth" worldviews. The fact that SCRs themselves are socially constructed means that there has to be something outside of SCRs that they are differentiated *from,* and so not all of the Universe can be said to be socially constructed. That's just a specific instance of the philosophical fact that saying there is no objective truth makes a claim of objective truth, and therefore is self-defeating. Of course, there are those today who do have different beliefs *about* the rules of logic, but there's no arguing with them.

17. We cannot, however, all go to the rainforest; in fact, if we did it would very soon cease being the authentic, pristine wilderness we want to experience in the first place, if it isn't already. On this see the section "Nature Versus Nurture" in James H. Gilmore and B. Joseph Pine II, *Authenticity: What Consumers Really Want* (Boston: Harvard Business Press, 2007), 84–87. But we can all go on a Web-surfing expedition or take a virtual jungle tour to bring elements of the rainforest to us, and while, no, they can never replicate the experience of being there, they can give us enough of an appreciation to want to support endeavors to save it for posterity.

18. In *Simulacra and Simulation* (Ann Arbor: The University of Michigan Press, 1994, originally published in French by Éditions Galilée, 1981), 1, Jean Baudrillard regards *simulacra* (with Disneyland foremost among them) as representations with no referent, "models of a real without origin or reality." However, all representations,

simulations, and virtual creations still refer to what people have experienced in the real world to provide context for whatever flights of fancy on which they wish to take people. You can't change the laws of physics, as Scottie often asserted on *Star Trek*, but even when a Virtuality experience does, it is recognized as a change, not a wholesale creation of something new. This is what Tolkien meant, as quoted in Chapter 6, "Virtuality," when he used the term "sub-creator." All of mankind's creations are *subordi-nate to the* creation. Janie B. Cheaney affirms this in her discussion of the awe-inspiring movie *Avatar*, in "Reel beauty," *World*, February 13, 2010, 30, when she says, "The truth is, everything in the movie was taken from real life and rearranged, enlarged, or color-enhanced. Every creator works from the original creation."

19. Stephen Wolfram, renowned scientist and creator of the Mathematica program, most famously stated this view in his book *A New Kind of Science* (Champaign, Illinois: Wolfram Media, 2002). As he attests on his website, "Quick Takes on Some Ideas and Discoveries in *A New Kind of Science*," *wolframscience.com*, wolframscience .com/reference/quick_takes.html:

> In its recent history, physics has tried to use increasingly elaborate mathematical models to reproduce the universe. But building on the discovery that even simple programs can yield highly complex behavior, *A New Kind of Science* shows that with appropriate kinds of rules, simple programs can give rise to behavior that reproduces a remarkable range of known features of our universe—leading to the bold assertion that there could be a simple short program that represents a truly fundamental model of the universe, and which if run for long enough would reproduce the behavior of our world in every detail.

Earlier, University of Texas architecture professor Dr. Michael L. Benedikt concludes his article "Cityspace, Cyberspace, and the Spatiology of Information," *Journal of Virtual Worlds Research*, vol. 1, no. 1, July 2008 (originally published in 1996), 19–20, by writing, "Finally, this is what cyberspace is about. . . . Even as the world we know becomes placeless . . . we must construct another one which we have not yet fully seen, a world in another image and from a material that is actually the universe's oldest and only material: *information itself.*"

This idea was first proposed by physicist John Wheeler in his paper, "Information, Physics, Quantum: The Search for Links," presented at the Santa Fe Institute in 1989 and published in Wojciech H. Zurek, editor, *Complexity, Entropy and the Physics of Information* (Boulder, Colorado: Westview Press, 1990), 3–28. His pithy summary of the entire idea: "It from bit."

And most recently, University of Oxford physics professor Vlatko Vedral, author of *Decoding Reality: The Universe as Quantum Information* (Oxford, England: Oxford University Press, 2010), contends, according to "A Quantum Calculation," *The Economist,* April 24, 2010, 81–2, "that bits of information are the universe's basic units, and the universe as a whole is a giant quantum computer." According to the article, "He argues that all of reality can be explained if readers accept that information is at the root of everything." We do find this view intriguing, for it seems to apply Occam's razor to the creation of the universe.

20. Virtuality not only underlies all our experiences of Reality but also life itself. As Hubert P. Yockey shows in *Information Theory, Evolution, and the Origin of Life*

(Cambridge, England: Cambridge University Press, 2005), ix–x, when James D. Watson and Francis Crick uncovered the structure of DNA as a double helix, they also discovered the digital underpinnings of life:

> [Watson and Crick] discovered that there is a genetic message, recorded in the digital sequence of nucleotides in DNA, that controls the formation of protein and of course all biological processes. The message in the genetic information system is *segregated, linear, and digital* and can be measured in *bits* and *bytes*. Computer users will notice the isomorphism between the program in computer memories and the genetic message recorded in DNA. . . . The genetic information system is essentially a digital data recording and processing system.

21. As Paul Harris, development psychologist and Harvard Graduate School of Education professor, puts it in regard to child development, "The imagination is absolutely vital for contemplating reality, not just those things we take to be mere fantasy"; quoted in Shirley S. Wang, "The Power of Magical Thinking," *Wall Street Journal,* December 22, 2009.

22. In a fascinating study of one Virtuality, *Coming of Age in Second Life: An Anthropologist Explores the Virtually Human* (Princeton: Princeton University Press, 2008), 5, Tom Boellstorff asserts, "Second Life culture is profoundly human. It is not only that virtual worlds borrow assumptions from real life; virtual worlds show us how, under our very noses, our 'real' lives have been 'virtual' all along. It is in being virtual that we are human: since it is human 'nature' to experience life through the prism of culture, human being has always been virtual being. Culture is our 'killer app': we are virtually human."

13. From Design to Deployment

1. Respectively: Nathan Shedroff, *Experience Design 1* (Indianapolis: New Riders, 2001); Mark Stephen Meadows, *Pause & Effect: The Art of Interactive Narrative* (Indianapolis: New Riders, 2003); Jesse Schell; *The Art of Game Design: A Book of Lenses* (Amsterdam: Elsevier, 2008); Dan Saffer; *Designing for Interaction: Creating Smart Applications and Clever Devices* (Indianapolis: New Riders, 2007); and David Lee King; *Designing the Digital Experience: How to Use Experience Design Tools & Techniques to Build Websites Customers Love* (Medford, New Jersey: CyberAge Books, 2008).

2. See Chapter 3, "The Show Must Go On," in B. Joseph Pine II and James H. Gilmore, *The Experience Economy* (Boston: Harvard Business Review Press, 2011), 64–105.

3. See Chapter 2, "Setting the Stage," ibid., 41–64.

4. See Chapter 5, "Experiencing Less Sacrifice," ibid., 123–143, as well as the previous chapter, "Get Your Act Together," 107–122, on mass customizing.

5. See Chapter 6, "The Real/Fake Reality," in James H. Gilmore and B. Joseph Pine II, *Authenticity: What Consumers Really Want* (Boston: Harvard Business Press, 2007), 95–114.

6. See Chapter 6, "Work Is Theatre," in Pine & Gilmore, *The Experience Economy,* 153–179. At its simplest, this means providing an engaging storyline with a beginning, middle, and end. We prefer the more complicated but incredibly rich form known as the Freytag diagram, which is covered here on 160–162, but explicated best

by Brenda Laurel in *Computers as Theatre* (Reading, MA: Addison-Wesley, 1993), 81–92 in particular. It involves seven stages: exposition, inciting incident, rising action, crisis, climax, falling action, and dénouement.

7. Marie-Laure Ryan, *Narrative as Virtual Reality: Immersion and Interactivity in Literature and Electronic Media* (Baltimore: The John Hopkins University Press, 2001), 15.

8. See, for example, Adam L. Penenberg, "Everyone's a Player," *Fast Company,* December 2010–January 2011, 135–141, and John Tierney, "On a Hunt for What Makes Gamers Keep Gaming," *New York Times,* December 7, 2010.

9. In "Games Theory," *New York Times Magazine,* September 19, 2010, 70, Sara Corbett quotes Paul Howard-Jones, a neuroscientist at the University of Bristol, as saying, "I think in 30 years' time we will marvel that we ever tried to deliver a curriculum without gaming." And in "The Play of Imagination: Extending the Literary Mind," *Games and Culture,* vol. 2, no. 2, April 2007, 169, Douglas Thomas and John Seely Brown conclude: "The model that virtual worlds provide offers a glimpse into the possibilities of what our classrooms might become: spaces where work and play, convergence and divergence, and reality and imagination intertwine in a dance where students grow to understand the importance of communities of practice and learn how to *be* the things they imagine."

10. Nonetheless, in the Google Tech Talks presentation "Putting the Fun in Functional: Applying Game Mechanics to Functional Software," *YouTube,* www.youtube.com/watch?v=ihUt-163gZI, Amy Jo Kim provides five essential game mechanics for social media: collecting, earning points, feedback, exchanges, and customization.

11. Note that "aesthetics" here—the elements of beauty—differs from "esthetic" above in the hit-the-sweet-spot design principle; the latter applies to passive-immersive environments, using the architectural term, heavily influenced by Michael Benedikt, *For an Architecture of Reality* (New York: Lumen Books, 1987), 4, where he says that "in our media-saturated times it falls to architecture to have the direct esthetic experience of the real at the center of its concerns."

12. Schell, *The Art of Game Design,* 42–43. For the inciting incident of much of this application of gaming to learning, work, and life, see Schell's presentation to the DICE 2010 conference, "Design Outside the Box," *G4,* g4tv.com/videos/44277/dice-2010-design-outside-the-box-presentation/. It should not be missed.

13. Alfie Kohn, *Punished by Rewards: The Trouble with Gold Stars, Incentive Plans, A's, Praise, and Other Bribes* (Boston: Houghton Mifflin Company, 1999), 189, citing Mihaly Csikszentmihalyi, "Intrinsic Rewards and Emergent Motivation," in Mark R. Lepper and David Greene, editors, *The Hidden Costs of Rewards: New Perspectives on the Psychology of Human Motivation* (Hillsdale, New Jersey: Erlbaum, 1978), 215. Schell echoes this element in the last of his one hundred lenses in *The Art of Game Design,* 461, "The Lens of Your Secret Purpose," which says: "To make sure you are working toward your own true purpose, ask yourself the only question that matters: Why am I doing this?"

14. Although we hasten to note that there is little evidence that violent games turn otherwise sedate players into perpetrators of violence. All change happens at the margin, as economists like to say, so surely in some cases, at least, it has made a difference in the personalities and actions of certain players.

15. You can find a model for doing so, Here-and-Now Space, in Chapter 9 of Gilmore and Pine, *Authenticity,* 179–218. Kim was helpful in developing this model, particularly the steps to operationalize it.

16. We are inspired here by James G. March, who in "Exploration and Exploitation in Organizational Learning," *Organizational Science,* vol. 2, no. 1, February 1991, 71, defines the two types of learning in organizations as "exploitation of old certainties" and "exploration of new possibilities." Our next book together, *Regenerative Management: Creating Persistent Advantage,* will tackle the issues of this section for all companies, showing how to orchestrate exploration and exploitation together in order to thrive.

17. S. Craig Watkins and H. Erin Lee, "Got Facebook? Investigating What's Social About Social Media," *The Young and the Digital,* www.theyoungandthedigital.com/wp-content/uploads/2010/11/watkins_lee_facebookstudy-nov-18.pdf.

18. William Powers, *Hamlet's BlackBerry: A Practical Philosophy for Building a Good Life in the Digital Age* (New York: Harper, 2010) and Thomas Hylland Eriksen, *The Tyranny of the Moment: Fast and Slow Time in the Information Age* (London: Pluto Press, 2001).

19. Nicholas Carr, *The Shallows: What the Internet Is Doing to Our Brains* (New York: W. W. Norton & Company, 2010).

20. Maggie Jackson, *Distracted: The Erosion of Attention and the Coming Dark Age* (Amherst, New York: Prometheus Books, 2008).

21. Mark Bauerlein, *The Dumbest Generation: How the Digital Age Stupefies Young Americans and Jeopardizes Our Future (Or, Don't Trust Anyone Under 30)* (New York: Jeremy P. Tarcher, 2008).

22. Steven Johnson, *Everything Bad Is Good for You: How Today's Popular Culture Is Actually Making Us Smarter* (New York: Riverhead Books, 2005), David Williamson Shaffer, *How Computer Games Help Children Learn* (New York: Palgrave Macmillan, 2006), and James Paul Gee, *What Video Games Have to Teach Us about Learning and Literacy* (New York: Palgrave Macmillan, 2007). See also John C. Beck and Mitchell Wade, *The Kids Are Alright: How the Gamer Generation Is Changing the Workplace* (Boston: Harvard Business School Press, 2006) and David Edery and Ethan Mollick, *Changing the Game: How Video Games Are Transforming the Future of Business* (Upper Saddle River, New Jersey: Pearson Education, 2009).

23. Neil Postman, *Amusing Ourselves to Death: Public Discourse in the Age of Show Business* (New York: Penguin Books, 1985), 4–5.

24. Neil Postman, *Technopoly: The Surrender of Culture to Technology* (New York: Vintage Books, 1992), 4–5 and 7, respectively.

25. Jaron Lanier, *You Are Not a Gadget: A Manifesto* (New York: Alfred A. Knopf, 2010), 33 and 4, respectively. In a similar, albeit more prescriptive, vein, see Douglas Rushkoff, *Program or Be Programmed: Ten Commands for a Digital Age* (New York: OR Books, 2010).

26. Pine & Gilmore, *The Experience Economy,* 269–270.

27. This is the summary of Sherry Turkle, *Life on the Screen: Identity in the Age of the Internet* (New York: Simon & Schuster, 1995), 258. For the original, see Robert Jay Lifton, *The Protean Self: Human Resilience in the Age of Fragmentation* (New York: Basic Books, 1993).

28. Erving Goffman, *The Presentation of Self in Everyday Life* (New York: Anchor Books, 1959). See also Pine & Gilmore, *The Experience Economy,* 153–164.

29. Turkle, *Life on the Screen,* 269.

30. Benedict Carey and John Markoff, "Students, Meet Your New Teacher, Mr. Robot," *New York Times,* July 11, 2010, and Anne Tergesen and Miho Inada, "It's Not a Stuffed Animal, It's a $6,000 Medical Device," *The Wall Street Journal,* June 21, 2010, respectively.

31. As Tom Boellstorff says in *Coming of Age in Second Life: An Anthropologist Explores the Virtually Human* (Princeton: Princeton University Press, 2008), 156, "One of the most surprising and consistent findings of cybersociality research has been that virtual worlds can not only transform actual-world intimacy but create real forms of online intimacy.... Second Life residents often saw it as 'an intimacy-making culture.'" Turkle, however, disputes this in *Alone Together: Why We Expect More from Technology and Less from Each Other* (New York: Basic Books, 2011).

32. Sherry Turkle, *Simulation and Its Discontents* (Cambridge, Massachusetts: MIT Press, 2009), 13.

33. Ibid, 21.

34. Lanier, *You Are Not a Gadget,* 4 (capitalization of this section head removed).

Afterword

1. *The Ultimate LEGO Book* (London: Dorling Kindersley, 1999), 8.

2. Søren Eilers, Mikkel Abrahamsen, and Bergfinnur Durhuus, "A LEGO Counting problem," *Institut for Matematiske Fag,* www.math.ku.dk/~eilers/lego.html. The professors show that the original LEGO number is off by four; the correct number is 102,981,504.

3. Ibid. This was calculated considering the efficiency level of their 2005 computer program.

4. Ibid. Their range of estimation lies between 78^N and 191^N.

5. All from "Company Profile: An introduction to the LEGO Group 2010," *LEGO,* 8 and 20, cache.lego.com/upload/contentTemplating/AboutUsFactsAndFiguresContent/otherfiles/download98E142631E71927FDD52304C1C0F1685.pdf.

6. Neither in Reality nor Virtuality can there be an actual collection of infinite objects (whether material or digital substances), nor an infinite progression of time (whether measured in millennia, centuries, years, seconds, or any other unit), nor an infinite expanse of space (whether measured in light-years, miles, feet, nanometers, or any other unit). Mathematician David Hilbert showed this with his concept now known as Hilbert's Hotel; see "Hilbert's Paradox of the Grand Hotel," *Wikipedia,* en.wikipedia.org/wiki/Hilbert%27s_hotel. For a good discussion of this and other ways in which actual infinities are impossible, see William Lane Craig, *Apologetics: An Introduction* (Chicago: Moody Press, 1984), 75–81.

7. "Eternal," *The Oxford English Dictionary,* Second Edition (Oxford: Clarendon Press, 1989), vol. V, 417.

index

about the authors

B. Joseph Pine II is cofounder of Strategic Horizons LLP, an Aurora, Ohio–based thinking studio dedicated to helping enterprises conceive and design innovative ways of adding value to their economic offerings via mass customizing, staging experiences, rendering authenticity, guiding transformations—and now using digital technology to create experiences that fuse the real and the virtual. He is coauthor of *Authenticity: What Consumers* Really *Want* (Harvard Business Press, 2007) and *The Experience Economy: Work Is Theatre & Every Business a Stage* (Harvard Business School Press, 1999, with an updated edition in 2011). Mr. Pine also wrote *Mass Customization: The New Frontier in Business Competition* (Harvard Business School Press, 1993) as well as numerous articles for the *Harvard Business Review,* the *Wall Street Journal, Chief Executive,* and *Strategy & Leadership,* among others. Prior to beginning his writing and speaking activities, Mr. Pine held a number of technical and managerial positions with IBM and is now is a Visiting Scholar with the MIT Design Lab as well as a Senior Fellow with both the Design Futures Council and the European Centre for the Experience Economy, which he cofounded.

Kim C. Korn helps companies unlock their potential to create advantage—and to re-create it again and again. As a management practitioner, Kim has been responsible for invention, innovation, strategy, operations, reengineering, information systems, product development, and business creation in his roles at Arthur Andersen (now Accenture) and Andersen Windows. He brings his consulting expertise, experience at guiding major change initiatives, and his practitioner eye to *Infinite Possibility,* leading development of the chapters on how to apply the core framework in actual business situations. Applying his skills and experience to the challenge of companies thriving indefinitely, Kim, in collaboration with Joe, is lead author on the forthcoming book *Regenerative Management: Creating Persistent Advantage.* This book guides companies in adopting the regenerative way of management, producing their own unique management prescription, and becoming capable of achieving persistent advantage.

Berrett–Koehler
Publishers

A community dedicated to creating
a world that works for all

Visit Our Website: www.bkconnection.com

Read book excerpts, see author videos and Internet movies, read our authors' blogs, join discussion groups, download book apps, find out about the BK Affiliate Network, browse subject-area libraries of books, get special discounts, and more!

Subscribe to Our Free E-Newsletter, the *BK Communiqué*

Be the first to hear about new publications, special discount offers, exclusive articles, news about bestsellers, and more! Get on the list for our free e-newsletter by going to **www.bkconnection.com**.

Get Quantity Discounts

Berrett-Koehler books are available at quantity discounts for orders of ten or more copies. Please call us toll-free at (800) 929-2929 or email us at **bkp .orders@aidcvt.com**.

Join the BK Community

BKcommunity.com is a virtual meeting place where people from around the world can engage with kindred spirits to create a world that works for all. BKcommunity.com members may create their own profiles, blog, start and participate in forums and discussion groups, post photos and videos, answer surveys, announce and register for upcoming events, and chat with others online in real time. Please join the conversation!